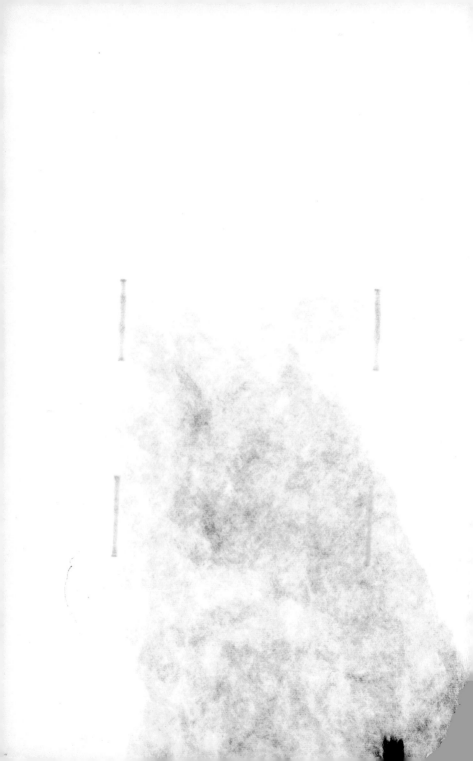

Alcoholism and Society

Alcoholism and Society

MORRIS E. CHAFETZ, M.D.

Clinical Associate in Psychiatry,
Harvard Medical School
Associate Psychiatrist and Director, Alcohol Clinic,
Massachusetts General Hospital

HAROLD W. DEMONE, JR.

Executive Director, The Medical Foundation, Inc.
Former Commissioner of Alcoholism,
Commonwealth of Massachusetts

Foreword by

HARRY C. SOLOMON, M.D.

New York   Oxford University Press   1962

To Stanley Cobb, M.D.
and A. Warren Stearns, M.D.

Foreword

It is flattering to be asked to write a foreword for this able treatise on alcoholics and alcoholism. My justification for accepting this commission is that I have had more than forty years of experience as a clinician in the care and treatment of alcoholics, and as a Professor of Psychiatry at the Harvard Medical School. On the basis of this experience I would say that the solution of the problem of alcoholism, or a complete understanding of the ecology of the condition, has not been reached. It is, therefore, valuable and timely that a comprehensive and critical review of the thinking and experience, the research approaches, and the treatment methods connected with alcoholism in conjunction with concrete suggestions for action should be made available. In this day of specialization it is refreshing that the authors have attempted to view man as a whole.

In retrospect, it would appear that each decade has added to the conceptual framework of the problem of alcoholism something that runs parallel to the social thinking and medical ideas of the period. For example the psychiatrist was involved early in the treatment of this problem. This arose out of the fact that many alcoholics developed serious mental disorders such as delirium tremens, alcoholic hallucinosis, and other psychotic symptoms requiring treatment in a mental hospital.

Also during the last century a large part of the interest of the personnel of mental hospitals centered on neuropathological studies attempting to define the pathological basis of mental disorders. By the beginning of this century the brain changes of certain alcoholic conditions had been well established; however, no pathological changes were found to explain delirium tremens and alcoholic hallucinosis. Knowledge concerning the role of vitamin deficiency in the development of alcoholic neuritis turned attention to a possible relationship between vitamin deficiencies and alcoholic psychosis. This was explored but without definitive results. With the development of biochemistry attention was turned to the possible place of protein metabolism. Here again the search was not highly significant.

As experience accumulated indicating that the delirium tremens patient and other patients with alcoholic psychosis tended to revert to their alcoholic habits after recovery from their acute episodes, psychiatrists and others became concerned about the problem of drinking in its other aspects, not simply the treatment of the acute psychiatric manifestations. In this context the studies of the causes of alcoholism and the methods of treatment began to receive the attention of both psychiatrists and practicing physicians. In fact, some psychiatrists specialized in the field of alcoholism. The concept that alcoholism was an illness became recognized. Curiously enough it is only recently that this idea has been publicized and generally accepted.

Along with the medical profession other disciplines and groups assumed a responsibility for the alcoholic. The Salvation Army, the Volunteers of America, and formal religious organizations became very active in attempting to aid the alcoholic. The clergy as individuals were consulted, and they made personal efforts to help. Social agencies found that alcoholism had a high incidence in the families of their clients. Industry learned of the high cost of alcoholism as related to their employees' absenteeism. Because of the disturbances in conduct produced by alcoholism, the correctional authorities, prison personnel, probation and parole authorities, and police, of necessity, had to deal with the problem. As the non-medical aspects of alcoholism became manifest the participation of the social and behavioral scientists became prominent, especially in research. With the growth of psychoanalysis the techniques of dynamic psychological investigation were added, an approach which plays a large role in current research and treatment. A recent successful method is that sponsored by Alcoholics Anonymous whereby one alcoholic helps another. It is interesting that the evidence gathered by all these different approaches has not as yet led to a solution of the problem.

It is a propitious circumstance that two individuals, one a psychiatrist and the other a social scientist, both with long experience and training in the investigation of the subject and in actual treatment efforts, should have collaborated in the production of an authoritative book which reviews the field and offers guidelines for future endeavors.

HARRY C. SOLOMON, M.D.

Commissioner of Mental Health, Commonwealth of Massachusetts; Professor of Psychiatry, Emeritus, Harvard Medical School

Preface

Our principal objective in this book is to make known to as large an audience as possible the information today available about the alcoholic, in the hope that we may help bring about a revolution in social attitudes toward alcoholism.

Alcoholism—third only to heart disease and cancer in incidence—is a major public health problem that we as a society have handled shamefully. Not only is an ignorant, moralistic, and punitive attitude rampant among lay people; it thrives among the caretaking professions as well. We are all familiar with the disparaging and even abusive labels used to describe and discuss the alcoholic. Society despises him; the medical profession shuns him.

If some of this hostile feeling toward the alcoholic can be dispelled and aid and understanding extended to him and his family, he may have more incentive to seek help. No one today can afford to be so smug or self-righteous as to say: "This problem cannot happen to me or to mine." Traditional attitudes of misunderstanding, rejection, disgust, moral preaching, and prohibition—even threat—have only made more difficult the solution of the problem. In addition, the rapid rate of acculturation in twentieth-century America seems likely to step up the spread of alcoholism. Only by facing the problem openly, as a mature, responsible society, can we begin to solve it.

We have tried to orient this book toward the lay as well as the professional audience; we would like the reader to see and know the alcoholic as we have. If a person ever has such an experience, the dimensions of his mind, as well as of his feelings, can never return to the restrictions imposed by his former ignorance and fear. Only when outmoded attitudes surrounding the alcoholic are discarded can progress in understanding alcoholism be made.

M. E. C.
H. W. D., Jr.

Boston, Massachusetts
December 1961

Acknowledgments

All authors are aware of their extensive debt to many in the creation and publication of a book. Most realize that important subtle influences remain unrecognized. For the more obvious contributions we give our thanks: to our chiefs, Dr. Erich Lindemann and Dr. Alfred Frechette, for their support and understanding; to Miss Lorraine Lyman for her devotion and interest in the preparation of the manuscript; to Miss Louise Harrigan, Mrs. Ruth Forstot, and Mrs. Helen Turner for secretarial assistance; to Mrs. Gwendolyn Williams for aid in bibliographical preparation; to Drs. Ruth Fox, Robert Straus, and John Philp and Mr. Ernest A. Shepherd for reading and commenting on the first draft; to Dr. Jack Mendelson for advice and counsel on the biochemical work; to Dr. Albert Ullman for aid in expressing learning theories; to Dr. Carl Binger for his advice and direction; to Mrs. Marty Mann for information on the National Council of Alcoholism; to Mr. Mark Keller and the Publications Division of the Yale Center of Alcohol Studies for information on the Yale Chapter and permission to quote material from their publications; to the *New England Journal of Medicine* for permission to use the material from an article by Dr.

Chafetz, "Alcoholism Problems and Programs in Czechoslovakia, Poland and the Soviet Union"; to Miss Elizabeth Lacy and Mrs. Susan Wheeler for editorial assistance; to the staff of the Oxford University Press, whose patience, efforts, and support were invaluable; and to our wives, Marion Chafetz and Marguerite Demone, for their constant encouragement and understanding.

M. E. C.
H. W. D., Jr.

Contents

I

Alcoholism and Society

Man's enjoyment of alcohol is ancient. Alcohol's historical influence, its present degree of cultural acceptance, and its pharmacological-physiological effects, together with the human need for equilibrium, are the crucial elements of the use and nonuse of alcohol. When these components are viewed together, an understanding of the causes of alcoholism is possible.

1

Orientation

Alcohol, like fire, was bound to exist. The mere storage of many products of the earth could result, under certain circumstances, in the formation of an alcoholic beverage. Alcohol, like fire, is a source of both good and evil. It can serve society meaningfully as a ritual symbol, as a means of enhancing food, as a tension releaser, and as a way of developing social ease. Yet man has, under its influence, committed crimes of all sorts and at all levels. Alcohol, like fire, symbolizes the paradox of the human condition.

In learning to understand alcohol use and alcoholism, the reader must bear one point in mind. All the factors that make for alcoholism are in a state of constant interaction. We are not examining static systems, but rather the dynamic interplay of many forces. Although we examine and elaborate certain events of alcoholism as though they were specific and immobile, they are like the frenzied activity of a valley of molten lava into which hundreds of streams empty. The wise reader, therefore, will not give unusual weight to any one aspect of alcoholism but will view it in relation to the whole.

This is all the more important because alcohol use and alcoholism have ramifications and implications which touch

3

upon almost everything in human behavior. For this reason, unless one sees the dynamic interplay constantly taking place between the various elements, the book will lose its meaning as an attempt to view man as a total organism. This chapter is intended to be a vantage point from which one gets a general picture of that interplay. The various factors will then be taken up in detail. Many facets of man's private and social life must be examined, and they must be correlated with a historical, physiological, and cultural view of alcohol.

We define alcoholism as a chronic behavioral disorder which is manifested by undue preoccupation with alcohol to the detriment of physical and mental health, by a loss of control when drinking has begun (although it may not be carried to the point of intoxication), and by a self-destructive attitude in dealing with personal relationships and life situations. Alcoholism, we believe, is the result of disturbance and deprivation in early infantile experience and the related alterations in basic physiochemical responsiveness; the identification by the alcoholic with significant figures who deal with life problems through the excessive use of alcohol; and a socio-cultural milieu which causes ambivalence, conflict, and guilt in the use of alcohol.

The discoverer of alcohol is unknown. Even the substance from which the first alcohol originated is not historically recorded, but most likely grape, grain, or honey served as the precursor. Evidence exists that alcohol has played a role in man's social development for many millions of years.[8] Explorers throughout the ages have reported local consumption of alcoholic beverages in new-found civilizations. Roueché [8] even suggests that in the Neolithic period agriculture "may have sprung from a desire to assure a regular supply of alcohol." A more reasonable assumption would be that the desire for alcohol was simply an added impetus toward increased agricultural productivity.

The early role of alcohol in human life is emphasized by its close relation to religion. One of the earliest uses of alcohol was in religious practices and ritualism. The Judeo-Christian and Greek religious practices employing wine are of ancient origin, and in the Bible and Greek literature references to wine are numerous. The concept has been advanced that, in part, alcohol's "baffling nature frightened man into his first fumbling steps toward systematized religion." [8] Our belief is that religion arises whenever man has to cope with forces he cannot understand, and certainly alcohol releases in us such forces. But there is a further connection between alcohol and religion. In the presence of the unknown, man seeks some explanation. By fitting the unknown into a comprehensible frame of reference, religion makes it possible for man to feel some security. Anxiety is diminished and it becomes easier to live with one's feelings. Alcohol, like religion, serves man in the sense that it (pharmacologically) changes his perspective and offers temporary relief.

Alcohol's ability to change man's perspective may help us understand its present increased use, since we feel that the use of alcohol is directly related to anxiety. (We define anxiety as an unpleasant feeling of apprehension arising from a threat from, or loss of control over, unknown and unpredictable danger, in contrast to a fear that arises from a known danger.) Primitive cultures contained the potential for considerable anxiety, but the sources of anxiety were relatively few. For example, if early man stumbled upon some new wild animal, its potential danger or usefulness to him could be ascertained fairly easily. Today we also face threats from our environment; however, because of the increased complexities of life and expanded boundaries of knowledge and communication, the sources of our anxiety are more numerous and less directly known to us, and the stimuli are less controllable and less predictable. Alcohol becomes, therefore, a social instrument in managing our feelings.

The question of why people drink has been the subject of many writers from many ages. William James in his *Varieties of Religious Experience* [7] wrote "... the sway of alcohol over mankind is unquestionably due to its power to stimulate the mystical faculties of human nature usually crushed to earth by the cold facts and dry criticisms of the sober hour ... the drunken consciousness is one bit of the mystic consciousness, and our total opinion of it must find its place in our opinion of the larger whole."

Horace [5] in ancient times wrote about alcohol usage in a more ebullient, but equally perceptive manner. "What wonders does not wine! It discloses secrets; ratifies and confirms our hopes; thrusts the coward forth to battle; eases the anxious mind of its burden; instructs in art. Whom has not a cheerful glass made eloquent; whom not quite free and easy from pinching poverty."

We see alcohol as an instrument used by a number of people with certain types of personalities and in certain social settings for many different purposes.

First, as a medicine for depression. Many individuals who suffer from a reactive depression or from a depression arising endogenously may take alcohol to lift their spirits. For these, alcohol is able to wash away ugliness even if only for a moment. The image of the rejected or disappointed individual heading for a bar is familiar. It is interesting, however, that alcohol for some may actually deepen depression.

Second, alcohol can blur perceptions when an individual is threatened. For instance, if a person is aroused homosexually, drinking will permit the expression of instincts that is unconsciously desired but repressed during sobriety. Thereby the individual, with drink, can engage in forbidden sexual activity and not consider himself responsible for his action.

Third, alcohol is often used to help support a system of defenses. In this category an "acting out" of the drinker's repressed conflicts is possible. With alcohol the individual who is latently hostile and aggressive may freely manifest his hostility and aggressiveness, being utterly unaware of his reactions. An example is the worker who will, when intoxicated, insult his employer as he would never dare to when sober. The difference between the second and third categories is that a person in the latter category, when sober, is incredulous of his contrary behavior with alcohol, whereas in the former, the individual whose perceptions are blurred is *aware* of his actions but does not blame himself.

The reader may well say that homosexual experience is acting out and that most of the examples we note can fit into any system of defenses. This is of course true. Our purpose, however, is to illustrate some of the many possible reasons for drinking. We recognize that no human behavior is motivated by a single force or single event. Behavior is the result of multiple influences and has many interrelated consequences.

The fourth use of alcohol is as an instrument to break down psychological barriers. People who use it this way need to drink to perform. In other words, anxiety and tension aroused by the prospect of writing, speaking before an audience, looking for a job, etc., is handled by drinking beforehand.

Fifth, as an emotional nutrient socially, in a healthy way, alcohol fulfills an important function in its ceremonial and ritualistic use. When alcohol is so used, as in the preliterate societies and in the Jewish culture, protection against pathological usage is built up. Using alcohol as an emotional nutrient, in an unhealthy way, an individual can get care from an otherwise rejecting mate. The mate, when the alcoholic is sober, could not and would not tolerate the dependent situation and demands.

In easing social situations alcohol fulfills its sixth and most effective role. The cocktail party would grind to a disastrous halt without liquor, as would some conversation and the ease of superficial relationships.

The seventh use of alcohol in our list is as a means of obtaining a state of bliss. People who use it in this form may seek a "dream state" or oblivion. They use alcohol as they might morphine. For example, a patient when sober took his wife to Skid Row. She was shocked by the sight of the intoxicated forms lying in the street. Noting this, her husband said, "What is even more shocking is that I envy them their oblivion."

The eighth way in which alcohol is used is in an environment where an intoxicated person is better tolerated than a sober one. This category involves the mates of some alcoholics. We, and others, have seen alcoholics whose marital partners have on the surface abhorred the drinking of their spouses. When, however, the alcoholic attempts to control drinking, the mate responds with opposition. If sobriety is achieved, the nonalcoholic becomes more and more disturbed. In such cases it is evident that the alcoholic's drinking, socially unacceptable and overt, was a defense and cover for the mate's own emotional difficulties. When the alcoholic improves, the problems of the nonalcoholic are exposed. The drinking of an individual under these circumstances is in part to satisfy the emotional needs of another.

Although most alcohol users drink to weaken controls, a rare group of individuals use alcohol to strengthen controls in order to prevent a psychotic breakdown. Alcohol allows them to maintain control over imminent personality disintegration. For example, a man who works effectively at his job refuses time off and vacations. He only leaves his work locale to sleep. Whenever he is impelled to spend waking time away from work, he can contain the threat to his contact with reality, and his distorted, frightening feelings, only by heavy drinking. As soon as he is back at work, he drinks no more. Such a patient should not be advised to stop drinking completely.

These categories, although they overlap, do offer some operational classification for understanding drinking behavior.

Beyond the reasons and categories just noted, superficial reasons for drinking may be: to keep warm, to cool off, to pep up, to relax, to enjoy the taste, and the smell, or, as a medicine, to fight a cold or increase the appetite. Of course, in some cultures, alcohol, especially wine, is used as a beverage accompanying meals.

Let us now look at the action of alcohol upon the human organism. Pharmacologically, alcohol is not the popularly envisioned stimulant, but rather a rapidly acting, continuous depressant. The apparent "stimulation" from alcohol is the result of the lower brain centers being released from higher brain controls. This reduces inhibitions, and behavior which is untoward when the individual is sober becomes acceptable. For example, the fastidious dresser may become sloppy after drinking heavily, or an always proper, ladylike woman may become obscene and promiscuous when intoxicated. The loss of learned social adaptive controls under the influence of alcohol led Horney [6] to say: "The superego is that part of the personality which is soluble in alcohol."

Alcohol begins its action once it has reached the stomach.[4] Like water and unlike most other foodstuffs, it does not require digestion. Although most alcohol is absorbed into the blood from the small intestine, a small amount is absorbed directly from the stomach. This direct absorption into the blood stream accounts for the rapid responses to alcohol. Once alcohol is in the blood, it is distributed throughout the body, but the area most sensitive to its action and effect is the brain.

Opposing alcohol's swift absorption is its slow elimination from the body. If one could slow the rate of alcohol's absorption or speed the rate of its elimination, not only would many unpleasant side effects (poor muscular control, slowed reaction, loss of control) be avoided but its pleasant social effects (lowered tension, feelings of well-being, ease of interpersonal relations) as well. With either slow absorption or rapid elimination the drinker would need so continuous and so plentiful a supply for so short a period of pleasant effect that it would not be worth the effort.

Delaying absorption of alcohol into the blood is possible. Accelerating elimination is not. One way to cause delay is to have food in the stomach, milk, fat, and meat being especially useful. Experienced partygoers know that drinking on an empty stomach produces a rapid and heightened effect. Another way of slowing absorption is by drinking slowly. The sipper never achieves the heightened response of the gulper, although both may drink the same amount. The third way absorption is influenced is related to the strength of the alcohol. In other words, if the amount of alcohol is the same, a 50 per cent alcohol concentration will have a greater effect than 35 per cent. (Concentration effects are complicated, however, by protective stomach secretions which slow absorption when high concentrations of alcohol are consumed.)

The main mechanism of the body's handling of alcohol is oxidation. Because of sluggish elimination of alcohol from the body, the individual who consumes large amounts fairly rapidly produces an initial high peak of alcohol in the blood, which may be sustained with a smaller input. The oxidation of alcohol, although a complex process, may be stated generally as follows: In stage one, ethyl alcohol reacts with oxygen in the blood, and the combination of the oxygen with two of the hydrogen molecules of alcohol results in the separation out of water and the formation of a new substance, acetylaldehyde. The liver is the chief site for the oxidation of alcohol to acetylaldehyde and water. Acetylaldehyde is a highly poisonous substance, but the body oxidizes it quickly (unless the liver has been damaged).

During stage two, oxidation takes place by the addition of oxygen to acetylaldehyde, without the formation of water, to form a new substance, acetic acid (vinegar). This stage of oxidation takes place in the liver and other body organs.

The ultimate stage of alcohol oxidation, like that of other foodstuffs, takes place throughout the body by local chemical action whereby acetic acid is oxidized to carbon dioxide, water, and calories (units of energy). A small percentage is excreted as unchanged and unoxidized alcohol from the kidneys and the lungs.

The energy derived from the oxidation of alcohol can be utilized by the body although it cannot be stored directly, as is the case with other calorie providers. This has resulted in the false belief that one cannot store fat from drinking. The fallacy exists because alcohol replaces other sources of calories in food. Because of the high caloric content of alcohol, the calories of other foods are not used, and *they* are stored as fat.

Bearing in mind some of the actions of alcohol, let us look briefly at cultural attitudes toward it. Crime of all varieties and irresponsible behavior of all degrees occur while persons are under some influence of alcohol. But alcohol has served society's purpose meaningfully as we mentioned earlier—in religion, and as a tension releaser, etc.

In spite of some of the better features of drinking, the knowledge that alcohol is a common denominator in all cases of alcoholism has led some to label it as the cause of alcoholism. Consequently the proposed cure is simple enough: eliminate alcohol. Many groups have considered this technique and will probably consider it in the future. Even if alcohol were the cause of alcoholism, it would still be unreasonable to believe it could be made to disappear suddenly and completely from the social scene. Even when obstacles of manufacture, supply, and cost are introduced, seekers of alcohol have little difficulty procuring it. Certainly we must remember that many more people enjoy the effects of alcohol in a healthy way than cling to it pathologically.

Mankind has generally looked upon alcohol with favor. Advertising, which serves to create desires and set values in most affluent societies, uses the mass media (movies, television, theater, the press, and radio) to sanction and approve its moderate use. As a source of social conviviality, religious ritual, and taxes, alcohol has been accepted in the present American culture. For example [3] two out of three adults in the United States make use of alcoholic beverages. Forty-nine of the fifty states permit the legal sale and consumption of beverage alcohol within stated limits. Even the one remaining "dry" state, Mississippi, permits the sale of low-alcohol-content beer. The vast majority of the one hundred million church members in the United States are affiliated with religious organizations which give moral sanction to moderate use of alcohol. In the prosperous year of 1956, American consumers spent 5 per cent of their over-all budget for alcoholic beverages. Compared with other individual purchases, this expenditure was exceeded only by the essentials of food, clothing and housing and is roughly the same amount as that spent on public education.

What does a look at the epidemiology of problem drinking reveal to us? Of seventy million alcohol users in the United States, it is estimated that there are five million alcoholics. The Federal Bureau of Investigation in its Uniform Crime Reports finds that the crime of drunkenness represents more than 40 per cent of all arrests, and is the nation's major single crime. Although not all who are arrested are alcoholics, many are. In Massachusetts, exclusive of minor traffic violations, more arrests and commitments to jail are made for drunkenness than for all other crimes combined. Studies of Massachusetts' tuberculosis sanatoriums and mental hospitals reveal that diagnosis of alcoholism, usually in conjunction with other diagnosis, can be made in roughly 30 per cent of all admissions. Chronic disease institutions, public welfare recipients, delinquents and their parents, divorcees, sex offenders, and other similar categories consistently provide higher percentages of alcoholics than should be expected in terms of the general population.

It has been generally held that alcoholics are usually men. We do not hold this opinion. Although we do not know the ratio of men versus women, the general figure quoted in the literature is 5½ to 1. As knowledge is disseminated that alcoholism is a disease and treatable, more and more women are seeking treatment. The impression about male versus female alcoholics may stem from the fact that the male alcoholic cannot "hide" as easily as the female. Men must go out into the business world, and their dependence upon alcohol is quickly noted. A woman, however, in the protected confines of her home, can, for long periods, escape social and even family detection. Our clinical observation leads us to believe that the tendency of women to use alcohol more freely than formerly in their social activity, coupled with their changing feminine role in society, may result in a greater incidence of alcoholic women in the near future.

Many people try out drinking when they are no longer living at home. College is a common trial spot. Although actual figures are unavailable, our experience suggests that only 3 to 4 per cent of students who indulge in protracted social drinking at college never succeed at becoming normal social drinkers. In other words, while the vast majority of young students will experiment with heavy drinking in college, most will stay within the confines of acceptable social drinking. The small percentage mentioned goes on from their heavy college alcohol intake to full-blown alcoholism, thus bypassing social drinking entirely.

A parallel phenomenon exists in our experience among elderly people. In retired groups, many individuals take up increased drinking but do, in time, revert to their preretirement pattern of drinking behavior. A small percentage goes on to alcoholism. It may be that for this small group the demands of work were sufficient to prevent their pathological dependence on alcohol from showing itself, and, once work was removed, alcoholism flared. The possibilities for "late-life alcoholism" should be taken into consideration in planning for retirement. Individuals who are "overinvolved" in their work, who seem to have no outside interests, and who use alcohol heavily at work or when alone are particularly vulnerable. Alcoholism can also occur when a spouse has died and the protection which he or she offered is removed. Treatment for these groups can be effected by social manipulation whereby an environment is developed after retirement in which the patient is made to feel needed and useful. The increasing of the social ties of these retired or widowed people often reduces their dependency problems.

Now that we have looked briefly at alcohol, its action, and some of the attitudes surrounding it, what about man? Why is alcohol, when placed in some hands, a drink of pleasure and communion, in others a form of slow suicide? If man is visualized as striving to maintain equilibruim within himself and in his relation to the outside world, alcohol can be seen to serve as a restitutive mechanism.

There exist physiologically, biochemically, psychically, and socially corrective systems counteracting states of disequilibrium. Claude Bernard [1] recognized this striving for equilibrium when he described his "milieu intérieur," Cannon,[2] when he discussed the mechanism for maintaining a steady, balanced internal constitution, and Wiener,[9] when he explained communication and control in the nervous system and in machines. By outpourings of hormones, by contraction and relaxation of blood vessels or muscles, and by stimulation of various body centers, man maintains a steady internal environment. Psychically, Freud's concept of id, ego, and superego was construed as a balancing of emotional forces. Psychiatric symptoms, although they may cause the individual discomfort and be socially destructive, tend to re-establish equilibrium, and they are restitutive. For example, the paranoid patient who feels alone and separated from the world may distort events so that he believes everyone is noticing him. Another patient may be overzealous in protecting the morals of society because deep in his mind he has strong drives to be promiscuous.

Socially, the striving toward equilibrium also exists. The individual who finds himself caught between two cultures cannot remain in his state of disequilibrium. He must either withdraw into himself or join the culture around him. By the actions of withdrawing or joining, the individual re-establishes his equilibrium.

As life becomes more complex and more troubled, as new sources of anxiety are introduced before old sources are eliminated, the individual in most cultures of today must seek for additional methods to maintain balance. This attempt is called "coping with life." What are the means of coping with psychological and social disequilibrium? There is psychological treatment: psychoanalysis or psychotherapy. By these techniques an individual attempts to correct behavioral abnormalities which have prevented his managing the new influx of stress and strain, and he seeks through therapy a new formula of adaptive behavior for the present and for the uncertain future. Others use tranquilizers and drugs. Still others become involved in organizational activity or create a background of noise through radio or television to prevent more threatening stimuli from coming into their awareness. Some are freed from stress by the onset of physical illness, while others develop neurotic symptoms or psychotic mechanisms. Some coping mechanisms are subtle; some are obvious; some are corrective and beneficial; some completely take over the individual destructively and become a way of life. One such response of the last-mentioned category is alcoholism. The alcoholic, in trying to maintain his state of equilibrium, becomes disastrously involved in his semi-suicidal attachment to his coping method, which results gradually in his complete rejection and social ostracism.

2

Causes of Alcoholism

In this chapter we shall express our own ideas as to the etiology of alcoholism. We have been unable, to date, to accept any single-factor etiological explanation. In general we feel that alcoholism is too far-reaching and diversified a condition to arise from a single cause. For that matter, we are unable to visualize much of the interaction of life and disease from the point of view of single cause and single effect. Many other studies have been made on the subject of the cause of alcoholism. Although we often agree in part with the theories that have been offered, we have found that many of them give an incomplete picture of the subject. We shall consider the etiology of alcoholism from a general perspective which will include consideration of prenatal influences, psychological, physiological, and biochemical factors of personality development, cultural influences, and individual and social attitudes toward alcohol.

A disturbed prenatal period, be the disturbance physical, chemical, or emotional, may establish the special personality foundation upon which alcoholism can develop. The fetus, like the infant, child, and adult, is affected by its environment.

Ashley Montagu [1] states that the "constitution is the sum

17

total of the structural, functional, and psychological characters of the organism." The genetic potentialities of the fetus, as of the child, are influenced by factors of environment. Therefore, we consider the constitution a dynamic process rather than a static state. Although genetic potentialities themselves may be limited, genes may be influenced to develop their potentialities in different ways with different end results as a consequence of the environmental influence in which they operate. Experiments show that the mother's physical, chemical, and emotional states affect the fetus. For example, if a pregnant woman contracts German measles, her child may well be born blind. Fatigue of the mother has been shown to affect the activity of the fetus. Drugs, infections, and nutrition, as well as maternal emotional stress, all influence fetus activity, and the newborn child reflects these conditions. Some babies at birth are irritable and cry excessively, while others seem placid and happy.

Now let us look at the newborn child. Born amid stretching, pain, and blood, propelled into a cold, strange world after nine months of protection and the essence of dependence, the new infant is ready to begin to build his personality upon the prenatal foundation. With the tying of the cord and the first breath profusing the lungs, the newborn is truly on his own. Not only must he do his own breathing, now air instead of water pressure bears upon his body. Temperature control becomes important for his well-being, the direction of his blood flow changes. For the first time he feels the need to fill a hollow stomach.

At the moment of birth the infant engages in the battle for survival. His first step toward healthy personality development is his capacity to sense and trust the love of another person to provide food, to keep him warm, and to give him gentle physical contact. If the infant is not fed immediately, he feels a new sensation of pain and hunger. The consistent warmth and tenderness of nurse or mother will be one sensation; coldness, rejection, and harshness of handling will evoke a different expectation and response; the giving of love and its withdrawal still another. Noise or its lack, physical contact or its absence, warmth or cold surrounding him—all these and other stimuli and sensations will direct and influence personality development.

The attitudes of the society into which the child has been born will affect his personality development. Prior to birth, guarded by uterine tissue, the fetus does not come into direct contact with another being. With the dilation of the cervix, social interaction begins. A nurse inserts a few drops of stinging fluid into the infant's eyes because medicine has taught that this may prevent gonorrheal infection. This is a social effect. Whether the baby is lined up in a large, brightly lit, dormitory-style nursery, or is put by the bedside of its mother, will be influenced by social factors. Whether circumcised or not, bound tightly or loosely in swaddling clothes, fed by bottle or breast, will be determined by social and cultural attitudes.

Before proceeding to individual attitudes of the alcoholic, let us review personality development in general. Fundamentally, our concept is one that involves unconscious modalities and influences; it adheres to the theories of infantile sexuality and oral, anal, and genital stages of development. These stages of personality development are the framework within which the evolving personality responds emotionally to early stimuli, thus creating and reinforcing patterns of behavior at a psychological and physiological level. We accept that these patterns of response as they develop become the baseline from which the individual views himself, and from which he eventually views the world; that these patterns tend to become established in the individual in time; and that they operate not only on a psychological level, but also on a physiological and biochemical one.

Physiological response and biochemical response are as much individual reaction as is the emotional response, with which they are intimately intertwined. The infant cannot consciously differentiate between the physical and the emotional. Therefore, as an adult he may have anxiety about not being fed, although he has ample money and food, because of the development of a pattern which started when he was not fed enough as a child. He will have anxiety and physiological and biochemical responses associated with these early patterns of not being fed. Emotional and physical life are tied together as a Gordian knot.

We cannot say at what age or how long it takes for the patterns of emotional and physiological response to become established, since this varies from person to person, but there is strong evidence that fixation occurs early in life. Patterns of response and behavior can be easily established in animal and man, as was demonstrated by the great Russian physiologist, Pavlov.[2] Since the infant starts out relatively free of these patterns and is open to direction, it is easier to influence his behavior than that of the already structured adult. A pathway chosen a number of times becomes familiar and safe; the tendency, then, is to follow it in the future.

Bearing in mind prenatal influences, cultural attitudes, psychological, biochemical, and physiological factors of personality development, let us now look at the make-up of the alcoholic. To help describe the individual attitudes of the alcoholic, we classify alcoholics into two broad categories: the reactive and the addicted.

Reactive or neurotic alcoholics have relatively healthy, integrated pre-alcoholic personalities. They use alcohol to excess when temporarily overwhelmed by external stress. They have made a reasonable adjustment to the demands of family, education, work, and society with reasonably progressive movements toward realistic goals. Excessive drinking is most often associated with observable, external stress situations, usually of short duration. The episode of excessive drinking has a determinable beginning, runs a course consistent with tension release, and may terminate through some measure of control exercised by the individual. Some reactive drinkers become so involved in their neurotic drinking that they approach a state approximating malignant or addicted alcoholism. The level of psychosexual development achieved prior to the onset of the pathological behavior will determine the severity of the alcoholism, the severity of regression, and the response to treatment. We believe anyone may use alcohol pathologically to alleviate anxiety, to make instinctual impulses acceptable, to strengthen defense measures, and to provide narcosis against painful reality; however, most people are protected from alcoholism by a strong personality and by strong cultural protective factors.

The addict, on the other hand, shows grave adjustment difficulties during the years before he became alcoholic, in relations within his family, in school, and in work. There is no clearly defined point where he lost control over drinking; usually a drinking bout is not traceable to any specific and immediate crisis. His "binges" seem to have no rhyme or reason; they usually continue until sickness or stupor ensues, and are usually self-destructive.

In psychoanalytic terms, addictive alcoholism is classified as an oral perversion. This perversion results from traumas that occurred during the earliest stage of psychosexual development, at the time when the individual's means of achieving security and release from tension was through stimulation of the oral cavity. Fixation at this oral level occurs, and it may be strengthened by constitutional factors tending toward increased intensity of oral drives. Much energy is directed toward excesses in drinking, eating, smoking, pill taking, and the like; there is emphasis on the mouth in sexual activity; and there is a predominance of orality in fantasy production. One patient who had been in therapy for five years, when asked by a friend what her therapist looked like, could remember only that he had a beautiful mouth. The alcohol addict gratifies his basic oral wishes directly and without anxiety, so psychiatrists label this method of gratification a perversion rather than a neurotic mechanism. (A neurotic mechanism is a disguised, anxiety-ridden converse of a perversion.)

The reader may well ask if the alcoholic is considered to be in the oral stage only because alcohol is taken through the mouth. The answer is no; the expression of orality in the alcoholic is much more than that. During the oral stage of infancy, the infant feels omnipotent. Whatever he wants, whenever he desires, fulfillment must occur. No person or thing exists outside this soul of the universe—himself. Through his mouth he derives sustenance, expresses hate and love, and exerts his power. It is as though the infant must totally devour all that dares come near. He does not perceive giving figures as separate individuals with separate needs. Rather, all who surround this lovely but selfish animal are there to serve him.

An alcoholic is not too different. Relations do not evolve which are derived from mutual respect, give and take, and recognition of individuality of the other. The relationships of the alcoholic are that of infantile demand. The alcoholic exhibits his oral fixation in his fantasies of omnipotence, his inability to perceive the outside world as a separate reality, his confusion of oral intake with hate and love, and his insatiability.

The fixation at this early level of emotional development is the result of deprivation of a warm, giving, meaningful relationship with a mother figure in infancy—usually because of death, or emotional or physical absence. Many addicted alcoholics we have seen were abandoned illegitimate children. Others were children of psychotic mothers, still others had had a parent die or disappear shortly before or after their own birth, some had parents who were severely alcoholic during the patients' early years. A few had indulgent, overly protective mothers with underlying disguised hostility. Although we are cautious about extrapolating from animal behavior to human reaction, we nevertheless are impressed with the work of Seitz.[3] Seitz reported that kittens suffering early deprivation from their mothers showed low tolerance to frustration and rage, emotional lability, poor adaptation to stress situations, and diminished learning capacity. These responses are not dissimilar to the reactions of alcoholics as we see them. Interestingly, schizophrenics have very similar histories, with similar fantasy and behavioral reactions to their early lives. One of the main reasons the addictive alcoholic does not use frank schizophrenic mechanisms to escape reality is because the significant members of his environment, with whom he relates and identifies, handle their desire to escape via alcohol.

The loss or lack of a meaningful relationship with a mother figure is crucial to our understanding of the motivating unconscious drives of the alcoholic, the first of which is gratification of his primary emotional hunger. Just as the infant seeks through ingestion to quiet the emptiness and soothe the pangs that threaten his security, so does the alcoholic seek this gratification by stimulating the oral mucosa, by absorbing massive amounts of alcohol, and by seeking peaceful oblivion. He thus symbolically attempts to achieve the blissful infantile state. Many patients, after their drinking has become controlled, express their envy of their intoxicated brethren who continue to achieve alcohol-induced oblivion. The main devastating unconscious wish with which the addicted alcoholic must deal is his passive-dependent wish (the helpless state of an infant) for reunion with an all-giving mother figure.

The loss early in life of someone with whom one can relate emotionally is responsible for *depression*, which is the main affect present in the addictive alcoholic. This severe underlying depression, expressed through feelings of emptiness, loneliness, "something important is missing," brings about the use of the main defense mechanism seen in alcoholism, that is, denial. Alcoholics deny their feelings of inferiority, depression, lack of self-respect, and dependence on alcohol. There is no more striking example of this than the intoxicated alcoholic denying that he has any problem. If asked whether he has had a drink, he replies "a little one," another denial. When he is confronted by his intoxicated state, the familiar response is, "I can stop any time I want to." Denial is his main method of dealing with life.

Depression, ever-present and deeply penetrating, pervades all the alcoholic's personality and all his reactions in the search for oblivion. Alcohol for the addict is a simple, easy method of achieving control over feelings of helplessness and deprivation. At the same time, it is a symbolic substitute, something that can be controlled. As one alcoholic put it, "Alcohol is adult mother's milk."

The loss or absence of an object of love during the oral stage of development results in primitive, excessive demands which are ultimately insatiable. Consequently, almost all interpersonal relations eventually result in rejection, which reawakens the original loss and rejection the subject experienced as an infant. The pain, depression, and loss of self-esteem which alcoholics experience reproduce and reawaken the rage experienced by a deprived infant, a rage so intense and all-consuming that the infant will seemingly destroy himself rather than relent. So it is with the alcoholic. The rage is of murderous ferocity and intent, and, rather than destroy another, the alcoholic turns his anger in on himself and consumes himself in drink. As one patient said, "It is more socially acceptable to get stinking drunk than to murder someone."

The addict's fixation at the oral stage suggests a possible explanation for his lack of satiation. In mature love, the instinctual wish is gratified but the object of love is preserved. In the oral stage, instinctual wishes are gratified by incorporation with the object of love, which is thereby destroyed. Each drink, therefore, gratifies the wish for love but at the same time destroys the object of love so that a new one must be found; satiation is never achieved. Hence, for the addictive alcoholic continuous consumption of alcohol is a symbolic acting out of the oral conflict; satisfaction of a basic wish is achieved only by the destruction of an object of love which must be repeatedly replaced.

When we view the psychological make-up of the alcoholic as we have done, we more readily understand his behavior. While from society's point of view behavior is either "good" or "bad," from the individual's point of view it always has some positive value, even though it may appear to others to be totally destructive. The behavior of any individual represents the best resolution of his conflicting drives that he is able at a given time to formulate.

What is the role that alcohol plays in the personality of the addict that goes beyond the superficial desire for tension release? (The fact that alcohol has a special role and fulfills a special need for the alcoholic precludes that all individuals can become alcoholic.) Alcohol fills not a small gap—not a crevasse, but an ocean of emptiness, a bottomless pit, a feeling tone of depression that, fortunately, is known to few. Into this abyss is poured alcohol. This "magical" substance dispels excessive tension and depression. It alleviates a sense of aloneness, provides readily available, instantaneous pleasure, permits a feeling of omnipotence and the mastery and expression of hostile feelings while providing a built-in guarantee of suffering, punishment, and alleviation of guilt. All this feeds back sufficient stress for continued drinking.

Another consideration in the development of alcoholism is the fact that alcoholics often have unusual responses to varying amounts of alcohol intake. (An alcoholic may become amnesic on two drinks or may consume a great amount and not show observable effects.) This has been attributed by others to various physiological aberrations, as yet undetermined, in alcoholism. Since attitudes toward drinking are developed early in life and since there is an intertwining of psycho-physiological responses in personality development, unusual physiological responses should not be surprising. Even before the first sip, the individual has expectations and attitudes toward his drink, and will accordingly respond physiologically and emotionally. An interesting analogy to this response is that of the orthodox Jew eating pork. The Jew may not only respond emotionally but may well have a physiological response of nausea, vomiting, and generalized illness. Certainly, the Jew has no basic disturbed physiological reactions to meat from pigs; his emotionally and culturally developed attitudes help produce them. Similarly, we believe, bizarre physiological responses to alcohol are related to psycho-physical and cultural factors.

It is not merely the role the beverage itself plays for the alcoholic which is important in the etiology of alcoholism, but also the constellation of attitudes surrounding its use. One such attitude is ambivalence. Ambivalence may be defined as the co-existence of opposite feelings which act entirely independently of each other (e.g. hate and love for the same object). Ambivalence exists where there is conflict about the use of alcohol. Where drinking is an integral part of the socialization process, where it is interrelated with moral symbolism and repeatedly practiced in group rites, there is no conflict and alcoholism is conspicuously absent. On the other hand, when a conflict about drinking exists and it is impossible to integrate drinking behavior into a pattern of healthy social drinking, and when drinking is performed outside social contexts (merely to solve emotional problems), the development of alcoholism has great potential.

To understand the force of this ambivalence about drinking,

it is necessary to see how deep rooted it is in American culture, having its origin in the Puritan ethic. The Puritans, who came to America in order to practice their own religion, condemned as evil all things bringing pleasure to the senses. The essence of the ascetic Puritan pattern was hostility toward spontaneous, impulsive enjoyment of life. Accompanying this attitude was the Puritan belief that drinking—even in moderation—led to sexual misbehavior. In spite of a decline in the religious ardor associated with Puritanism, the personality type based on these values became an ideal. The Puritanical ideas were superimposed upon the Anglo-Saxon cultural attitudes (as a whole characterized by heavy alcohol use) of other settlers in America, and produced a conflict in values. This ambivalence, with resulting pressure on the individual, was increased later by the gradual destruction of old cultural barriers coupled with an increase in communication of ideas and attitudes.

The Puritan ethic of conscious control of will, personal sin, and responsibility allows no deviant behavior. Hence, a problem with alcohol results in the individual's rejection and separation from the social group. Group opinion is often a deterrent against excessive drinking; therefore, once isolated, a potential alcoholic is propelled into further unhealthy drinking practices (for example, clandestine drinking) to meet life's problems. The choice of alcohol as a way to deal with these problems can often be traced, as was noted earlier, to the alcoholic's having seen significant members of his environment, emotionally important to him, use alcohol pathologically to handle life's difficulties.

We consider that alcoholism exists when alcohol becomes the main focus of a person's thoughts and emotions, physiology, and environment. The alcoholic will spend an inordinate time in planning where, when, and how he will drink and will go to enormous expense and effort to obtain liquor. He will destroy himself rather than give up alcohol. He will destroy all relation-

POSSIBLE GENETIC FACTORS
AND FACTORS OF PRENATAL
ENVIRONMENT

↓

PSYCHOLOGICAL FACTORS

Trauma of deprivation at oral stage: destruction of self and relationships, anger,
depression, denial, alcohol usage, inability
to reach satiety, attempt to return to infantile
helplessness and passivity through oral gratification and alcoholic depression of nervous
system

↓ ↑

PHYSIOLOGICAL-BIOCHEMICAL
FACTORS

Morbid pattern of physiological and social
stimulation

↓ ↑

INFLUENCE OF MODELS

Seeing significant figures use alcohol in an
unhealthy way

↑ ↓

SOCIO-CULTURAL FACTORS

Practices and attitudes encouraging ambivalence, conflict, and guilt about alcohol use

↑

FUNCTIONS OF ALCOHOL

Expels tension, depression, loneliness; provides immediate pleasure and a means of
expressing and mastering hostility; provides
suffering, punishment, the alleviation of guilt
over hostility, and stress for continued drinking.

ADDICTIVE
ALCOHOLISM

ships, be they family, friend, occupational, or social. Alcohol is his all-consuming goal and everything else including staying alive is secondary. Alcoholism arises from a dynamic interaction of several factors: possible prenatal influences, a personality disturbance of early life, a bizarre physiological response to alcohol, the experience of having seen a significant figure use alcohol in an unhealthy way, and cultural attitudes of conflict and ambivalence toward its use.

II

A Review of Previous Work

Many theorists have claimed that alcoholism is traceable to a specific cause. We strongly believe that no single factor, be it a psychological, physiological, biochemical, or sociological one, can explain addiction. In the previous chapter we discussed the many factors which we believe combine in varying proportions to promote a person's addiction. However, thousands of studies have been made on this subject by anthropologists, sociologists, physiologists, psychologists, and psychiatrists. Definitions and theories have been presented which differ (sometimes just in part) from ours and contradict other theories. We hope it will be interesting for the reader to see how we examined and evaluated these and also how the data studied broadened our understanding of the origins and prevention of alcoholism.

3

Theories of Alcoholism

a. Definitions of Alcoholism

Researchers have sought a definition of alcoholism for some time. In 1879 Maudsley [14] in his book *The Pathology of Mind* discussed "alcoholic insanity," "chronic alcoholism," and "dipsomania." "Dipsomania" he described as a "well-marked form of mental degradation, if not of actual mental derangement, which shows itself in a fierce morbid craving for alcoholic stimulants and is greatly aggravated by indulgence." Although modern workers would question Maudsley's references to degradation, craving, stimulants, and indulgence, the general attitude of his remarks is significant even today.

There are three basic types of definitions of alcoholism, not always clearly differentiated: one deals with causes, and focuses on psychological and/or physiological factors; the second is mainly descriptive and uses social influences as its frame of reference; the third combines the first two and attempts to divide alcoholics into categories.

Typical of the quotations from the literature emphasizing psychological characteristics are the following: "Alcoholism is a type of abnormal mental reaction; alcohol has been found to be an antidote for some obsessions or emotional depressions." [5]

Alcoholism is a "habit of uncontrolled drinking which shows the characteristics of 'malignancy' in relation to the total personality, as comparable to the malignancy of a tumor in relation to the physical organism." [20] The term compulsive drinking is used often. To Menninger [15] alcohol addiction is "a form of self-destruction used to avert a greater self-destruction, deriving from elements of aggressiveness excited by thwarting, ungratified eroticism, and the feeling of a need for punishment from a sense of guilt relative to the aggressiveness." Menninger goes on to point out that the accomplishment of the self-destruction occurs *"in spite of* and at the same time *by means of* the very device used by the sufferer to relieve his pain and avert this feared destruction." Similarly, Knight's [12] definition, presents alcoholism as a psychogenic symptom of a serious personality disorder. In contrast Isikowitz [10] defines alcoholism as a limited pathologic hunger for alcohol.

More and more present-day definitions of alcoholism speak in descriptive social terms rather than causal terms. For example, Seliger [18] in 1941 described alcoholics as people who do not stop drinking either because they are unable or they do not wish to do so, and whose behavior consequently interferes with their life activities. In 1933 Ernst [6] noted that alcoholism is not an isolated unitary disease but a symptom of a general personality and social disturbance. To the American Medical Association, [1] "Alcoholism is a disease which is characterized by a compulsive drinking of alcohol in some form. It is an addiction to alcohol. The drinking of alcohol produces continuing or repeated problems in the patient's life."

Definitions which combine psycho-physiological and social influences are now being offered increasingly: Fleming [7] sees two kinds of excessive drinking: symptomatic drinking and true alcoholic addiction. Barham [3] gives three main clinical divisions: pseudodipsomania, true periodic dipsomania, and chronic alcoholism. Similarly Brocklehurst [4] classifies alcohol addiction into three groups: primary idiosyncrasy to alcohol, secondary compensatory alcoholism, and bipartite alcoholism. Simmel [19] uses his terms quite differently: the social drinker, the reactive drinker, the neurotic drinker, and the alcohol addict. For the social and reactive drinker, Simmel sees alcohol defending the ego against the mental impact of external circumstances. For the neurotic and addict, alcohol defends the ego against the threat of inner unconscious conflicts which only secondarily impair the ego's capacity for coping with reality. Bacon [2] feels that the vast majority of alcoholics fall into two groups: primary and secondary compulsive drinkers.

An illustration of the attempt to divide alcoholics into categories is seen in the recent sophisticated definition of alcoholism in the book *The Disease Concept of Alcoholism* by Jellinek.[11] He has devised a new classification of alcoholics: Alpha, Beta, Gamma, Delta, and Epsilon. Alpha alcoholism is seen by Jellinek as "a purely psychological continual reliance on the effect of alcohol to relieve bodily or emotional pain." Although the drinking of the Alpha alcoholic exceeds the bounds of society, he still has the ability to control his drinking and to abstain. Signs of progression are not evident.

Beta alcoholism represents to Jellinek that species "in which such alcoholic complications as polyneuropathy, gastritis and cirrhosis of the liver may occur without either physical or psychological dependence upon alcohol."

Gamma alcoholism is described as "(1) acquired increased tissue tolerance to alcohol, (2) adaptive cell metabolism, (3) withdrawal symptoms and 'craving,' i.e. . . . physical dependence, and (4) loss of control." Whereas Alpha and Beta alcoholism might not progress, "in Gamma alcoholism there is a definite progression from psychological to physical dependence." This form of alcoholism is the most destructive, personally and socially, and is typical of the patients seen in American alcoholism clinics and AA groups.

Delta alcoholism includes the first three characteristics described in Gamma alcoholism "as well as a less marked form of the fourth characteristic—instead of loss of control there is inability to abstain." Alcoholics who can control the amount of intake but cannot abstain are common in wine-drinking countries, such as France.

Epsilon alcoholism, that is, periodic alcoholism, is described by Jellinek as the least known form of alcoholism. Although Jellinek's study of alcoholism definitions is scholastically valuable, it perpetuates the trend to categorize alcoholics into static groups. We feel that it is more important to visualize alcoholism as arising from multiple and varied components which overlap.

Since many authors refer to the alcoholic as an alcohol addict, an elaboration of the concept of addiction is necessary. Although we have presented briefly our own concept of addiction as it applies to alcoholism, we must examine the views of others before we go on to other aspects of the problem. We have chosen a few studies that seem pertinent.

Wikler,[21, 22] who has done outstanding work in the field of addiction, has differentiated in psychodynamic terms the effects of alcohol and opiates. He suggests that the particular effect of each drug in conjunction with the cultural attitudes will determine the relative prevalence of the type of addiction in a particular setting. For example, in an Occidental culture in which a moderate expression of aggression is valued highly, alcohol intoxication is viewed with amusement, whereas the placidity and diminished aggression induced by opiates are viewed with contempt. In the Chinese culture where Confucian placidity and repressed aggression are highly valued, violence and competitiveness disdained, alcohol intoxication is an abhorrence.

Pfeffer [17] regards alcoholism as an addiction because of these factors: loss of control over alcohol usage, tolerance change, a withdrawal syndrome, and a total relinquishing of all interests in favor of a preoccupation with alcohol and its effects. This viewpoint, as far as it goes, agrees with ours, except for the emphasis on tolerance. Our reason for de-emphasizing tolerance may be illustrated by a short case history. A 35-year-old female alcoholic reported that her first experience with alcohol had been when she was age 8. At that time her mother had concocted a "home brew," and had permitted the patient and her sister, a year younger, to drink some. Her sister became violently sick. The patient, on the other hand, waited until the coast was clear and quickly consumed the entire brew, becoming severely intoxicated. From that early age on, her response was the same. Alcohol intake spelled loss of control, heavy intoxication, and a preoccupation with alcohol and its effects to the total exclusion of everything else. At no time was there any evidence of the development of a tolerance phenomenon. This patient was an alcoholic from the very first sip. This is not an unusual case. When one uncovers and examines the first response of an alcoholic to his first drink, one can usually see that the groundwork for alcoholism already existed.

The above may lend support to Lemere's [13] concept of a "cellular craving for alcohol" (although we do not believe in it). For the minority of alcoholics who have had difficulty with alcohol from the onset of their drinking history, Lemere raises the possibility of hereditary predisposition. For the rest, however, he formulates the cellular craving theory from the idea that the sudden withdrawal of alcohol after prolonged use throws the brain into disequilibrium. He contends that with prolonged use there is an alteration in the metabolic pattern of brain cells, and alcohol may become a necessity for optimum brain function. We feel that Lemere is really describing behavior after a prolonged alcoholic bout, and not the fundamental question of addiction.

Mitscherlich [16] suggests that alcohol addiction is the result of psychopathological disturbances which give rise to exorbitant thirst, and this thirst is psychodynamically substitutive in function. Torturing thirst and excessive drinking are in turn the atonement for and expiation of guilt.

Goldberg [8] feels that alcoholic habituation results from increased tolerance due to a rise of the intoxication threshold in the alcoholic's blood. As we stated earlier with our case history, we do not feel that tolerance plays the significant role ascribed to it in alcohol addiction.

Isbell [9] has probably devoted more effort toward studying addictive processes than any other individual in the United States. He considers addiction as an overpowering desire, need, or compulsion to continue taking a drug, a willingness to obtain it by any means, a tendency to increased dosage, and a psychological and occasionally physical dependence on the drug. Addiction to Isbell is the use of a substance to such a degree that it is detrimental to either the individual or society. The characteristics of addiction as he sees it are tolerance phenomenon (a decreasing effect from repetition of the same drug dose), physical dependence (an altered physiological state requiring continuous consumption of a substance to prevent the appearance of an "abstinent syndrome"), and emotional dependence (the substitution of a substance for other types of adaptive behavior). That emotional dependence is fundamental in the alcohol addict we readily affirm; tolerance and physical dependence, however, do not always seem to us to play a role.

In reviewing the basic definitions and concepts of alcoholism, we have discovered that a wide range of attitudes exist. We now restate our own definition as a point of comparison and frame of reference before proceeding to psychological theories of alcoholism.

Alcoholism, we feel, is a chronic behavioral disorder manifested by undue preoccupation with alcohol to the detriment of physical and mental health; by a loss of control when drinking has begun although it may net be carried to the point of intoxication; and by a self-destructive attitude in dealing with relationships and life situations. Alcoholism is the result of: a disturbance and deprivation in early infantile relations accompanied by related alterations in basic physiochemical responsiveness; the identification by the alcoholic with significant figures who deal with life problems through the excessive use of alcohol; and a socio-cultural milieu that causes ambivalence, conflict, and guilt in the use of alcohol.

b. Psychological Theories of Alcoholism

Freud's charting of a formerly unknown part of the mind to show the role sex or sexual forces play in unconscious motivation left an impact on twentieth-century thinking that is still being felt. One is hard put to attend the theater, read a modern novel, watch a television program, or listen to everyday conversation without encountering the results of his work. When Freud uncovered the unconscious, man could no longer hide from himself. Whether or not one agrees with Freudian concepts of infantile sexuality, Oedipus complex, transference phenomena, one is nevertheless involved with them. To seek below the obvious has become a way of life, expression, and communication.

Freud [6,7] early in his observations turned to the alcoholic. Strong oral influences of childhood (the oral stage being the first stage of psychosexual development) were cited by Freud as a major cause of excessive drinking, and he viewed the alteration of mood by alcohol as its most valuable contribution to the drinker. The mood change, according to Freud, resulted from a redirection of thought processes in the alcoholic, the alcohol providing the impetus for regression to childhood levels of thinking. The individual thereby achieved gratification from thinking that was uncontrolled by logic. This theory considers the use of alcohol as an escape from reality.

The escape concept has taken hold and is described by many authors, and by the many alcoholics who acknowledge it in a self-incriminating way. Jellife,[10] in 1919, developed the escape theory by maintaining that alcohol permits indulgence in the "autoerotic ecstasy of dreaming" instead of facing "tortures which arise from the reality." Parland,[18] in 1957, equated escape in alcoholism with escape in homosexuality.

Both kinds of escape, we agree, in women as well as men, stem from desire to flee one's normal sexual role. But we think that emphasis of the escape phenomenon as the major etiological component of alcoholism is an oversimplification. The alcoholic, like all of us, wants to escape from unpleasant reality. What but escapes are our defenses, our rationalizations? The critical questions are why the choice of alcohol as a means, and why does the escape method cripple the whole personality.

As is the case with any inquiring mind, Freud was not satisfied to rest on his formulation and in later years revised his thinking about the alcoholic.[8] He equated with alcoholism the model of repressed homosexual traits he had used to describe the development of paranoid symptoms, and these traits illustrated the prime psychological turmoil of the addict. Freud maintained that because of the unconscious homosexual wish (related to strong oral influences of childhood), a man succumbed to the pull of the public house, getting from the company of men the emotional satisfaction he could not get from his wife. It was Freud's contention that disappointment by women (wives, mothers, lovers) drove men to drink. Whenever the alcoholic's latent homosexual feelings came to the surface, he repressed them by returning to his wife. In turn, he then suspected his wife of sexual activity with those men he unconsciously loved, thereby developing paranoid symptoms.

Contemporary and later analysts utilized this Freudian formulation and elaborated upon it. For example, Karl Abraham [1] considered the alcoholic as severely frustrated by his mother early in life and hence forced to turn to his father for solace. This resulted in overidentification with his father and the development of homosexual tendencies.

Since alcohol consumption is related to increased sexual excitement, Abraham formulated a popular equation: drinking prowess is the equivalent of sexual prowess. To this day a man who does not drink is viewed by many with suspicion and distrust. Abraham further pointed out that alcohol may substitute for sex, and he likened this substitution to certain sexual perversions such as voyeurism and fetishism. In perversions, stimuli that normally are a part of the foreplay of sex become its major gratification; there is fixation at this preliminary sexual stage. For example, viewing the desired sexual object is but a means of forepleasure leading to culmination in sexual union. For the voyeur, however, complete satisfaction is achieved merely by the looking. Abraham believed the sexual development of the alcoholic was fixated in forepleasure (oral stimulation). Alcohol thus becomes the means of effortless gratification whereby the alcoholic exchanges women for wine.

Although latent homosexuality and confusion in sexual identity may play a significant role in the evolution of problems associated with alcoholism, they do not offer sufficient impetus for the development of so devastating a condition. Much of the psychopathology of alcoholism may be tied to factors commonly seen in the patient with homosexual problems, but these are not only insufficient to be the sole etiological agent for alcoholism; they are often misinterpreted. Since the fixation at the oral stage is so early in psychosexual development, the alcoholic has never achieved a genital level of differentiation and is so desirous of receiving love, he does not differentiate the sex of the provider.

Another important psychoanalytic component of alcoholism often advanced is the self-destructive drive of alcoholics. Menninger [16] in his best seller *Man Against Himself* raised this much-disputed point. It was his contention that generally alcoholics unconsciously have a powerful desire to destroy themselves. Addiction is one means of expressing this unconscious urge which is the result of the child's feeling betrayed by his parents. The frustration arising from the betrayal results in an intense rage toward his parents which in turn causes interpersonal conflict. He wishes to destroy his parents yet he fears losing them. Later in life, alcohol becomes a means of achieving both gratification and revenge against the parents. The feeling of hostility toward parents creates a desire for punishment to alleviate guilt. Therefore, Menninger viewed alcohol addiction as a form of slow suicide used to avert a greater self-destruction.

The concept of self-destructive urges in alcoholism has recently been challenged by McCord [14] and his group in their longitudinal studies of pre-alcoholics and non-alcoholics. They expected to find, if the self-destructive etiological concept was correct, a higher incidence of suicidal trends in the pre-alcoholic than in the non-alcoholic. This was not borne out in their study.

Irrespective of these findings about suicide, our experience with alcoholics has revealed that most of their relations, endeavors, and goals have been self-destructive. The continuous, unbroken thread always runs in the direction of the alcoholic's unconsciously doing himself harm. Hence, it is not the alcohol wedded specifically to suicidal attempts or thoughts which emphasizes the alcoholic's self-destructive drives, but rather the total life pattern of aggression and hostility directed inward. Only by taking into consideration this all-encompassing self-destructiveness that pervades every facet of the alcoholic's personality can one understand the total intensity of this etiological factor.

Many theorists have elaborated on Freud's original oral concept, and oral fixation has also been incriminated as the sole cause of alcoholism. For example, Knight [12,13] was of the opinion that the predominance of oral craving is especially significant in the alcoholic. He attributes the oral fixation to specific early family experiences: an indulgent mother and an inconsistent father he sees as the most common family configuration. A child overly indulged by a permissive mother, according to Knight, cannot learn self-control and reacts with intense rage to every frustration. This capacity for rage is fed by an inconsistent father who unpredictably gratifies at one time and denies at another. In such a family the attitudes of the mother and father tend to reinforce one another. This pattern of dependence, rejection, and intense desire for indulgence is built into the personality, associated with deep feelings of inferiority and guilt. During puberty, there is an intensification of envy of masculine prowess as exemplified by the father, and drinking becomes regarded as "manly." The child begins to drink, and his drinking in time becomes anti-social with concomitant defiance of parental wishes. This pathological behavior develops out of an unresolved adolescent revolt. The pharmacological effects of alcohol reinforce irresponsible behavior, and ultimately others are forced to take care of the imbiber in his passive, drunken stupor.

If Knight's contentions concerning the typical family producing alcoholics are correct, then we must prepare for an invasion of alcoholics in unbelievable numbers. In mid-twentieth-century America (and, we suspect, in other affluent societies as well), mothers are primarily directed toward overindulging the needs of their children. With the commuting father in and out of the home like a surreptitious lover, his influence and attitude are limited and inconsistent. Fortunately such parental influences appear not to be a major contributing factor in alcoholism.

Tiebout [21] incriminated the unconscious need to dominate as a strong motivating force of the alcoholic. Along with this need are found hostile attitudes, feelings of loneliness and isolation, and ambivalent perceptions of inferiority and superiority. With these deprived and conflicting feelings the alcoholic, according to Tiebout, strives for perfection and craves "ecstatic peaks." The striving for perfection we feel is an important concept, as it may be the means by which the alcoholic assures himself of certain and continuous failure.

The Adlerian school of "individual psychology" evolved their own concept of the alcoholic.[3] They attributed addiction to a desire of the individual to remove powerful feelings of inferiority while escaping responsibilities. To Adler,[2] feelings of inferiority were the root of all alcoholic problems. Inferiority might be overtly expressed or be hidden behind the screen of superiority. Marked shyness, a preference for isolation, impatience, irritability, anxiety, depression, hypersensitivity, and sexual insufficiency may herald the onset of an addiction. "Boastfulness, malicious criminal tendency, a longing for power," Adler maintained might be the symptoms of addiction when the superiority complex was the adaptive mechanism employed. He contended that alcoholism is the result of childhood pampering. Overindulgence and excessive coddling result in the individual's inability to face up to the frustrations of adult reality, and this in turn leads to inferiority feelings. The alcoholic then attempts to counter the demands of society by the use of alcohol. It is not difficult to see that the traits Adler listed are quite universal and in no way specific to alcoholism.

The contention that alcoholics are children of pampering

mothers has been the theme of many psychologists and psychiatrists. Although overindulgence may be seen to play a role in some histories of alcoholics, our experiences and that of others do not support the thesis that it plays the major role. On the contrary, the addicted alcoholics we have studied have more often come from neglecting mothers. Emotional and physical deprivation were the order of the day, pampering a less frequent occurrence. Since analytical investigation has been economically feasible only for the higher socio-economic groups and our clinic patients are from the middle and lower social classes, the different findings may be a concomitant of social class variables.

An elaboration of the Adlerian view by Schilder [19] attributes alcoholism to a perpetual state of insecurity from earliest childhood. This insecurity is related to parental associations. The child, in Schilder's formulation, has been pushed deeper and deeper into an insecure abyss by ridicule, by passivity, by threat, by corporal punishment, and by degradation. Although the threats originally came from one or both parents, the child learns to expect them, and soon sees the community as threatening him in a similar way. Social tension and insecurity are thereby heightened. In adult life, alcohol dissolves this painful situation, generating feelings of social acceptability and security while the individual is intoxicated. With the disappearance of that mood, the original feelings return with increased vigor and demand renewed drinking. Schilder felt that the alcoholic suffers deeply from his social insufficiency. He is unable to establish a close relationship with other human beings and is aware of it. He claims and expects special favors, appreciation, and love. Schilder says the love the alcoholic feels for his own body and intellect he hungers for from others. The constant social tension developed from this desire is only relieved through alcohol, which permits him the feelings of being lovable and loved. The Schilder thesis concerning social insecurity does not answer why all socially insecure people who drink do not become addictive drinkers.

Strecker [20] fits alcoholism into an introvert-extrovert axis. The introverted personality, with its inwardly directed drives accompanied by social uneasiness, is able to lubricate with alcohol its social capacities. By the continuous use of alcohol in social interaction, an alcohol addiction based on an introverted psychoneurosis develops. Although there is admittedly a great deal of drinking by the outward-oriented extrovert with social ease, Strecker considers this a use of alcohol to heighten pleasures of reality. Strecker believes that "even in more or less normal social drinking, alcohol quickly dissolves for the drinker the garments of social responsibility and years." With addictive drinking, regression is to more primitive levels of helplessness, with loss of control and fantasy involvement.

This thesis implies that the potential for alcohol addiction exists for all individuals, that given sufficient, continuous intake of alcohol, regression may occur to make anyone alcoholic. This does not agree with many interdisciplinary observations of the problem. The Jewish and Italian cultures have their fair share of introverts and extroverts and continuous alcohol users, yet as the numerous studies we shall note reveal, they have negligible alcoholism. We know that alcohol lubricates social intercourse in most cultures. If alcohol consumption is the cause of alcoholism, no one is safe, and we had best bring back the Prohibition era. It seems to us that Strecker confuses the alcoholic with the heavy social drinker, as well as with the schizoid individual who uses alcohol as one of many defenses.

Björk [4] introduces a new concept in the etiology of alcoholism when he considers addiction as a defect of superego development and therefore as a moral question. He contends that the alcoholic has a partial responsibility for his illness, which should be viewed in its sado-destructive aspects as a crime. On the surface it would appear that the municipal and state governments in the United States agree with him, since "drunkenness" is our most frequent criminal offense.

It seems strange that we must still bring moral questions into the etiology of alcoholism. The role of scientific investigation is to make observations and derive facts. To introduce moral judgment serves only to lower the self-respect of patients who are already practically deprived of it. We cannot understand how anyone can blame the alcoholic for being what he is any more than the cardiac, tubercular, diabetic, or mentally ill patient. Individuals have no control over the circumstances that give them their heredity, sex, physical being, environment, religion, and ethnic group. We do not wish to ignore issues of morality where they are germane, but we feel that they do not enter into the etiology of alcoholism or any other disease.

The "craving concept" of alcoholism introduces another major theory. Meerloo [15] described certain steps culminating in addiction when he maintained that the initial intake of alcohol is associated with a general urge for pleasure, elation, and release. With continued consumption of the drug, there develops an artificial ecstasy, a craving and a compulsion to repeat the experience symbolized by intoxication. When craving becomes specific and is reinforced by pharmacological dependence, then addiction exists. Meerloo maintains that the personality of alcoholics is usually of the manic-depressive type. The common bonds of all addiction are a craving for ecstatic experience, an unconscious drive for self-destruction, and an unresolved unconscious need for oral dependency. Ecstasy is defined as a feeling of pleasure increased beyond a certain "threshold of rationality."

The particular concept of craving for alcohol was the subject of the World Health Organization Expert Committee on Mental Health and Alcohol symposium held in 1954. We will discuss the views of seven members of the committee. Jellinek,[11] in this symposium, pointed out that psychiatrists tend to avoid the word craving because of the strong connotation of narcotic addiction. To avoid blunting the meaning, the psychiatrists have settled on the word compulsion to indicate the specific desire for alcohol exhibited by the alcoholic. This specific concept of craving in alcoholism derives from the observation that when the alcoholic takes one drink, the aftermath frequently is a drinking bout or bouts associated with insatiable and uncontrollable desire. On the other hand, Jellinek feels that rather than seeking a specific substance, the alcoholic seeks intoxicating effects, and that any other substance might satiate him equally successfully. This would negate the idea of a specific appetite for alcohol. Instead, the alcoholic builds up a desire to feel different, to experience a seemingly glorious effect, knowing that alcohol can do this for him. As added proof against specific craving, Jellinek paints the well-known picture of the alcoholic during custodial care having most of his dependency needs gratified, seeming no longer to desire alcohol, but, upon release from care, needing it again.

Isbell [11] on the other hand took an opposing view to Jellinek's idea of craving. Isbell firmly believes that alcohol withdrawal symptoms are physiologically determined and it is only the coloring or shading of these symptoms that results from psychological factors. He also states that after prolonged abstinence there may no longer exist a physiological requisite for alcohol. The psychological craving arises from a combination of psychiatric and cultural factors with particular emphasis on the latter. An individual with a given set of psychological problems, raised in a culture which frowns upon alcohol, will be less likely to use it to excess than the individual with the same problems raised in a culture which openly tolerates its excess. In other words, although psychiatric factors are of prime import, less exposure to alcohol will result in less intake. Therefore, according to Isbell, the craving for alcohol occurs by chance and because of its ready availability. This contention is supported by the observation that not everyone with personality problems becomes alcoholic, since not everyone uses the same adaptive mechanisms.

The third panel member, Lundquist,[11] approached the concept of craving with the premise that alcohol is used universally because it is a tension reducer. He stated that any activity which easily lessens anxiety tends to become a habit. The ultimate strength of the habit according to Lundquist will depend on the degree of anxiety prompting a search for tension release. Therefore, under appropriate circumstances, a psychological need may intensify to such an extent as to establish a real craving for alcohol. To Lundquist the craving for alcohol is not a continuous but a variable phenomenon. Drinkers—with or without addiction—have a critical point beyond which craving will become manifest; the same individual will reach his particular critical craving point with varying amounts at varying times. Consequently, craving for alcohol in Lundquist's formulation is a learned need, and the intra-individual resistance to the craving depends on the "psychic powers of resistance and on the strength of motives which can be mobilized against drinking." He therefore maintains that the individual's state of health and social or environmental circumstances will play significant roles in the development of a craving for alcohol.

The craving concept for alcohol is completely and utterly rejected by Tiebout.[11] His approach, therapeutic in orientation, is that the concept of craving can be used by alcoholics disadvantageously as an excuse to drink, or to maintain that they suffer an uncontrollable hunger. Therefore, in Tiebout's eyes, the word *craving* implies a conscious longing, a disastrous succumbing to superficial temptation. He would rather describe this need as a compulsion because this term introduces and emphasizes the powerful unconscious elements which Tiebout feels are operating. To him, conscious craving has little to do with addictive drinking.

Duchêne,[11] another member of the symposium, assigns the major role in craving to a personality disorder, while to Mardones,[11] craving is an "overpowering, urgent desire," to obtain a supply of energy or to alleviate withdrawal symptoms. MacLeod [11] completed the symposium by noting the possibilities for research in craving.

We have presented the views of the symposium without comment. This is to allow the reader to see the pendulum swings of ideas even among learned and experienced men. Jellinek and Tiebout on one hand reject craving as a concept in alcoholism. Isbell holds a dual banner—psychological and physiological craving—while Lundquist and Duchêne incriminate mainly psychological forces in the craving controversy. Mardones and MacLeod emphasize the physio-pathological processes as the soil of craving. And so it goes. The final conclusion of the committee, with which we agree, was that craving is a poor concept since, owing to its everyday connotation, significant meaning is lost. We agree that a more effective approach would be to look at the need for alcohol with respect to the onset of excessive alcohol use, drinking patterns during the acute alcohol bout, relapses into new bouts after long abstinence, continuous daily drinking, and loss of control.

The ever-present female has been indicted in the etiology of male alcoholism. Duchêne [5] has shown that significant numbers of male alcoholics are married to women chronologically older than themselves. This phenomenon illustrates the need for mothering or a return to the breast in alcoholism. Navratil [17] carried the female role further. He states that the mother relationship of alcoholics was either one of early deprivation or of excessive indulgence. When a wife was eventually chosen, she was usually one who was motherly and domineering.

Sexual life with her was sparse, with either frigidity, lack of interest, or active dislike. Therefore, Navratil considers alcoholism a psychological disturbance of married life, rooted in a psychological disturbance of childhood.

Multifactored influences in alcoholism are considered by Gibbins and Zwerling. Gibbins [9] relates alcoholism to an abnormal relationship with parents—an over-abundance of love for one, terror of the other, with rejection or overprotection of the child. Gibbins considers that the "psychological crime of 'parental loving-dominance' is perpetrated against the child." When the child reaches an age where society expects maturity and adult behavior, his emotional stunting has resulted in unsuccessful adaptive attempts. According to Gibbins, alcohol is chosen by chance to ease the psychological pain of social maladjustment. Since alcohol is the least socially reprehensible and most readily available evader of reality, it is chosen by the deviant over other tabooed behavior.

Zwerling [22] also chooses a multiple-factor approach to alcoholism. He views the traits of the alcoholic as "dynamic intertwined character processes constituting a single pattern, variable both in severity and in the relative prominence of the constituent elements." A disruptive mother-child relationship in the early part of life sets in motion abnormal developmental trends and is a prime mover in alcoholism. These trends culminate in the multiple characterological symptoms associated with the alcoholic. The characterological structure is not unique to alcoholism, and Zwerling believes it to be "necessary, but not sufficient, in the etiology." "Variations in cultural attitudes towards drinking are conceived as the crucial co-variable. Where permissive and utilitarian attitudes prevail, then relatively mild adaptive disorders may progress into an addictive cycle; where, conversely, cultural attitudes arouse powerful counteranxiety, more severe character disorders are required to initiate an addictive cycle. Physiological factors may additionally enter in as factors altering the initial readiness to addiction through a state which is specifically relieved by alcohol. It is far less doubtful that prolonged drinking produces distressing physiological symptoms which are relieved by further drinking, and that these physiological disturbances enter significantly into the total pathology of the addictive cycle."

The panoramic sweep of psychological theories we have presented reveals some ill-thought-through impressions, speculations, and condemnations, and some far-reaching and perceptive theories. We have integrated into our theory of etiology those concepts which we feel are pertinent to an understanding of alcoholism. We shall show that through this understanding the rehabilitative method is strengthened, and more effective means of prevention are possible.

c. Learning Theories and Biochemical Studies in Alcoholism

In this section we discuss the contributions of the learning theorists and biochemists to the etiology of alcoholism. The learning theorist and the biochemist have in common the frequent use of animal experimentation. We do not imply that learning theorists are not concerned with emotions and feelings but merely that their approach to understanding personality development is different from those psychodynamic ones examined in the previous section. Since their studies are related to animal experimentation, we shall discuss them with biochemical studies.

LEARNING THEORY

In examining observations of the learning theorists, we feel it essential to point out that the learning theorists who have written on alcoholism are of the "reinforcement school." The theorists focusing on cognitive factors have not yet written about alcoholism.

Before examining more intensively the contribution of learning theorists to the etiology of alcoholism, we shall mention briefly a few of the basic concepts of the system. The general factors of the reinforcement school are: A drive sets in motion responses, which are also influenced by cues from other stimuli not sufficiently strong to operate as drives but more specifically differentiated than a drive. When a response is not rewarded by a reaction diminishing the drive, this response has a tendency to disappear, letting others materialize. "The extinction of successive non-rewarded responses produces so-called random behavior." When a response is succeeded by a reward, the relation between cue and this response is strengthened. As a result the next time an identical drive and other cues are present, this response will more likely occur. "This strengthening of the cue-response connection is the essence of learning."

Dollard and Miller,[2] both of the Hullian school of psychology, view a neurosis as "functional" and a result of experience rather than of damage to instincts. The learning theorist, according to Dollard and Miller, prefers the principle of reinforcement (reward) to Freud's pleasure principle.

In discussing alcoholism, they point out that alcohol tends to result in a temporary reduction of fear and conflict, although ultimately it produces a state of "misery." Therefore, reinforcement theories hold that the attempt to adapt to fear and conflict may be the cause of an alcoholic's drinking. They do state, however, that reinforcement theory as it is presently understood does not furnish all the necessary answers for the question of alcoholism development. We agree with their hesitation. It has been our experience that in some social drinkers and alcoholics, alcohol has tended to increase rather than to decrease tension.

The reinforcement principle in alcoholism is elaborated by Schoben [13] who feels alcohol is used to handle anxiety because of its ready availability and the learned response of the first drinking experience. Conger [1] sees reinforcement occurring when alcohol removes "fear-motivated restraints" while Kinghan [4] theorizes that alcohol disintegrates complicated neurotic patterns, permitting simple "goal-oriented" responses to take over.

Ullman [15] contributed significantly by suggesting that the formation of addiction depends upon a psychological state created in part by the sociological variables involved in attitudes toward drinking. This is coupled, according to Ullman, with the "physiological fact" of the tension-reducing effect of alcohol. Ullman proposes that an individual who is highly motivated to drink will become addicted, that is, an individual who suffers emotional arousal (ambivalence) in regard to drinking, who often drinks during stressful situations, and who achieves a tension-reducing effect by drinking. Ullman goes on to suggest that altering the habit systems of the alcoholic by substituting other tension-reducing activities for drink can help the alcoholic. He adds that this will eliminate the need to search for " 'underlying causes' of alcoholism which probably do not exist."

We have presented the views of some learning theorists as they apply to alcoholism. We agree that there are phases of learning in the development of alcoholism. The alcoholic must have had a pre-alcoholic period of learning during which attitudes toward alcohol and drinking were formulated from his external environment. Also, with the first, and with subsequent drinking experiences, there is further "learning" in relation to his internal environment as well as the external. What we object to, however, is the concept of alcoholism as a simple habit, conditioned reflex, or purely learned response. If this concept were accurate, then we could very likely habituate, condition, or teach many people to become alcoholic. Such a possibility does not correlate with our clinical observations. As we shall see from preliterate and literate societies, there are many communities with potential for "learning" alcoholism—some produce alcoholics, some do not. Furthermore, if habit, reflex, or response were the sole cause, then treatment would be simple. We could then create the habit of abstinence. Any observer of alcoholics knows that once an individual has been an alcoholic, he must always guard against alcohol. This is true after he has abstained five, ten, twenty, or thirty years. Certainly, if habit, conditioning, or learning and reinforcement were the major components, it should be possible for the learned response of controlled drinking to replace the learned response of uncontrolled drinking.

Ullman's contention that "underlying causes" probably do not exist and that drinking is for release of tension only, also appears to be limited. No individual who works with alcoholics can help but be impressed with the multitude of serious emotional problems that existed in the alcoholic prior to his addiction. Although alcohol may relieve tension for the social drinker, its role in alcoholism, as we have noted, is far more serious and significant. The devastation resulting from the alcoholic's use of alcohol far surpasses any possible relief he may derive from tension release, when long-range effects are considered.

In reviewing briefly the work of learning theorists in alcoholism, we have noted that those who focus on cognitive factors are not represented because they have not written on the subject. We suggest that if cognitive factors were introduced into an understanding of alcoholism, the needed linkage between the psychoanalytic, the learning, and other personality theories might evolve.

One other area of research, seemingly the province of learning theorists, has not been dealt with: the whole area of habit extinction. In other words, if alcoholism is a consequence of habit formation, the proper therapeutic approach might be "deconditioning" or habit extinction. Since there is no evidence that such a therapeutic endeavor has been attempted, we should like to recommend that it be considered by those psychologists best able to manage the problem, the learning theorists.

Our final conclusion is that, although the learning theorists have contributed much to an understanding of alcoholism, they have neglected to pay sufficient attention to other forces operating in the alcoholic.

PHYSIOLOGICAL THEORIES AND ANIMAL STUDIES

As the learning theorists, the biochemists have received much of their experimental support from animal studies. The classical experiment of Masserman and Yum [7,8] is the one most frequently cited, and hence we shall describe it in detail. Sixteen cats were trained to open a box for food pellets. Since a delay was introduced into the opening of the box, the cats were trained to manipulate another switch which activated the necessary signals. The periods of training ranged from six to twenty days, and the cats were used in pairs. One cat of a pair always became dominant. After behavior and dominant-submissive patterns were well established, alcohol was given in various doses, and the behavior of the animals was studied under a shock and under the influence of alcohol. Subsequently stimuli were introduced to develop hunger-fear motivational conflict, and once the conflict and "cat neuroses" were established, alcohol was again given.

Masserman and Yum's results show that in the normal, or "preneurotic" cat, alcohol causes excitement and exaggerated movements; fewer learned responses were displayed. As the effects of the varied doses wore off, prior responsiveness returned by stages. Sober cats were considered to be neurotic when they refused to manipulate the switch or approach the food, or when they lost interest in capturing mice placed in the apparatus. With alcohol, however, amelioration of neurotic behavior occurred, i.e. the latest learned, neurotic patterns were forgotten and the cats could flip the switch without suspicion. Alcohol produced in the "neurotic" cats the same disorganization and regression to primitive goal-directed responses as in the "normal" cats. As the alcohol effect disappeared, neurotic reactions reappeared.

In a choice between plain milk or milk with alcohol, the cats showed interesting responses. Neurotic cats chose the container with alcohol more often than did the normal ones. After recovery from their neuroses, their desire for alcohol abated. With reinstitution of their neuroses, the cats showed a renewed preference for alcohol.

Masserman and Yum's conclusions from these experiments were that an organism had to experience satisfaction of a need before "behavior directed toward its recurrent satiation became adaptively patterned." They acknowledge the pharmacological effect of alcohol as a cortical depressant, and the fact that a neurotic animal whose environment has become threatening may welcome relief by any drug that blurs anxiety-creating apperceptions. These authors also discuss prolonged tension release resulting in addiction. It is at this point that most behaviorists have interpreted the findings of these workers as a confirmation for habit formation in addiction. We emphasize the initial need which incorporates alcohol into the dynamic emotional system of the individual as well as into the complex social milieu in which he lives.

Masserman [9] in a more recent article discussed alcohol's role in preventing trauma. He stressed the point, with which we agree, that a great many factors influence the effects of any single drug on an organism at a particular moment. Therefore, the action of a given dose of a drug is believed to vary not only in different animals, but in the same animal at different times. Masserman suggests: "It is impossible to state the effects of any drug on any organism without considering the latter's genetic characteristics, past experiences, and biological status, and its perceptions about motivations toward and evaluations of its current physical and social milieu. Clinical considerations indicate that these qualifications and contingencies as to all pharmacological action apply particularly to the problems of alcoholism in humans."

A similar study was done by Conger.[1] He designed his experiment to test the assumption that the behavior observed by Masserman and Yum was simply an approach-avoidance conflict, and that alcohol reduces the fear that motivates avoidance. In Conger's experiments he trained and tested rats in a simple approach-avoidance situation (a lighted alley with food, ultimately giving them an electric shock at their goals). Five minutes after a placebo injection, the rats would not approach the food-shock end of the alley. Five minutes after an injection of alcohol, the rats ran up to get the food.

Conger further tested his thesis to determine whether the alcohol-strengthened approach was habit for alcohol or was based on hunger, on a weakened-avoidance habit, or on fear. By a technique of harnessing the rats and measuring their pulls toward or away from a goal, he was able to deduce that alcohol reduced the strength of the fear without significantly affecting hunger.

Conger, therefore, contends that alcohol may produce a decrease in the learned drive for fear-motivated avoidance, while having little effect upon the primary drive of hunger-motivated approach. Further, Conger feels that alcohol tends to decrease the strength of learned drives by leaving primary drives essentially unaffected.

Other animal experimenters drew different conclusions.

Weiss [16] found that rats intoxicated by alcohol are better able to resolve a conflict than non-intoxicated rats. Richter [12] was unsuccessful in his attempt to produce addiction in rats by forced prolonged ingestion of alcohol.

The idea of nutritional disturbances has played an important role in the thinking of animal experimenters in the etiology of alcoholism. Westerfield [17] reports that restricted food intake of rats resulted in a marked increase in the voluntary consumption of alcohol, while Mardones [6] found that rats who suffered a deficiency of vitamin B increased their intake of alcohol. To Mardones, these findings confirmed the "genetotropic" theory of the etiology of alcoholism advanced by Williams and his group. [19,20] Because Williams and his co-workers found that they could control the appetite for alcohol of mice and rats, they concluded that alcoholism developed as a result of nutritional deficiencies, widely different deficiencies contributing directly or indirectly in the appetite for alcohol. Williams goes on to maintain that abundant satisfaction of every nutritional need abolishes this appetite. He says that the satisfaction of every need will yield better "results" and that consistently good nutrition from childhood on seems to lessen the likelihood of the development of alcoholism. People who become alcoholics at an early age are those with unusually high requirements for some specific food factor, and their deficiencies show up earlier. Williams believes that refined foods contribute to "physiological perversion." Popham [10] and Wexberg,[18] among others, have criticized this formulation. In terms of evaluation of supporting data, statistical analysis, and methodological approach, Williams's work leaves much to be desired.

Lester and Greenberg [5] attempted to test nutritional deficiencies and alcohol intake. They felt that the nutritional or genetotropic hypothesis of alcoholism was drawn from inadequate evidence. They pointed out that even when the alcohol intake of rats is large, they space their drinking so as to avoid reaching intoxication. The authors conclude that if there is a basis for the genesis of alcoholism in man, "it will probably not be found in concepts restricted to the field of nutrition." These authors point out the dangers of drawing conclusions too readily from animal studies and applying them uncritically to the field of human behavior.

Other physiological theories are expressed by Himwich,[3] who regards alcoholism as resulting from structural physiological aberrations whereby the cells of the body and particularly those of the brain appear to function better in the presence of alcohol than in its absence. Randolph [11] incriminates a "masked food allergy" (a decrease or abolition of unpleasant symptoms immediately following ingestion of a food to which a patient is sensitive). He feels that in a masked allergy the individual develops a craving for foods to which he is specifically sensitized because their intake temporarily relieves his symptoms of discomfort. Our clinical experience does not support in any way an allergic cause of alcoholism, nor do we subscribe to the theory.

Smith [14] has proposed a theory which contends that alcoholism is a genetically transmitted metabolic defect of the adrenal glands.

We have attempted in this section to scan briefly theories other than the sociological and psychological pertaining to the etiology of alcoholism. We recognize that others have been excluded, but the sample presented here should illustrate to the reader the diversity of opinion as to the cause of alcoholism. We feel that so wide and diversified a body of opinion on possible etiological factors merely reflects that alcoholism is still an open field of inquiry. This chapter further emphasizes the difficulties in establishing single-cause theories.

In closing this discussion, one other point about the use of alcohol seems pertinent. Some individuals contend that they are unable to drink because their physiological system rejects alcohol. We know of no data which substantiate disturbed physiological responses. Our opinion is that such reactions are psychological defenses, that the individual has a psychological conflict about the use of alcohol, and rejects alcohol by means of a physical symptom.

4

Drinking and Alcoholism in Different Cultures

By using cultural histories, we wish to show the reader the range of alcohol use and non-use in various ethnic and religious groups. From this perusal, it will be obvious that how, where, when, why, with whom, and how much we drink are factors that cannot be fixed as individually significant in alcoholism. Because many of the so-called signs of alcoholism are part of the acceptable drinking patterns of some cultures, an examination of these patterns is useful in understanding how alcohol is fitted into a system of maintaining psychological and social equilibrium. Such a study will also throw light on preventive approaches to be discussed later.

a. Preliterate Societies

Alcohol is readily available to any society. We have assumed that the invention of alcoholic beverages probably occurred at about the same time as the discovery of agriculture. Wine may accidentally have become available prior to the evolution of agriculture merely from the storage of wild grapes, with their fermentation and resulting crude exudate. Distillation of spirits, on the other hand, is a relatively modern undertaking, only some 2000 years old.

Many substances have been used as sources of alcoholic beverages.[3] For example, fruit, honey, various saps of plants, milk, and grains have at one time or another been used. The maguey plant of Mexico not only is useful in making rope and medicines, but also is the source of tequila and pulque, a bitter beer. So we can see how the preliterate could turn to alcohol even in a roaming and herding stage of development, but especially when he settled down to an agricultural level of civilization.

In our study of drinking patterns, we shall begin by looking at preliterate primitive societies. We cannot look at all of them so we have taken a sample. The direction of our study runs like a line through the American continents, beginning at the north, ending in the south.

THE ALEUTS

Living in the barren, frigid locale of Nikoleski, the Aleuts,[1] or Eskimos of the Arctic, form a small and isolated community. Their economy, dependent on the sea, is occasionally supplemented by sheep ranching, and is essentially unstable; their health is generally poor. In everyday, sober life they are tactful, circumspect, and emphasize control of emotions.

During the eighteenth and nineteenth centuries, the Russians introduced alcohol to the Aleuts. In spite of Aleut folklore, which refers to beverages that may have had an alcohol content, no evidence has been unearthed to indicate that they had it before this. Piva, the Russian beverage adopted, is a malt beer fermented from a vegetable called mitten.

Ordinarily the Aleuts drink only at parties attended by men and women, who are usually the same age. Since piva must be prepared ahead of time, planning is necessary. When party time finally comes, the objective is to get drunk. Weeping, laughing, showing of affection and resentment, and even physical violence are common, contrary to acceptable sober behavior. Since children and sober people guard the drinkers, accidents rarely occur, and if they do they are minor. Eventually the partygoers pass out. If when they awaken piva remains, the drinking begins again.

The Aleut's first drink usually takes place in early adolescence at a party and usually at the urging of friends. This first experience is followed by increasing participation in parties between ages 15 and 18. Drinking is always for fun, yet most Aleuts express concern for the indirect effects of noise, inconvenience, and possible damage and injuries which might result. There is no social pressure to discontinue drinking, but some Aleuts voluntarily resolve to give it up; this is seldom more than temporary.

Alcohol use by the Aleuts is primarily integrative, in that it allows for the relaxation of inhibitions without moral condemnation. It is one of the few forms of acceptable, readily available relief of tension. The Aleuts have adopted a Russian alcohol beverage and the Russian custom of drinking to excess (without Russian pathology).

According to Berreman [1] it would seem that Aleuts, like many other preliterate groups, are less intoxicated than they appear. In any case there is no known alcoholism. Sometimes relatively mild disapproval is expressed when drinking results in behavioral excesses, but as best ascertained, no guilt feelings or ambivalence about drinking exist.

A new factor has recently come into play which may have significance for the future of the Aleuts' drinking behavior. In recent years the United States government has been sending them school teachers, some of whom condemn the drinking behavior of the parents as immoral and uncivilized. This attitude, if accepted by the Aleuts, may lead to feelings of resentment, fear, and shame, ultimately creating unfavorable group attitudes of ambivalence and guilt, and thus opening one of the doors to alcoholism.

THE SALISH INDIANS

Following our line southward, we come upon three Salish Indian tribes of British Columbia studied by Lemert.[4] These tribes support themselves by fishing and logging. Their resources are meager.

The role model for children is one of restrained behavior. This is coupled with passive, shy, and timid attitudes, although aggressiveness persists and may become visible. Most problems arise out of family interaction, especially in husband-wife conflict. This marital conflict, forming an integral part of Salish life, has been heightened recently by a growing independence of women. The Salish society has been plagued, however, by the superordinate status of the white man and his superimposed bureaucratic and governmental control. The white men were responsible for the introduction of alcohol in the forms of whiskey and rum. Today, with their limited means, the Salish tribes use mostly home brew of a low alcohol content.

Alcohol became integrated with Salish culture in the competitive standards of the potlatch ceremony.[9] The potlatch was a winter ceremony, during which gifts were given. The person giving the most received the most respect and status, because for these people prestige comes from public disposal of wealth. The ceremony was accompanied by drinking, dancing, feasting, and boasting. With the influx of Roman Catholic missionaries, the role of alcohol changed; the potlatch ceremony was condemned as socially destructive. As a consequence new drinking behavior developed which combines the with the new.

The Salish drink to get drunk. Drinking is informal ar

sional. At the New Year, all caution is thrown to the winds; drinking and dancing go on from three to six days. The Indians pass their brew from person to person, until the supply is exhausted. They stagger, sway, laugh, and shout, with a boisterousness very opposite to their sober state. Most striking are outbursts of aggression even after small amounts of alcohol intake, especially among younger Indians. These have on occasion resulted in violent deaths. Uncommon sexual misbehavior sometimes accompanies intoxication.

Among these Indians, the ability to obtain and consume alcoholic beverages brings high status and prestige, and purchase of distilled spirits symbolizes the height of economic success. Local white opinion is highly critical of Indian drinking practices, but the Indian community itself does not ordinarily impose penalties on extreme drinking behavior, since all adults are at times involved in drunken episodes.

Drinking parties for the Salish offer opportunities for collective undertakings and experiences and permit continuity with old cultural values. Since drinking is essentially an in-group activity, myths and folklore are retold, and songs with strong cultural significance are sung. Old pagan practices return and conflict directly with newer Roman Catholic ones.

The Salish tribes are groups in conflict. Complete integration with the dominant white culture has been avoided, and though many old behavioral patterns have been discarded, only in part have new cultural values been established. Drinking is an attempt to adopt the behavior of the whites, except that the Indians over-react and exaggerate the response. Although there has been no specific mention of alcoholism among the Salish, the tendency toward a compulsive need for alcohol with intoxication could well be near alcoholism. What most likely exists are some pathological excesses mixed with some anti-social drinking behavior.

THE MOHAVE

The next group we study is the Mohave society, an Indian tribe, located in a part of Arizona that borders on Mexico. The Mohaves are primarily farmers. As Devereux [2] has stated, the Mohave gives great respect to the man who combines gentleness with stoic courage. For the Mohave, sexual indulgence is of major interest and is a culturally accepted pattern of behavior. Generosity is a cardinal virtue. Aggression is not displayed against whites.

Alcohol came to the Mohave as an important commodity during the latter half of the nineteenth century. White settlers introduced it, although later the United States government prohibited its sale to Indians. As the Indians seldom had much money, they were rarely able to ignore the prohibition law and purchase large amounts of illegal alcohol. Consequently, there has never been enough alcohol available to intoxicate many of the tribe at one time. Economics and laws aside, no Mohave would think of taking a drink in public without offering the treasured bottle to anyone who is around.

In the social attitude toward drinking behavior, intoxication and aggressive anti-social behavior are not the usual end result. This is in part due to a rapid "passing out," since a scarce supply limits the Indians' experience with alcohol. It is most often procured for parties or dances, and these are usually orderly affairs.

Closely connected with the hospitality pattern described above is drinking connected with sexual activities. If, at a dance or a party, a male shares a bottle with a woman, the implication is that he desires sex. By accepting several drinks, the woman indicates her acquiescence. This is different from using alcohol for seduction, which is unheard of in Mohave circles; nor is it considered promiscuity or payment in advance. The

Mohave sexual ethic is different from the dominant Judeo-Christian sexual ethic of our culture. The Mohaves consider what we could call promiscuous sexual relations to be neither vile nor antisocial. The main sexual stimulus is opportunity. Alcohol can readily be accommodated into such a scheme, and intoxicated Mohave women are aware of the sexual implications of their condition. Their husbands may exploit them sexually; other men may also take advantage of the situation.

The intoxicated Mohave acts as he always does, only more so. Changes may be judged as quantitative rather than qualitative. The maudlin and mawkish behavior common in so many other intoxicated groups is not evident. Brawls are rare, and aggressiveness is infrequent. Drinking, in a culture where the people are brave, need not be utilized to enhance masculinity. The Mohave does not regard drinking as a manly act, but he considers a moderate intake under prescribed social conditions a normal, pleasurable form of relaxation. There is no offense implied when nondrinkers refuse to indulge. The Mohave will, however, criticize excess. He will attempt to help the rare alcohol addict, whom he pities rather than condemns. The Mohave will more readily condemn the disorderly behavior of the sober than the drunk. He believes that every human being deserves respect and that no one should be denied the opportunity to regain the esteem of his fellow man.

What does the Mohave culture reveal to us about alcohol and alcoholism? Intoxication exaggerates the more obvious characteristics of an individual and suppresses his minor ones. The continuity of behavior and affect is likely due to the superficial and minimal intensity of Mohave repressive forces. Because of the high degree of cultural continuity, superego aspects are not as pervasive and punitive as in other cultures in conflict. The behavior of the intoxicated Mohave Indian reveals important components of Mohave ego psychology. A striking fact is that Mohave society has withstood the ravages of alcoholism common to some other American Indian tribes and attests to the union of successful drinking practices with the tribe's psychology and culture. Strengthening this situation is an absence of anxiety and, again, the strict preservation of basic cultural attitudes.

Where alcoholism does exist in a Mohave, the evidence suggests a linkage between an obsessive preoccupation with death and intense oral fixation. Devereux [2] considered the oral fixation data as confirmation for Freud's thesis of the oral erotic and latent homosexual aspects in addiction. The finding in the Mohave alcoholic of repressed aggressions and incestuous wishes, orally expressed, is quite striking, since on the whole, the average Mohave has attained a reasonably high and rare degree of sexual maturity.

SOUTHERN COLOMBIA

We now look into a rural farm district in southern Colombia in South America. In this small part of the world live three separate cultural groups: the Coconuco Indians, the Mestizos of the Pueblo, and the Zarzal.[7]

The Coconuco Indians are part Mestizo, part native Indian, making up roughly two-fifths of the total district population of 2000 families. Alien values imposed by neighboring cultures produce great conflict in their lives. They believe that nature is all powerful and that any satisfaction of personal ambition is presumptuous.

The Mestizos also represent two-fifths of the total population, and they counterbalance the Coconuco not only in numbers but also in cultural goals. Descendants of non-Indian pioneers, they are the active businessmen of the district. Contrary to the Coconuco belief in control by all-powerful nature, the Mestizo believes that the individual controls his environment, and that personal ambitions are desirable and worthy, producing a culture in which aspirations exceed possible levels of achievement.

The third group, the remaining one-fifth of the population, is the Zarzal. Racially mixed, descendants of forced native laborers, they are torn and bewildered. Their value systems and cultural orientations lie between the Indian and Mestizo and are accepted by neither. In addition, they fail to reward appropriate behavior by members of their own group.

All three cultural groups have free access to commercial alcoholic beverages. Although all three prefer a distilled beverage, aguardiente, they also buy beer, wine, and rum. A sugar cane and corn brew is produced in their homes.

In the three communities the Roman Catholic Calendar with its various rites—baptism, confirmation, communion, marriage, death—is the guide for ritual drinking. Alcohol, considered healthful, is used in healing rituals.

Nonritualistic drinking behavior, however, reveals differences in the three groups. Among the Coconucos drinking is a diversionary, friendly, masculine act occurring on weekends and at fiestas. Although intoxication occurs, it brings the group together, is well controlled, and alcoholism is unknown.

For the Mestizo, alcohol is an outlet for frustration. Some women and all men drink during the week, day or night. Not only does the Mestizo drink more than the Coconuco, but intoxication results in fights. Nevertheless, there is no alcoholism.

The Zarzal drinks alone more than the other two groups. All males and more women than in the Mestizo culture imbibe, and drunkenness, greatest in this group, results in wild behavior and some severe alcohol problems, for example, compulsive drinking.

Although there is some cultural variation in the three groups, the general attitude toward drinking is relatively consistent. Among the three, ritual drinking must be controlled. Intoxication is undesirable when it results in aggressiveness and inter-feres with work. To receive the label of drunkard is to invite exclusion from ritual drinking gatherings. Alcoholism is con-demned, and, for the most part, problem drinking is rare.

ECUADOR

To the south of Colombia are the Indians of the Ecuadorian Sierra.[6] Alcohol is essential to all their social events—marriage, baptism, religious fiestas, sowing of the fields, and harvest time. It may also be a balm for shock or fright, or it may be used to express prestige, pride, and vanity. An Indian of this society would never begin or finish an important undertaking without first fortifying himself with alcohol.

Here in the high Sierras, a different attitude toward the use of alcohol arises. The local world knows when drinking has occurred. When market is over, it is important to return home swaying and shouting. In spite of only two or three glasses a pretense of drunkenness is desired and affected. Such behavior is important in a culture where drinking is never done alone, where alcohol is considered a pleasure to be shared with others.

These Ecuadorian Indians, as described by Sandoval,[6] have definite ideas about alcohol usage. Women and minors should not generally drink, and if they do, must not become or act drunk. Males are not to remain drunk continuously.

With attitudes and limits such as these, alcoholism should be, and is, rare.

PERU

In Lunahuana, Peru,[8] there is a rural Mestizo community of 10,000. A cultural fusion of Spanish and Indian elements, it has a contemporary American and European overlay. Now a gen-eration removed from economic dependence on wine and brandy production, these Mestizo have as the principal means of support grapes, cotton, fruits, and vegetables. Locally produced wine (24 proof) and brandy (94–100 proof) are readily available and frequently consumed.

The previous culture emphasized the superiority of the male, but since then women are more independent, many owning land and earning more than their husbands. Males of fifteen and over drink and become drunk. Women rarely drink and never participate in the drinking activities of men.

Drinking occurs everywhere except in church (Roman Catholic). The goal of drinking is to get the partner intoxicated. Since a drink cannot be refused, a man's mettle is easily tested. The occasional solitary drinker is regarded with suspicion and subjected to disapproval. A spree drinker, however, is tolerated.

The typical sober male is timorous, but, when intoxicated, becomes verbal, repetitious, maudlin, and claims everyone to be his friend. Alcohol is an appropriate means of diminishing anxiety and relieving tensions. Violence rarely occurs under its influence, and aggression is generally turned inward. This is because correctness is the social goal, and these Indians are sensitive to unfavorable criticism.

Drinking among these Peruvian Indians is permissive and positive. No abstinence movement exists; no definition of drinking as a problem exists. Drinking and drunkenness have no sinful connotations and consequently produce no guilt. It is not because the Indians have no sense of guilt; guilt would manifest itself if a man were to mistreat his wife, child, or friend. Alcohol, essentially integrative in the culture, fosters social participation rather than withdrawal, and therefore alcoholism is rare.

ANDES

Culturally isolated in the high Andes Mountains, there resides a rural Indian tribe of some 1800 people.[5] Isolation is relatively complete, so identification is only with their local community; children are assured of achieving most goals if they act in a prescribed and reasonable manner, as expectations are feasible. Drunk or sober, the people of the community interact easily, using sorcery and gossip as the most common outlet for aggression and tension release.

Corn beer, wine, and distilled spirits are their alcohol beverages, all readily available. Corn beer is often shared with young children, and universal drinking occurs in all over sixteen. Adult drinking, especially that of the male, usually ends with drunkenness. Vomiting, passing out, and a succession of drunken days are socially acceptable. Even a morning drink may be taken in the proper social context. The frequency and amount of alcohol consumption are high.

Intoxication in this culture is merely an exaggeration of one's sober state. Most drinking shared with friends, neighbors, and relatives is group-directed and carried out in the guise of a fiesta. Any social situation outside of the ordinary obligates these Indians to drink. No formal social barriers exist as to who may drink together. Rather, drinking and social customs are well integrated with basic institutions of the culture, and in spite of much drinking and drunkenness, there is no breakdown of either interpersonal relations or social roles.

Alcohol is used positively and for these Indians plays an integrative role. No abstinence movement threatens their drinking. Since alcohol is not used for personal adjustment or for exploitive purposes, there is little ambivalence or guilt connected with it. Consequently, in this small community, pathological drinking does not occur.

Our preliterate society investigation would not be complete without a look at one classical study. By culling data from the cross-cultural files of Yale University, Horton [3] investigated 118 societies. The files on seventy-seven of these contained information on drinking customs.

The range of cultures was varied and wide: hunters, herdsmen, farmers among others. They were located in the Asiatic,

African, Oceanic, North and South American areas. Thirteen were undergoing a process of acculturation at the time their drinking behavior was observed.

In 20 per cent of the 118 cultures studied, alcohol is unknown or unused. The absence is a result of either a failure of invention, legal prohibition, religious prohibition, or taboos of local societies. Native manufacture is the source of alcoholic beverage for three-fourths of those societies using alcohol; the others use outside sources. In over half the cultures men and women partake equally and together. In others, women drink less often than men and with less incidence of intoxication. Also, in most of these drinking societies parents freely share with their children the customary alcoholic beverages. The members of many of these societies would endure ill health and social disorganization in the continued quest for alcohol, although alcohol is seldom allowed to interfere with *essential* social and economic activities.

Among these primitive people, drinking to get drunk and drinking to excess are the goals; moderate drinking is rare. Aggression, ranging from verbal quarrels to murderous assault, is a frequent response. Consequently, regulative controls have developed to try to prevent or curb drinking. Nevertheless, aggression resulting from drinking is rarely punished or even penalized severely, thus allowing tension release. Although most of these primitive societies are permissive toward drunkenness and even consider it a desirable goal, a negative attitude co-exists toward sexually aggressive behavior released by it. Chronic intoxication, when it occurs, is usually a mass phenomenon rather than an individual one and is an outgrowth of the disastrous process (for them) of acculturation.

As a consequence of his studies, Horton developed theorems and corollaries which he tested. The two receiving the greatest support from the data collected were Theorems One and Two.

THEOREM ONE: "The drinking of alcohol tends to be accompanied by release of sexual and aggressive impulses."

He contends that this was directly and indirectly verified.

THEOREM TWO: "The strength of the drinking response in any society tends to vary directly with the level of anxiety in that society."

This was tentatively verified, since insobriety varied directly with the anxiety as measured indirectly. Anxiety was measured in terms of subsistence insecurity and acculturation.

We feel Horton's emphasis on the anxiety-reducing function of alcohol as its basic value is oversimplified. The social and commercial use of alcohol and its use to gratify oral needs are equally important, if not more so.

What may we conclude now that we have examined a series of preliterate societies? First, that the drinking behavior of certain preliterates is related to acculturation, as shown in the Salish and Aleuts. Second, that most preliterates had developed their own alcoholic beverages, usually of a low alcohol content. Third, that contact with white societies provided for many the first experience with distilled spirits. Fourth, that the group drinking behavior so common among preliterates, despite its extremes, seems to be a protecting device, since alcoholism is seldom found. The preliterate individual uses alcohol more to enhance social relations than as a means of meeting life's problems. Fifth, that in spite of a low standard of living, many primitives expend a substantial portion of their meager resources on alcohol. Sixth, that Indians who do not have Western culture's philosophy of personal sin or blame do not incriminate alcohol for difficulties arising from excesses. Here, we see no ambivalence, no indigenous directives against alcohol, and, hence, reduced alcohol addiction. It is, in fact, a rarity. Although by American standards the Indians' drinking may be extreme, even pathological, it is not compulsive to the point of destruction, and there is no violation of *their* group standards. It is the rare individual who is incapacitated for long. Seventh, that in those preliterate cultures where alcohol usage is a problem, we suspect not alcoholism as we know it, but rather a dependent alcoholic needing alcohol but controlling it. Eighth, that prohibition attempts with preliterates have been as unsuccessful as in our contemporary societies.

By way of conclusion, let us compare preliterates and suburban Americans. The latter's group protection is less well structured and less intense. Also, the extent of social controls and pressure brought upon the deviant American is greater. Definitions, attitudes, and controls established by preliterate societies are more easily learned and managed than those of the modern American, whose social values are often ill-defined, deriving as they do from distant societies. In spite of alcohol's obvious liabilities, most preliterate societies seem to have decided that its advantages when used in a social group outweigh its liabilities.

b. Literate Groups

In our examination of literate cultures we include the Irish, Jewish, Italian, Methodist, Mormon, and Moslem. The first three represent drinking cultures; the Methodists, Moslems, and Mormons, nondrinking cultures. Since cultural ideals are in constant change, we describe first the basic drinking attitude and then indicate cultural modifications.

THE IRISH

Many authors have made pertinent references to the Irish intimacy with alcohol. Bales [3] quoted an Irish priest writing in 1840 as follows: "... In truth, not only were our countrymen remarkable for the intemperate use of intoxicating liquors, but intemperance has already entered into, and formed a part of the national character. An Irishman and a drunkard had become synonymous terms. Wherever he was to be introduced in character, either in the theater or in the pages of the novelist, he should be represented habited in rags, blooding at the nose, and waving a shillelagh. Whiskey was everywhere regarded as our idol." Percival [19] in 1955 pictured average Irishmen in their homeland accepting the inevitability of excessive drinking among their people. As a consequence, they were suspicious and resistant to any action that might curtail the right to drink, and were unfavorably disposed to Alcoholics Anonymous.

Statistics confirm these statements. Skolnick [21] in 1951, reviewed figures of arrests in the United States in which inebriety was a factor. The Irish had a high incidence. Bales [3] reveals that the incidence of Irish-American alcohol problems runs rather consistently two to three times higher than any other ethnic group in America. Myerson [18] in a 1952 review of a series of Skid-Row alcoholics in a Boston halfway house found that the Irish made up 74 per cent of his sample, a significant figure even considering the high percentage of Irish in Boston. A World War I study of American draftees and volunteers suffering neuropsychiatric disorders revealed that the Irish led all other ethnic groups diagnosed alcoholic. The Irish rate was twenty times that of the Italian or Jewish. When Hyde and Chisholm [12] evaluated neuropsychiatric rejections for army service during World War II, the Irish led all other ethnic groups in chronic alcoholism as the reason for rejection for service.

There are supplementary reports suggesting variations in Irish alcoholism rates. Glad [9] suggests that alcoholism rates in Ireland are not as high as Irish-American rates in the United States. He bases his suggestion on a statement by Dawson: "when we compare the drunkenness rate of the individual counties (in Ireland) ... it is found that drunkenness is actually less prevalent, upon the whole, in those containing the largest towns than in the rural counties." Since analysis of Irish emigration shows a high incidence from rural areas, it follows that the Irish immigrant population is not representative of Ireland as a whole but represents instead a high risk group for alcoholism.

The influence of Catholicism has been suggested as a major causative factor in Irish alcoholism. Since both the Irish and Italians are primarily Roman Catholic and their alcoholism rates are in significant contrast (the Italian rate is very low), it becomes clear that religion is not the controlling factor. We find that the Irish are closely wedded to alcohol in their cultural life, and that many drinking problems emanate from this. Bales's [3, 4] study is excellent and we rely on him as a source.

We noted that alcohol problems have been common to the Irish for many years, perhaps centuries. A historical understanding of Irish-American drinking behavior must begin in Ireland itself. Until recently the English controlled Ireland and used it as a source of food. It was important for English economic expansion elsewhere that Ireland remain agricultural. Because of this, transportation and communication were not developed. The Irish were exploited by an absentee landlord system which placed the farmer on a subsistence level. Consequently, the Irish farmer, who assured a steady source of agricultural manpower, could not readily leave the farm. A high population density with an extended family system resulted. When grandparents retired, space was made for them in already meager quarters. Farmer, wife, and children were absorbed by problems of mere subsistence. Most families had to live within a single room; however, it is worth noting that rigid separation of the sexes was maintained.

In child rearing, the Irish have been ambivalent and contradictory. Unmerciful teasing of boys by their elders was usual. This, combined with displays of lavish affection and extravagant love, would be contrasted at other times by parental attitudes of intense anger and hostility. Inconsistent and vacillating love and punishment were the means of control. Families living so intimately suffered extreme conflict. National poverty resulted in anxiety in the children over parental ties and economic conditions.

The Irish farms were small, and subdivision was economically illogical. Farming was the main source of income; a boy could not marry and support a family until his father retired or died. Only one son was able to inherit a farm and since he was not usually designated in advance, most of the sons would remain on the farm. With the settling of the inheritance, the other brothers and sisters were expected to leave. Possibilities were limited: emigrate, become apprentices, or enter the church. An occasional girl might receive a dowry to marry.

On the other hand, since the father rarely retired, the sons who remained on the farm continued to be dependent upon his benevolence; unable to marry, they found themselves treated as boys until they were aged forty-five or fifty. Marriage was impossible because of the economic realities. Sexual activity outside of marriage was strictly prohibited by the church. To control a potentially explosive sexual situation, social contacts between the sexes were kept at a minimum. Males gathered with males, females with females.

Males, bachelor as well as married, met frequently in small groups either on a farm or in a local tavern. The horseplay encouraged in male children was continued into adulthood, and intermixed with drinking. The nondrinker was suspect. Since he was not spending his leisure time with the boys, the implication was that he must be molesting unmarried girls. Alcohol was also used to cement business relationships, and at baptisms, births, engagements, marriages, and funerals, it flowed freely.

The Irish do not strongly disapprove of drunkenness. Many

a good wife might even treat her husband to a morning drink. In fact, the drunken man is frequently envied rather than pitied.

These family, economic, and drinking patterns form the nucleus from which alcoholism of Irish-Americans evolved. Then the immigrant Irish suffered socially, economically, and religiously in their new environs. Their Catholic religion was under challenge by the dominant Protestants in the new country. Under American cultural influences, the strong role in the family came to be exercised by the mother, and the three-generation family was difficult to maintain. Their status was at a new low. Protections were few, challenges many, stresses continuous.

Certainly when the new stresses were combined with a built-in cultural attitude accepting drink as fulfilling a functional need, the prerequisites for the development of alcoholism existed. Bales,[4] in describing the utilitarian attitude of Irish drinking, points out "There is no counter-anxiety attached to the process of drinking ... and there is every suggestion for the individual to adopt drinking as the means of dealing with his particular maladjustment."

What is evidenced is that Irish-American drinking is utilitarian and unritualistic, there are feelings of envy for drunkenness and also ambivalence toward alcohol's use; this drinking is reinforced by cultural upheavals.

THE ITALIANS

Essentially all adult Italians drink, yet the rate of alcoholism in Italy is only one-eighth the rate in the United States.[16] This rate is contrasted with the adult population in the United States where only two-thirds drink. Why do the Italians drink so widely, yet suffer so little from alcoholism? Information about their drinking behavior will clarify this question.[16]

Most Italians drink, taking wine with meals primarily and

thereby making it a staple in their diet. Beyond this observation we find that Italians generally consume great quantities of fluids. For their Italo-American descendants wine is no longer an important staple in the diet. Total fluid intake, however, of second and third generation Italo-Americans is more than twice that of their Italian counterparts. Although the Italo-American alcoholism rate is apparently increasing, we question whether a higher fluid intake need is a prerequisite for addiction. Observers note that the Italian dilutes his wine generously with water, to make it go further and to make the water, possibly impure, safe to drink. The Italo-American's alcohol concentration is considerably greater than that of the Italian. In terms of the ratio of total daily calories from alcoholic beverages to total calorie intake, the rate was significantly higher for the Italian. This shows that alcohol is much more important as a food for Italians than for Italo-Americans.

Alcohol consumption is integrated into the Italian's daily way of life and viewed positively. Its legitimacy stems from a culture where water was often in short supply or, on occasion, polluted. Alcohol has been defined by the Catholic Church in Italy as a gift from God. When this attitude is combined with the use of alcohol as a medicine as well as a means of strengthening family ties by its consumption at meals, the basis for healthy attitudes is provided.

As Lolli [16] and others have noted, divorce, even separation, is rare in Italy. There is no anxiety stemming from broken families. Italian society is also patriarchal and equality of husband and wife has never been accepted. Roles are clearly delineated, dissatisfaction from marriage is less likely, and thus an anxiety-provoking factor common in American culture is avoided.

We referred earlier to the oral needs of alcoholics. Since obesity is considered partial evidence of orality, examination of obesity data in Italians is pertinent. Among them 29 per cent of the males and 55 per cent of the females are significantly above the ideal weight. Among second- and third-generation Italo-Americans this is true of 56 per cent of the men and 34 per cent of the women. The Italian and his American counterpart have major weight problems, which makes it clear that they can manifest oral symptoms.

Italians and Italo-Americans are deeply religious. Almost all Italians, in Italy and the United States, receive the emotional support that an organized religion supplies.

Lolli [16] from his studies of Italians and Italo-Americans finds that regular consumption of alcohol does not necessarily lead to poor health. In fact Lolli has found *only* one subject, an Italo-American woman, who reported never tasting alcohol. Those who recall their first drink, in both Italian and Italo-American groups, had it between six and ten years of age. Wine was commonly the first drink. With two-thirds of the Italians, wine was the exclusive beverage used, while only rarely did second-generation Italo-Americans use wine exclusively. One-half of the latter group drank wine, beer, distilled spirits, and aperitifs, while only 2 per cent of the former drank anything other than wine. Clearly, the drinking habits of the Italians—both men and women—alter sharply when brought under American cultural influences.

Not only has drinking behavior been altered, but also the rationale for drinking has changed and is different in the United States from what it is in Italy. Italians drink for pleasure, for health purposes, and for traditional reasons. Second- and third-generation Italo-Americans prefer to drink mainly for sociability and taste.

The use of alcohol with meals differs strikingly between the two cultures. Lolli found that 82 per cent of the Italians he studied drank with their meals exclusively, while only 8 per cent of second-generation Italo-Americans maintained this practice. As we noted before, it is safer to drink with meals.

Drinking then receives psychological support as a group activity; its rationale is established physiologically in terms of delayed absorption. Furthermore, when it is related to daily eating practices, there is psychologically less tendency to assign alcohol a magical role. Without special psychological significance, there is less possibility for alcohol to be fitted into an emotional system as a defense or symptom mechanism. Lolli states that with the Italians alcohol contributed little to the development of neurotic traits which, when present, seldom led to excessive drinking.

Few of the parents—Italian or Italo-American—oppose the use of alcohol. The average Italian describes the typical paternal attitude as indifferent whereas second-generation Italo-Americans describe it as approving. This may be a possible reflection on an American's need for approval for drinking in a culture where it remains questionable.

Even intoxication is more an American than Italian trait, and more likely a male than female response. In Lolli's study 60 per cent of the male and 16 per cent of the female Italians reported one or more incidents of intoxication. Of the second-generation Italo-Americans 84 per cent of the men and 51 per cent of the women reported episodes of intoxication. Significantly, not only do many more Italo-American women become intoxicated, but 20 per cent report five or more episodes as compared to none among Italians.

Drunkenness, when it occurs, is a *group* phenomenon of Italians and their American counterparts. When an Italian becomes intoxicated he does so under a blueprint for safe drunkenness: at festive occasions where others are present, including the opposite sex (contrary to the Irish who become intoxicated in bars and in the presence of other men only).

From this examination of Italians and their drinking behavior, we must conclude that Italians in Italy are not likely to have alcohol problems. Their American cousins, adopting

American familial, occupational, and recreational customs and drinking patterns, begin to lose the protection of the Italian drinking tradition and demonstrate new drinking problems. But their rate of addiction is still significantly low compared to the average American.

THE JEWS

When we look at the Jew and his drinking behavior, much that is pertinent to alcohol etiology comes into focus. If one asks Jews whether they drink, many deny it. They equate "drinking" with Gentiles and do not consider their use of alcohol as "drinking." The fact is, however, that Jews do drink, but without pathological consequences. Various studies demonstrate with amazing consistency extremely low rates of alcoholism among Jews—Orthodox to Reform, east or west European, urban or rural, educated or uneducated, laborer or professional.

We may well ask, why the low rate of addictive drinking among Jews? According to Glad,[9] the Jew tends to regard drinking as "socially practical and . . . religiously symbolic and communicative." Glad postulates a low rate of Jewish alcoholism because of this tendency toward social drinking and drinking for the achievement of symbolic gratification.

Rosenman[20] attributes the rare alcoholism among the Jews to their religious orientation. Judaism, according to him, unites all gods and divinities into a single image of God. Lacking, therefore, is an image of alcohol as a tool of Satan; rather, alcohol is a gift of God and must be used as such. This can be contrasted with certain Christian views (see Methodists and Mormons) that alcohol is a vehicle of the devil and therefore should be condemned.

Bales[4] sees the controls against alcoholism emanating from the early experience of every Jewish child. He points out that alcohol is given to the child in the ritual of circumcision, serving a communicative and symbolic purpose. Alcohol, the family, religion, and God are intimately involved in this ceremony as well as in others throughout life. Powerful sanctions develop about early drinking experiences. Drinking for effect becomes alien and profane as a result of them.

To understand further Jewish drinking, let us examine the drinking experience of infants and children during religious rituals and ceremonies. Our model is the Orthodox Jew, since Conservative and Reform groups are primarily offshoots from their orthodox brothers. Jewish ritual falls into three categories; rites of passage, the Sabbath, and holidays and festivals.

One of the most important rites of passage occurs for the male Jew eight days after his birth. During the circumcision ceremony, a festive and religiously symbolic occurrence is the *makel's* (operator's) recitation of a benediction over a cup of wine, from which the infant is given a few drops. The wine is then shared by both parents. If the male child is the first-born son, twenty-two days later the important rite of Redemption from God of the first son is symbolically blessed with wine. Other important Jewish events, such as Bar Mitzvah, and marriage, are similarly endorsed with wine.

During the Sabbath, drinking is an integral part of the ritual. At a Jewish home, in the evening after synagogue, the father recites the "Prayer of Separation" at the dinner table, and wine is used. No Jewish child reared in a home where the family is drawn together each Sabbath with wine and food can feel drink is evil. These are moments of warmth and closeness not achieved under other circumstances; all members of the family share the wine.

In the Jewish religion, as in others, there are certain holy days and festivals. Among the more important are Rosh Hashonah (New Year), Yom Kippur (Day of Atonement), Chanukah (Feast of the Lights), Purim (Triumph over Haman), and Passover (The Flight from Egypt). Yom Kippur ends the Ten Days of Penitence. Strict fasting for twenty-four hours is mandatory. Labor and bathing are forbidden. Water, alcohol, food, and tobacco are not used. This is the rare moment in Jewish life where alcohol does not fulfill a positive function, but then, abstinence and penance are the goals of Yom Kippur.

Purim, on the other hand, is a glorious day. It celebrates the triumph of the Jews over Haman. Although business and work are permitted, it is a time for exchanging gifts and assisting the poor. In the Book of Esther, the Schulchan Aroch states: "the whole miracle was occasioned through wine ... one should drink more than he is accustomed to of wine or of another intoxicating beverage." Interestingly enough, exceptions are made for those who might get in trouble. Alcohol "will cause him to despise some precept ... lead him to levity ... it is best not to become intoxicated."

Successful cultural controls can and do emanate from the integration of drinking with religion and family. Alcohol is taken consistently and meaningfully by the Jews, and all are permitted to share in its use. Jews drink all beverages and often. Because of the wine ritual, that is the most popular drink. As the regular observance of the Sabbath declines, however, so does the use of wine. Jews as a group tend to drink less often than others in public except on business.

Admissions for alcoholic psychosis among Jews in New York hospitals has revealed that in 1920 there were none, in 1930 there were four admissions, and in 1940 eleven admissions. To Malzberg (in Bales [4]) this suggested an alcoholism rate change. The impressions of observers are that as Jews assimilate into the American pattern, they leave orthodoxy and its restraining influence, and increasingly turn toward alcoholism. However, more recently, Malzberg [27] found that for the years 1949–51 Jews made up only 1 per cent of all white patients admitted for the first time to New York state mental hospitals with alcoholic psychosis. Since the estimate for the percentage of Jews in the New York state population is 15 per cent of the

white population,[28] it may be concluded that the contrast between Jews and non-Jews still remains rather striking.

Snyder [23] concludes: "Our findings strongly suggest that the
sobriety for which Jews have long been noted depends upon
the continuity and vitality of the Orthodox religious tradition;
and that participation in Orthodox religious activities substan-
tially insures moderation in drinking regardless of frequency."
He allows also that "the thread of Orthodox life may be woven
into many regional culture fabrics without losing its sobering
influence on the Jews." The degree of orthodoxy varies according to broader socio-cultural influences—the Polish, Russian, or
German.

Snyder refers to Jews who bring moral strengths to drinking
which counter intoxication. Although these factors may not
have resulted from personal experience of the individual, they
are nevertheless the standard Jewish orientation toward drinking behavior. Jews learn to drink in a controlled manner through
the religious, ceremonial use of alcohol. Jews learn how *not*
to drink by continual comparison of the Gentile's hedonistic
drives with their own broader pattern of religious, ethnocentric
ideas and sentiments.

Data on possible Jewish alcoholism are nonexistent. Jews are
simply not members of the alcoholic population of clinics and
hospitals. For example, at the Massachusetts General Hospital
in Boston, in over 1000 patients seen in the Alcohol Clinic, only
two Jewish patients have appeared. Interestingly enough, the
absence of diagnoses of alcoholism among Jews is contrasted
sharply with studies of neuroses which show a high percentage
of Jews undergoing treatment.

Snyder [23] extends his findings into another generation by
studying carefully the Straus–Bacon [24] group of college students. He concluded that the drinking behavior of Jewish
students removed from orthodoxy tends to resemble in certain
respects that of the general population. We feel, on the other

hand, that even among young, non-Orthodox Jews the personal identification to Judaism continues to act as a protective device against alcoholism, but perhaps to a lesser degree than with orthodoxy. We must never lose sight of a main Jewish goal—to maintain a separate Jewish identity. For this reason, the Jew never has actively sought converts to his religion, and frequently manipulates the social scene as a means of maintaining and strengthening Jewish identity.

In conclusion, we emphasize that Jews drink, often and early, with negligible departure from sobriety. Where drinking is an integral part of socialization, interrelated with moral symbolism and repeatedly practiced in group rites, alcoholism is rare.

Earlier in this chapter we presented a description of the drinking practices of three literate societies, two Christian and one non-Christian. In describing *nondrinking* literate cultures, we shall use again three groups, Methodists, Mormons, and Moslems.

METHODISTS

The largest American church proscribing alcohol is the Methodist Church. Methodists claim a membership of over 9 million (as compared with Jews: 5 million; Episcopalians: 2.5 million) and are a significant social force in the United States. Their members are involved in a cultural conflict because they live in a milieu where drinking is an accepted social custom and yet they are admonished not to drink. This culture conflict is bringing about changes in the attitude of the Methodist Church toward alcohol.

This attitude originated early in the history of the denomination. John Wesley [26] the founder of the Methodist Church, speaking in the mid-eighteenth century, denounced the liquor trade: "We must not sell anything which tends to impair health. Such is eminently all the liquid fire commonly called drams or spiritous liquors." Wesley, however, permitted the use of alcohol as a medication in cases of "extreme necessity," but not as a beverage. According to Skolnick,[22] Wesley also differentiated sharply between spirits and beer or wine. Wesley himself used beer. As a strong adherent of frequent communion, he also took wine. Today in the United States, Methodists use grape juice rather than wine in their service.

Parenthood of ideas or national movements is often difficult to determine. Scholars have tended to credit Bishop Francis Asbury of the Methodist Church as the father of the American prohibition movement. As his grandson and biographer Herbert Asbury [1] wrote of the bishop, "from the beginning of his American Ministry, Asbury was the inveterate foe of the 'Rum Demon' although he himself drank ale and legal wine 'for my health.' . . . Under his instructions and leadership the Methodists were the first sect to make drinking a matter of concern to the Lord."

In time, concern with the use of alcohol resulted in a more militant attitude by the Methodists. By 1892 the church was vehemently proclaiming: [8] "We do record our deliberate judgment that no political party has a right to expect, nor ought it to receive, the support of Christian Men so long as it stands committed to the license policy, or refuses to put itself on record in an attitude of open hostility to the saloon."

Methodist attitudes of 1960 were similar. Then the General Conference of the Methodist Church stated: [17] "The Methodist Church is in militant opposition to the liquor traffic. Our appeal is for total abstinence from all uses of intoxicants." The church then strongly recommended: "Positive education for a life free from beverage alcohol"; "Commitment to Abstinence"; "Rehabilitation of those who suffer because of beverage alcohol"; "Legislation as an effective means to outlaw beverage alcohol."

To hold high office and to assume leadership in the Methodist Church, one must refrain from the use of intoxicating beverages. This has resulted in a church mobilized for action against alcohol. The year 1880 saw the institution of the Permanent Committees on Temperance and Prohibition. Year after year, since that date, the Committees have reaffirmed temperance as a special goal of church activities. Only in 1960 did the church incorporate temperance interests into the General Board of Christian Social Concerns.

The Methodist Church of late has altered its approach to alcohol. As Caradine Hooton,[10] General Secretary of the temperance program since 1949, states, the church is attempting "a positive attitude . . . a proclamation of the positive benefits of Christian living instead of a negative condemnation of alcohol and drinkers." He suggests a need for an understanding of the motivation to drink and for the use of scientific knowledge in the education for temperance. Hooton and others in the church represent new voices in the hierarchy of the movement and raise the possibility of changed Methodist attitudes in the future.

In *Stumbling Block*, by the Reverend Douglas Jackson,[13] a leading Methodist educator, differences in attitude toward alcohol among religious and social groups in the United States are emphasized. Jackson points out that "all good citizens and all good Christians can agree that clearly established misuse of alcohol which endangers society and innocent persons must be stopped." He disapproves of moralistic lectures to the alcoholic and suggests that it is necessary for the church to become interested in the rehabilitation of alcoholics. He decries the "dogmatism and confidence in their own sanctity" displayed by temperance workers, claiming that such dogmatism hinders effective work with alcoholics.

Other church postures on alcohol involve stressing its relation to crime and accidents and its ill effects on physical fitness. Skolnick [22] derived from these the Methodist attitudes on social drinking. Social drinking leads to problems: crime and personal and social disorganization. If one accepts the concept that childhood learning experiences influence adult behavior, then, as Skolnick hypothesizes, "Methodists who drink will, in line with their childhood learning about the consequences of drinking, tend to show greater problems ... in the area of drinking than either Jews or Episcopalians."

When one looks closely at his excellent dissertation, one discovers certain interesting information. Using the Straus-Bacon college student study, Skolnick found that Methodist students were forced to learn about alcohol outside their homes in spite of the fact that a majority of their parents drank. Consequently, the group or familial use of alcohol common in Jewish and Italian drinking practices was unavailable.

Beyond this, two-thirds of the fathers of the Methodist students did not know of their sons' drinking. Of the one-third who knew, most had expressed some form of disapproval. This is to be contrasted with the 10 per cent of Jewish fathers who were unaware of their sons' drinking. Methodist drinkers, showing a striking similarity to Irish drinkers, do most of their drinking in commercial establishments and usually in the company of males, where social controls are most relaxed.

Methodist students report using alcohol as an aid to forget disappointments, to deal with crises, to get along better on dates, or to overcome shyness. Along with incorporating alcohol into their emotional coping mechanism, more Methodist students drink to get intoxicated than any other group of students. The latter practice may emanate from church attitudes giving abstinence as an ideal while implying that any drinking indicates the extreme of insobriety. The only advice to abstain, outside the church, that had effect was parental admonition. Abstinence, a desirable social characteristic, found high support. Friends of users were likely to be users; friends of abstainers, abstainers.

What does this information show us? First, as Skolnick [22]

noted, the Methodists' adoption of total abstinence came not from scriptural injunction, but was a response to a major social problem of the nineteenth century (excessive drinking). This was reinforced by a negative teaching approach: if we drink, trouble is sure to follow. Either abstinence or excessive drinking behavior was the result of such teaching.

Skolnick claims that the philosophical and theological proscription of drinking was adopted primarily to solve the problem of excessive drinking. When total abstinence has been taught by using negative approaches, then extremes of drinking occur among those who eventually drink, as compared to the more moderate drinking found among drinkers who have matured in an environment with a more positive orientation to alcohol. Finally, Skolnick contended that those Methodists who were frequent and deeply committed churchgoers were the ones who practiced total abstinence. His prediction, based on his study, is "that a significantly larger proportion of persons reared with an abstinence orientation will become alcoholics as compared to, for example, persons reared with a ritual orientation."

Although there is considerable substance in Skolnick's formulation, we feel that it is oversimplified. Not all Methodists who drink become alcoholics—not even the majority. There is no evidence to date that Methodists have a disproportionate problem with alcoholism. Skolnick, we fear, in spite of his brilliant observations, bases his hypothesis too strongly on *one* factor and this, like any single-cause formulation, is unrealistic. Alcoholism is the result of many factors. Any other view tends to preclude the bulk of the striking information from other disciplines.

The low incidence of alcoholism among Methodists in spite of possible unhealthy cultural attitudes we feel is the result of three things: personal maturity (unlike the Irish, the Methodists are not hampered by family structures that retard growing up); learning about alcohol in other places besides the church; and a wide variation in emphasis on drinking within the church itself.

The Methodist Church in its attitude toward drinking faces a major problem, since drinking is accepted by the culture in which Methodism exists and by many other Protestant denominations. More and more younger Methodists are using alcohol. Therefore, the church is faced with the necessity of describing as deviant behavior that behavior which is actually practiced by many of its members. Moreover, abstinence as an ideal seems to produce two results that are contrary to each other: on one hand, it fortifies a repugnance to drink; on the other, by identifying the act of drinking with intemperance, it suggests that one drink is equivalent to drunkenness, thereby encouraging the extreme behavior the Methodist Church most deplores. In the resolution of this conflict, we support Dr. Hooton [10] in his efforts to bring about a "positive attitude" rather than a "negative condemnation" of alcohol and drinkers in the Methodist Church.

MORMONS

The attitude of the Mormons (Church of Jesus Christ of the Latter-Day Saints) toward alcohol is similar to that of the Methodists. Strong recommendation and urging is made against alcohol use, but ordinarily a member will not be expelled because of drinking. Social pressures, however, are applied; abstinence campaigns are vigorously conducted. Campaigns have been conducted not only against alcohol but also against other stimulants (tobacco, coffee, and tea). In spite of a strong abstinence attitude, the Mormons have been and are active and energetic supporters of Utah's alcoholism treatment programs. Utah was one of the earliest states promoting aid to the alcoholic, as we shall discuss later.

There is much less published material on Mormon drinking than on the drinking of the Methodists. Fortunately, we have data from two studies of students, one a high school group in Utah,[14] the other a college group.[24] The high school study was conducted in 1956 by Evan Jones,[14] who investigated 19 Utah high schools and 8507 students (85 per cent Mormon). The study of Straus and Bacon [24] in 1949-51 is the source for the college material.

Of the high school students (ages 14 to 19), 38 per cent described themselves as having had drinking experiences. Since it was shown that less than half of these drinking Mormon students were permitted to drink at home, it would seem that 25 per cent of all Mormon students drink in violation of religious and familial taboos. Apparently the familial taboo is not great, since 40 per cent of the Mormon parents also drank.

Mormon high school students who drink usually do so in a car, a friend's home, their own home when alone, while hunting and fishing, in some isolated locale, or in a beer parlor. Utah has a state-controlled system that operates all liquor stores. Only beer is sold at a bar; beer is also available in grocery stores.

Among Mormon male college students, 54 per cent reported themselves users of alcohol. Among other male college students, 94 per cent of the Jews, 90 per cent of the Catholics, and 77 per cent of the Protestants used alcohol. Religious practice and custom as related to alcohol use show reverse effects according to religious group: only 21 per cent of the Mormon males who attend weekly church use alcohol, whereas among devout Jewish males, 100 per cent are users.

If we look at the first drinking experiences of Mormons, we can class many of them as unhealthy experiences. The largest category drinks first with school friends. Though the second largest first takes alcohol with parents, the other categories' first drink is with nonschool friends, older persons, or alone, in that order.

According to these studies, Mormon college and high school students drink less frequently than any other religious group. However, 12 per cent of the Mormon high school students who drank reported engaging in activities after drinking which they would not otherwise have engaged in. In the college group almost half the Mormons reported social complications (failure to meet obligations, damage to friendships, accident or injury, and formal punishment or discipline) as a consequence of drinking. This high rate of Mormon social complications is especially striking when contrasted to the few Mormon users who drink heavily—fewer than most religious groups as a whole. Apparently even moderate drinking can result in problems in interpersonal relationships when negative sanctions are strong. This is emphasized by the findings in the high school population that half the junior and senior class users of alcohol had at least one incident of intoxication. Among the college students, Mormon male users of alcohol are more likely to have been tight, been drunk, or have passed out than male students of other religious groups. These findings illustrate relatively high rates of intoxication in a group who do not drink as often as others. Straus and Bacon [24] correlate this high rate of drunkenness with "a reaction against the prohibitive pressures of the church. By their mere drinking, Mormon male students may in a sense be rebelling against these restrictions, and rebellion once turned loose often takes the form of extreme rather than mild reaction." Bacon [2] suggests that for Mormons who do drink, the alcoholism rate is high.

One-half the Mormon students express admiration or approval toward militant abstainers, while only one-fourth express disapproval, resentment, or scorn toward abstainers trying to influence others. Moreover, Mormons are more prone than any other group, to express a definite opinion (pro or con) regarding drinking and abstinence. In contrast, only 10 per cent of the Jews voice approval of the proselytizing abstainer.

Among the students studied, abstainers in various religious groups expressed many reasons for their abstinence, but reasons of religion and morality were highly valued by Mormons. This corresponds with Christensen's [7] study of Mormon student views on mate selection, where of twenty-one traits rated, drinking was cited most frequently as an objectionable characteristic. Mormon students freely express less tolerance and more disgust toward drunkenness than any other religious group studied.

In summary, we feel that Mormon injunctions against drinking apparently have some effect, although half their adherents have rationalized away such proscriptions. The crucial variable depends upon the effectiveness of the rationalization. As with the Methodists, the roles of drinkers are clearly defined; they either abstain or drink to excess. Drinking and personal problems are inevitably intertwined. Since American culture in general gives alcohol a positive sanction, and since communication increases the difficulty of maintaining isolation from such ideas, rebellion among young Mormons when it occurs tends to focus on the alcohol taboo. Methodists and Mormons are too numerous to control their adherents as effectively as small sects or cults; this increases the potential for experimentation with forbidden attitudes. The geographical isolation in Utah associated with the historical hostility of other groups toward the Mormons has permitted them to be more effective than the Methodists in maintaining a consistent, nondrinking custom.

As is the case with the Jews, maintaining a consistent attitude toward alcohol may be one way by which the Mormon keeps and fortifies his identity.

MOSLEMS

When we came to our last nondrinking culture, the Moslem, we were surprised by the lack of published information available. This contrast with the availability of information on drinkers reflects the interest of investigators in why people drink and points out their lack of concern with why and how other people do not drink. Study of abstinent or nondrinking cultures may reveal much-needed information, since we often do not understand their mechanisms of social control. The Moslem religion prohibits the use of wine and thus offers investigators in alcohol problems a rich field of study, to date sadly neglected.

The alcohol taboo among Moslems is religious.[4] During the flight from Mecca, Mohammed and his followers fought with various tribes. Apparently, one battle was lost because some of Mohammed's lieutenants had been gambling and drinking and were unable to function. As a result Mohammed forbade both drinking and gambling. He supported this injunction by reference to the fable of two drunken angels who disobeyed God's commandments and were punished. Following this action, God forbade the use of wine by His Servants forever.

Similar to the abstinence attitudes of the Methodists, Moslem alcohol taboos were born out of excesses and then invested and legitimized by religious support.

How effective were and are wine taboos? What about other alcoholic beverages? What happens to users? Throughout the Moslem world, are there historical changes, variations by ethnic, geographical, and national origins; social class, occupation, and education? What about the impact of western civilization, improved communication and transportation? Are there urban-rural variations? Although we can raise many questions about Moslem alcohol attitudes and practices, we can answer few.

If the stories in the *Thousand and One Nights* have any validity, the prohibition of wine has not been entirely effective. Other tales of the use of alcohol have occurred in the literature for centuries, indicating that there is some basis of accuracy in descriptions of ineffective prohibition. Lane,[15] in an 1883 article, described a type of wine which the Moslems permitted to be used, and he even described wine addicts. It was Lane's contention that coffee served as a substitute for fermented beverages.

Bales [4] has also described certain flexibilities in cultural attitudes among the Moslems. He believes that cultures must provide mechanisms to meet inner tensions. If not alcohol, what else? Bales reports that Moslems "are users of hashish and seem to be habituated to very strong tea and coffee." Others have noted that certain manipulations of Mohammed's edict have existed. Mislabeling of wine containers is common. Others contend that Mohammed's reference only excluded the use of wine, not beer and distilled spirits. Still others interpret the injunction as condemning only excessive drinking. Bales concluded that total prohibition among the Moslems "can hardly be regarded as a model of success."

There are a few other reports about Moslems drinking. The Chopras [5,6] state that drinking among the upper and middle classes in India "is uncommon except in moderation; this is especially the case among those who take to European habits and customs, such as the Mohammedans." The Chopras also state that in the western Himalayas (primarily Moslem) fermented beverages are seldom used. They further suggest that occupation is "perhaps a more important factor than caste or religion in influencing the consumption of alcoholic drinking," for urbanization tends to break down the controls exercised more effectively in agricultural regions. Industrial employment and adequate income seem to combine to increase use of alcohol. "A floating population" at certain fairs or festivals brings about a heavy consumption of alcohol. Medicinal values of alcohol are often used as the reason for imbibing among Indian Moslems.

We have recently heard that if one wants a large drink in the Middle East one asks for a "Mohammedan." This is purported to be a double shot of alcohol. It finds use in apparent nondrinking cultures and allows a large amount to be ordered and hastily consumed before one's neighbor arrives on the scene. Horton,[11] speaking of China, India, Mesopotamia, and the Incas and Aztecs, all of whom prohibited alcoholic beverages, claims "these attempts invariably failed." *Time* Magazine [25] suggests that tourists longing for the gaiety of the 1920's in the United States can find a similar mood in modern-day New Delhi in the prohibition practiced there. Speakeasies, bootleggers, stills, gangsters, and runners are common phenomena. *Time* says that illegal brewing is India's "busiest cottage industry."

Unfortunately these have to remain isolated observations and the material from stories and tales unchecked, for there does not exist for comparison any systematic study of the Moslem drinking patterns similar to studies of Irish, Italians, and Jewish.

5

A Review of Etiological Factors

As we have noted, we cannot accept one-factor explanations of alcoholism.

In review, what are some of these rejected single-cause hypotheses? Economic deprivation has been offered. Yet the Aleuts and the Salish, for example, are economically deprived and suffer no alcoholism. Furthermore, Jews and Italians, who have low alcoholism rates as racial and ethnic groups, are found in all economic classes.

An unpredictable economy associated with unachievable economic goals has been put forth as a possible cause. Here again the Aleuts, the Salish, the Mestizos, and the Jews serve as examples. All seldom respond to their unpredictable economy by resorting to alcoholism.

Poor health has been implicated. The Aleut, Italian, and Jew experience all ranges of good to bad health without evidence of alteration of alcoholism rates.

The habit of drinking to drunkenness has been condemned as the cause of alcoholism. But Aleuts, Salish, Coconucos, and Ecuadorian Indians all drink to get drunk; yet there is no alcoholism among them. As Horton [1] has pointed out, drinking to excess is a typical goal in many cultures; it is usually a group phenomenon and unrelated to alcoholism.

Some theorists have blamed the type and supply of alcohol. The limited supply of alcohol for the Aleuts, Salish, and Mohave has not so far resulted in alcoholism as a problem, whereas the Coconuco Indians, the Mestizos, the Zarsals, the Andean Indians, the Jews, and the Italians have free access to all kinds of alcohol with infrequent addiction.

A purely hedonistic desire for alcohol has been considered a factor in the cause of alcoholism. The Aleuts and Mohave certainly are hedonistic in their goals, yet neither have problems with alcoholism.

There is no alcoholism in a culture where alcohol is used as an outlet for frustration (the Colombian Mestizo); pathological drinking is rare where alcohol is used as a balm to sooth shock or fright or to express prestige, pride, or vanity (Ecuadorian Indians); nor does alcoholism appear among the Mestizos of Peru when alcohol is used to diminish anxieties and relieve tensions.

What other single-factor cultural characteristics may be implicated in the etiology? Some blame marked behavioral changes after drinking. Yet the sober, tactful, circumspect Aleuts, who emphasize continual control of emotions, after drinking enjoy great emotional outflow entirely contrary to their sober state. And the Salish, passive, shy, restrained, and timid become laughing, aggressive, shouting, and boisterous after drinking. In both alcoholism is rare. As Horton [1] has noted in the societies he studied, aggression is a frequent response to alcohol imbibing which does not result in high alcoholism rates.

A culturally subordinate status has been hypothesized as a cause. The Salish, subordinate to whites, and the South Colombian Coconuco, subordinate to the Mestizo, suffer no alcoholism. The Mestizos of Peru, where the men claim superiority in position but where the women are independent, owning land and earning more than their husbands, are not afflicted. If subordinate status were a major factor, the shunned and often lowly positioned Jew should be fighting off alcoholism.

Of late, cultural conflict has been incriminated. The Aleuts, Salish, and Mohave, who seem to possess all the single-factor causes for alcoholism, are increasingly in conflict with the white man and yet remain without the problem of alcoholism. It is true that the Zarsals, bewildered and pulled in different directions, have just begun to suffer from alcoholism. On the other hand the Peruvian Mestizos, who are a fusion of Spanish and Indian with an overlay of contemporary American and European influences, do not show alcoholism. The constant cultural conflict of the Jew, although perhaps precipitating other abnormal responses, has never resulted in alcoholism.

The hypothesis that prohibition makes more desirable the forbidden fruit and is necessarily accompanied by excessive drinking has been offered as the cause of alcoholism. For this thesis we have little evidence for refutation or acceptance. The Mohave who has had alcohol prohibited to him gets intoxicated but does not become alcoholic. On the other hand, the Mormon to whom alcohol has been prohibited has problems when he drinks. The relation between prohibition and alcoholism needs further elaboration and clarification. Like all other single factors we are convinced that this too can not stand alone as a cause, although data are limited at present.

Drinking during the day and at odd hours, it is said, results in alcoholism. Among the South Colombian Mestizo some women and all men drink during day or night to a state of intoxication without addiction. Even the early morning drink may be taken in proper social context by Andean Indians or by Orthodox Jews without pathological dependence on it.

Because of high alcoholism rates among the Irish, it has been suggested that it is related to Catholicism; however, the low rate of alcoholism of Italian Catholics immediately negates this view.

Neurosis has been a handy culprit in explaining away alcoholism as well as other ills. As Lolli [2] notes, however, Italian drinking habits, "when neurotic traits are present, seldom or never lead to excessive and uncontrolled use of alcohol." Of course, the Jew is reported to suffer more than his fair share of neuroses, and yet he avoids the scourge of alcoholism.

The pharmacological effect of alcohol as a reducer of tension has been frequently implicated as a causative factor. It is obvious that pharmacological properties and potentialities of alcohol are constant. Tension reduction can become meaningful only as it relates to specific individuals and specific cultures. As we have noted earlier, alcohol does not always reduce tension, but sometimes increases it. All people who experience tension release from alcohol do not become addicted. The excessive drinker, hungering for pleasure rather than satisfaction, is said to be in a potentially addicting situation. Yet many hedonistic pleasure-seekers have relaxed with alcohol without succumbing to an alcoholic way of life.

Others have suggested strong oral influences in childhood, and yet patients or major ethnic groups with oral problems who drink (i.e. Jews) are seen every day by psychiatrists for other disorders and are not alcoholics.

Latent homosexuality as a single cause of alcoholism has been a main and recurring theme among many psychiatrists. Latent homosexual problems manifest themselves in many individuals and in many ways without the complication of alcoholism. We feel that the unconscious, strong desire of the alcoholic to be in a passive role has been misunderstood as homosexuality. If, as we noted earlier, the alcoholic has as *one* part of his multifaceted condition a defect and deprivation stemming from his earliest relationship with his mother, then it is logical (and his behavior and reactions tend to confirm the logic) that he should strive for situations where he can achieve what he feels he missed. If the one main motivating force in the alcoholic is to achieve symbolically gratification at an infantile level, it would not be surprising to find absent a defined sexual identity. If the alcoholic has a fixation at an early emotional level, he cannot see himself clearly in either sexual role and may assume any stance in order to satisfy his all-consuming desire to be loved. We feel that this passivity is mistaken for homosexuality.

Others have suggested the desire for escape as the cause of alcoholism. Escape from reality is a reactive phenomenon rather than a causative one. Some escape from reality is a reaction of all people and is not solely the province of the alcoholic. We might make the same criticism of other single psychological constructs: disappointment by women, "castration," anxiety, feelings of inferiority, childhood pampering, feelings of inadequacy, self-destructive drives, and fixation on forepleasure. These and many more emotional disturbances are present in a vast number of recognized and unrecognized psychiatric states (as well as the so-called normal). In combination with many other factors some have a contributary function in constructing the alcoholic. Cited alone as *the* germ of alcoholism, they serve only to confuse.

We should like to contest Strecker's [3] contention that the potential for addiction exists in us all. Although temporary regressive behavior may occur in everyone under the influence of alcohol, this does not imply that everyone could become addicted. The potential can exist only if the genetic, psychophysiological, and socio-cultural elements necessary to creating the severe disturbance of alcohol addiction are already present.

Genetic factors alone must also be rejected because as various psycho-physiological and socio-cultural alterations occur, problems of alcoholism tend also to change.

Nor could a conditioned reflex involving increased tolerance and withdrawal effects be solely causative. Once the bout was over, once the patient was "deconditioned" or "conditioned to sobriety" there would be no further difficulty. No matter how long a time the alcoholic is sober, the overwhelming evidence to date is that if he begins to drink again, his responses with alcohol will be pathological.

Nutritional deficiencies and metabolic diseases associated with disturbed adrenocortical function also have been offered as single-cause factors. We feel, and evidence seems to confirm, that these are secondary to poor nutrition associated with alcoholism as well as secondary to liver damage.

It is not surprising that we have had to reject all single factors offered as sole etiological agents of alcoholism. We can accept single-factor causality only rarely in any kind of problem, medical or otherwise. Tuberculosis, for example, is not caused by the tubercle bacillus alone. More people have been exposed to tubercle bacillus *without* becoming tuberculous than have developed the condition. What appears to be the case is that environmental, physiological, social, cultural, and psychological factors combine with the necessary tubercle bacillus to cause tuberculosis. A similar complex of psycho-physiological and socio-cultural disturbances must operate in the individual to produce an alcoholic.

III

Contemporary Alcoholism Programs

Man's responses to social and medical problems are uneven. Often damage is extensive before society reacts. Alcoholics continue to be morally shunned and punitively treated. In this section, we will examine society's efforts in behalf of the alcoholic, wherein the major impetus has been one alcoholic helping treat another.

6

Governmental Alcoholism Programs

Legend and superstition, action and reaction, have been prevailing responses to alcohol throughout the ages. Slavic legends attribute the invention of distillation to the devil. The czars of Russia made taverns a substantial source of their income by exercising a monopoly over them; in the early years of Communism the Russians tossed their unemployable alcoholics into work camps and rehabilitated them by working them to death. But many people have recognized a responsibility to limit alcoholism in their society, and in this chapter we shall try to trace their developing attitudes and responses to the problem.

The first written codes of law make reference to the necessity for a workable liquor control system. In the code of Hammurabi, a king of Babylon,[7] written almost four thousand years ago, prices were fixed for alcoholic beverages served in taverns. In Sparta, death was the penalty for warriors unfit to wage war because of drunkenness. Although the Chinese have had notably few alcohol problems, they seem to have responded erratically to alcohol, having enacted and then repealed laws dealing with the manufacture, sale, and consumption of wine forty-one times during the period from 1100 B.C. through A.D. 1400.[8]

Ambivalent reactions to alcoholism have been prevalent in America. The massive Washingtonian Movement of the nineteenth century (treatment oriented toward self-help) was preceded and followed by a myriad of legal decrees dealing with alcoholism. When in February 1872 the Commonwealth of Virginia established its Board of Health, among the five major Board requirements was the following: [12] "It shall be the duty of the Board ... to examine into and report what ... is the effect of the use of intoxicating liquor as a beverage, upon the industry, happiness, health and lives of the citizens of the state, and also what legislation, if any, is necessary in the premises." It took seventy-six years (until 1948) to initiate an alcoholism program following the passage of special legislation.

In the United States, Virginia was not first in its legislative interest in alcoholism, for in 1870, California similarly instructed its new Board of Health. The First Biennial Report of California (1870–71) commented on the seriousness of the problem, recommending "encouragement of those preventive measures brought about by individual will, aided by and at the same time aiding voluntarily associations with others, rather than by legislative enactment." As did Virginia and other states, California delayed actual action.[5, 10]

Scanning the history of government alcohol programs, we see that during the first fifty years only one approach was tried at any one time: legal, moral, punitive, even therapeutic at times—they were rarely combined. A many-sided approach did not evolve until after the failure and repeal of Prohibition and the lessons learned by two private organizations in battling alcoholism, Alcoholics Anonymous and Yale University Center of Alcohol Studies. Alcoholics Anonymous emphasized the approach of one alcoholic trying to help another, since society had not been able to deal effectively with the problem. Yale focused on alcohol and alcoholism scientifically. These two groups were followed by the first state-sponsored activities in alcoholism (Utah and Oregon, 1943), the organization of the first voluntary citizens association (1944), now the National Council on Alcoholism, and the organization of members of alcoholics' families into the Al-Anon Movement (1949). The twentieth-century approach to alcoholism now incorporates the earlier methods of treatment and citizen support, and adds to them the scientific method.

In 1943 Oregon and Utah were the first to establish programs through legislative action. In succeeding years, other states (37 states by 1961) instituted legislation on behalf of the alcoholic. (Hawaii's and Nevada's programs are so new they have been excluded from the following analysis.)

Eighteen state alcoholism programs came into being as independent, autonomous state agencies and had to stand or fall on their own success. Eight claimed a Department of Public Health as their parent figure, four were under Mental Health Departments, and three were located in a Department of Institutions as an appendage of public welfare. Four programs had special identities: a Liquor Control Board, a Department of Social Welfare, a Public Welfare Department, and an agency structurally related to a college of medicine.

The institutional pattern for alcoholism programs was established early in 1945 by Connecticut, which created a separate board having three major functions: research, education, and treatment, with the emphasis on treatment. The out-patient clinic program followed that of the Yale Clinic plan and in turn was the basis for out-patient programs throughout the nation.

As one looks back on the origins of the state alcoholism programs, one discovers antagonistic attitudes. One-half the programs came into being independently of other state departments. Existing community agencies seemed to want no part of state alcohol programs, and vice versa. On the part of the existing agencies, the rejection of these programs reflected the general hopelessness felt toward alcohol problems as well as the lack of community motivation toward positive action usually associated with alcoholism. For their part, the innovators of alcohol programs guarded their independence. Those who were recovered alcoholics felt that alcoholism was a special and unique problem not to be trusted to existing agencies. Professional workers who took the initiative were able to see the advantages of the community's hostility toward alcoholics as permitting themselves more flexibility.

Nevertheless the first two states in this new movement began their work in existing departments: Oregon, in the still extant Liquor Control Board; Utah, in the State Public Welfare Department. Virginia, in 1948, started a trend in state agencies which appears to be growing—its alcoholism program became part of the Department of Public Health.

Though at present alcoholism boards are maintained in twenty-eight states, their evolution illustrates the trend set by Virginia toward removing control of alcoholism programs from the concerned but untrained layman to the professional health department. The tendency is to substitute advisory functions for the alcoholism board's policymaking powers which are then transferred to the health department. This move is reinforced by legislation requiring qualifications for alcoholism-board membership. These gradual changes are not only introducing more professional workers to the field but also emphasizing a new willingness to consider alcoholism a sickness and a concern of public health.

Legislators have been trying earnestly to come to grips with alcoholism in these terms. Fourteen states have given it a label. Three call it a "disease," six, an "illness and public health problem," two, a "sickness," and one, a "public health problem," one speaks of "victims," another, of "sufferers." Seventeen states are even more ambitious; they try to define alcoholism. Most describe it as "any condition of abnormal behavior or illness resulting directly and indirectly from the chronic and habitual use of alcoholic beverages." [2] These efforts are important. By suggesting the illness concept they reinforce the treatment programs, giving them much needed prestige and social sanction. This makes it easier for the alcoholic to seek treatment.

There has been a change in the sources of funds for alcoholism programs. Formerly, eleven states raised the funds from taxes on alcoholic beverages. Now only seven do. The trend is to procure appropriations from general funds, as with other existing health efforts. This is another indication of alcoholism's increased "respectability."

Pressure against the former special funds has come from two sources. The first, a powerful one, is the alcohol beverage industry. Although it has not been overtly active in its lobbying activities, steady and subtle pressure is exerted to eliminate these special taxes where they exist. The motivation of the industry is to keep the retail price as low as possible, and, at the same time avoid the harmful association of alcoholism with tax income derived from their product. The second major source of opposition comes from state executive departments who wish to stem the tide of special funds. The larger the percentage of earmarked revenue, the more complicated and awkward the administrative fabric.

To date, state programs have shown a steady and constant growth in appropriations. In 1944, the first complete year of operation for state programs, a total of $30,572 was appropriated. Four years later, in 1948, total state expenditures had increased to $430,000. In 1952 the total had risen to $1,700,000, in 1956 to $3,800,000, and in 1960, $6,000,000. In the first sixteen years of state program operation (1944–60), $32,000,000 have been spent by the specialized alcohol agencies. In terms of the magnitude of the problem, this is a pittance, but certainly better than nothing.

Alcoholism programs now reflect the traditional public health structure of treatment, research, and education, another indication that government action in alcoholism has come of age. In some alcoholism programs co-ordination has been added as a fourth component. Although we shall review these four functions separately, in operation they overlap.

TREATMENT

Legislative action in this country was first directed toward treatment. The pioneer public out-patient alcoholism clinic was established by the District of Columbia's Department of Public Health in 1945. This primary effort was bolstered two years later by Congress, when it officially established a special alcoholism agency in the District of Columbia Department of Public Health.

The increased expenditures for alcoholism programs, while associated with a concomitant rise in the population, resulted primarily from an increased interest in the problem. This may be illustrated by a four-year sampling. In 1948, in state alcoholism programs, 473 patients were seen for treatment, while in 1952 the number had climbed to 7858. By 1956 there were 20,235 patients enrolled in state treatment efforts, and 26,000 patients in 1960. By the end of 1960, after twelve full years of state interest in the treatment of the alcoholic, about 177,000 patients have been seen, some intensively, some only once, in treatment facilities operated or supported by state agencies.

Referral sources to state facilities for treatment occur in the following order of frequency (this is a five-year nation-wide average): physicians, Alcoholics Anonymous members, self-referrals, family and friends, courts and police, and social agencies. The motivation for referral and treatment varies. In some cases treatment is undertaken deliberately by the alcoholic; in others it has occurred by happenstance, while some people are brought in for treatment by legal pressure. The early focus of most programs on treatment is emphasized by the following statement of the Connecticut Commission on Alcoholism: "until there is concrete evidence available to the people of the state that alcoholism is a remediable illness, programs directed at public education on problems of alcoholism and at prevention of alcoholism will have little effect; thus focus on treatment demonstrates that alcoholics can be helped."

An illustration of the difficulty in motivating the alcoholic to seek help is exemplified by the fact that fourteen states have special commitment procedures in their law. Legally oriented, coercive approaches are still important in persuading some alcoholics to undertake treatment.

Clinical treatment in all states is mainly by out-patient therapy. All states operating a program have at least one facility designated as an out-patient alcoholism clinic. They are usually located and operated within the confines of a general hospital or in rented facilities independent of other health services. These clinics are usually staffed by a part-time psychiatrist and a full-time social worker. In some clinics the basic staffing is implemented by psychologists, internists, public health nurses, and recovered alcoholics.

Certain states (Connecticut, New Hampshire, North Carolina, Georgia, and Florida) go beyond out-patient facilities and provide special and separate in-service hospital programs. Other states complement their out-patient activity by using general or psychiatric hospitals for their hospitalization needs. Those states having in-service programs were in the alcoholism movement early, and since 1953 no state has established special hospital facilities. Although there are many reasons for this, the expense of operating special hospitals and the recommendation for use of general hospitals by the Committee on Alcoholism of the American Medical Association have been dominating factors. This can, of course, benefit the alcoholic. Too often special alcoholic wards or hospitals have been thought of as areas for the delinquent or incorrigible, and they tend to foster ancient, punitive, and moralizing ideas about alcoholism. Only by incorporating alcoholism treatment programs within existing treatment facilities can the identification and recognition of alcoholism as a public health problem be accomplished and result in improvement in the quality of care.

A major progressive movement of recent years is that of the "halfway houses." They serve in addition to special hospitals and out-patient facilities. They are primarily for the homeless alcoholic who does not require complete custodial care, but rather long-term protective support while he gradually re-establishes his contacts and responsibilities with the community. From the halfway house he may venture out to work and return to the protection of this supportive establishment, at the same time receiving whatever help is needed.[9]

The treatment regimes of state programs range through the gamut of rehabilitative endeavors. They include individual and group psychotherapy (supportive or insight-oriented), case work, psychodrama and sociodrama, recreational and occupational therapy, medical care, pastoral counseling, and Alcoholics Anonymous.

RESEARCH

In the area of research, state attitudes have vacillated. With the exception of Oregon, all programs are permitted to participate in and support research. Yet only a handful of people are involved in research associated with state programs, and even that research is generally an extension of and secondary to treatment. In 1958 only eighty research projects, representing 16 per cent of the state budget, were under state auspices.

When one analyzes the reasons for the lack of research support by state governments (all give it their blessings as long as state money is not the issue), one is left with an answer pertinent for government activities as a whole. State programs are as a rule "today-oriented." The politician and legislator who has his left eye on the present needs of the state and his right eye on the next election cannot be expected to buy or support activities which are "future-oriented." Research necessarily deals with future possibilities and probabilities. One cannot predict whether it will succeed or fail, and much of it, if honest, must fail.

EDUCATION

Most legislators have accepted in principle alcohol education efforts because they equate education with prevention. This equation and the acceptance of education and prevention as a goal for state activities are worth special emphasis. The prevention of alcoholism necessitates an understanding of the etiological factors. Yet lack of interest, ignorant attitudes and myths, and gross absence of research activities persist. In addition, these ancient attitudes have driven the alcoholic underground. Consequently, not only have we been left in ignorance about factors contributing to the condition, we have also lost contact with the people who might be treated and studied. For these two reasons alone, the dissemination to the public of educational information directed toward understanding and uncovering prospective patients is essential. It produces a more positive attitude toward the alcoholic, so that with a measure of self-respect he may ask for help with his problem.

State programs have participated vigorously in all phases of dissemination, distributing over a million pieces of literature each year and utilizing films, radio, television, and speakers' bureaus. It is a psychological axiom as well as a clinical observation that barriers—especially barriers constructed out of ignorance and myth—are easily erected but removed only with great difficulty. So it is with alcoholism. The moral, punitive, ancient walls around the drinker and his problems, which isolate him, are not easily scaled or breached. Workers seeking to break down these walls have been few, and much of the motivation to do so has had to be generated by the alcoholic himself, in his own behalf. In order to expand the number of workers in alcoholism, special training programs for both professional and lay audiences have been sponsored by states. Yet only 10 per cent of state alcoholism program budgets are allocated to the area of education and very few full-time specialists are employed in this capacity.

CO-ORDINATION

A recent innovation in alcoholism programing is that of coordination. This function is never explicitly spelled out, and is only realized in association with the other major procedures and goals, treatment, research, and education.[3] The Massachusetts legislature tried to define the role of co-ordination as follows: [6]

> ... seek to coordinate the work of all departments and agencies dealing with the care and treatment of alcoholics ... (and) ... receive ... reports from all such departments and agencies ...

Co-ordination serves to meet the needs of existing organizations and institutions, develop new methodological approaches, and facilitate treatment, research, and education.

One thing is certain, state alcoholism programs are born against resistance, live surrounded by hostile and threatening forces, and only continue to survive by a constant interest and effort. In the uphill struggle for the creation of state alcoholism efforts, three attempts have fallen by the wayside. Death by budget strangulation was the fate meted out in Wisconsin in 1955, in Kansas in 1956, and in Tennessee in 1959. The reasons were not obvious, for all three were permitted to function in the major areas of treatment, research, and education. In no startling way were these three programs different from all other state programs. Perhaps a general retrenchment of state activities or the dominance by temperance-oriented devotees of legal, rather than rehabilitative, measures was the cause. Certainly the power groups in the community must have lost interest in the problem. New life may be breathed into them, since the enabling legislation remains unchanged. Alcoholism programs as the most recent addition to public health movements are still on very shaky ground. They could easily disappear following the ancient order of seniority: the last to be started, the first to go.

Although there is no typical process or timing in the creation of state alcoholism programs, the activities of Texas may be considered "average." Its constitution, enacted in 1876 (Article XVI, Section 42), provides that "the legislature may establish an inebriate asylum for the care of drunkenness and the reform of 'inebriates.'" In 1893, a law was promulgated requiring that the effects of alcohol and narcotics be taught in all schools, colleges, and universities that are wholly or in part supported by state funds. Fifty-eight years later, in 1951, legislation was enacted permitting the admission of voluntary alcoholic patients to state hospitals. Two years later came the creation of a State Commission on Alcoholism to operate in the three major areas of alcoholism. However, as has been the case in other states, no funds were allocated. In 1955, a special appropriation was made to the state hospital system to aid in the treatment and care of alcoholics in state hospitals, and only in 1957 was a special appropriation of $150,000 made to give the commission life and vigor. This case history emphasizes the ebb and flow of attempts to convince states of their responsibility to this major health problem.

A beneficial effect of state interest has been the development of municipal action. For a long time municipalities have acknowledged alcoholism as a problem only peripheral to others, for example, correction, probation, welfare, tuberculosis, and chronic disease. However, with the evolution of specialized state endeavors for alcoholics, some of the larger cities and counties have developed their own programs (New York, Minneapolis, Cleveland, San Francisco, Worcester, Boston, and Columbus). This municipal activity foreshadows a spreading activity at a more local level of government assumption of responsibility for alcoholism programs.

Early in the creation and development of state programs, the need for the strength that unity provides was demonstrated in the creation of the North American Association of Alcoholism Programs. This group (NAAAP) came into being when ten states, plus the District of Columbia, and the Province of Ontario, banded together to form the National States Council on Alcoholism, which later became the NAAAP. The objectives of the earlier and present organization, as stated in its by-laws, are as follows:

1. To provide a medium for the exchange of ideas and information regarding organization, policies and methods relating to state, provincial, territorial, and the District of Columbia programs of alcoholism.
2. To establish standards for the classification of problem drinkers and for the evaluation of therapeutic procedures in order to compare and appraise program results in the various states, provinces, territories, and the District of Columbia.
3. To establish standards for educational, clinical, and related services for the guidance of states, provinces, and territories, now entering the field of alcoholism and for the self-evaluation of states, provinces, territo-

ries, and the District of Columbia already administering such programs.

4. To encourage and co-operate with national, voluntary and official agencies and with institutions engaged in research and other activities concerning alcoholism.

This united effort has permitted the NAAAP to approach the national government, through the United States Public Health Service granting agencies, for financial aid in supporting special meetings and for the initiation of research projects. Projects have involved evaluation of efficacy of state treatment programs, efforts toward delineation of the vast nomenclature difficulties associated with alcoholism, and most recently a survey of past and present efforts.

As we view governmental alcoholism efforts in the United States we have mixed feelings. That there has been effective effort in recent years is gratifying. Yet this is not enough. More funds and more experimentation are needed in alcoholism programs if real progress is to be made. Those programs directed exclusively toward treatment alone are doomed to failure because sufficient trained personnel do not and cannot exist. Only when treatment is combined with research and education, and new techniques are explored and developed, can real progress ensue.

For the future we envision a growth of municipally operated programs, an integration of independent state programs with public health departments, an increased focus on research, education, and co-ordination, and finally a closer collaboration between alcoholism programs and existing health agencies and personnel.

GOVERNMENTAL EFFORTS IN OTHER NATIONS

The Canadian provinces' programs began shortly after those of the American states, and have shown amazing growth, in general exceeding the American states in average per capita appropriation. As in the United States, no national program exists. In Ontario the Alcoholism Research Foundation is probably the outstanding governmental alcoholism program in the world.

Although the Scandinavian countries, the Benelux Nations, France, and Switzerland have all enacted legislation pertaining to alcoholism [1] (Sweden began in 1913),[4] we have chosen to discuss here three iron-curtain countries, Czechoslovakia, Poland, and Russia, since little information is available in the United States about their efforts.

In these three countries, as in most nations throughout the world which operate alcoholism programs, all alcoholism activities are directed by the national government.

In Czechoslovakia, the area of alcoholism work is extended to any complications or problems arising from the excessive use of alcohol. By alcohol excesses the Czechs mean using alcohol at unsuitable times (at work), in an unsuitable form (too high a concentration), at an unsuitable age (childhood), and at unsuitable times of life (pregnancy and illness). The Czechs carefully emphasize that they are not making efforts to enforce prohibition or abstinence for the general population but merely desire to deal with the ravages of excesses. Quite wisely they add that prohibitionary aims would meet with strong opposition and would most likely defeat anti-alcoholism programs. Czechoslovakia is a socialized, industrial country where large groups gather together socially, and much drinking occurs at these gatherings.

Consumption of alcohol in Czechoslovakia has increased fully one-third in the last reported year of 1956 in comparison with consumption fifteen years before in 1941. This increase in alcohol usage has brought increasing problems of alcoholic excesses despite the fact that the Czechs say that many economic causes leading to alcoholism have been removed by the socialistic state. Figures also show an increase of 33 to 50 per cent for problems involving the drunk driver, and a 43 per cent increase in convictions and prison sentences for crimes involving alcohol.

As in the United States, more money is spent in Czechoslovakia on alcohol than on books, movies, and theater. For example, in 1946 the Czechs spent 300,000,000 Czech crowns on the cultural goals mentioned, whereas they spent 1,900,000,000 Czech crowns on alcoholic beverages, 720,000,000 of which was on hard liquor (this is significant in a major beer producing and consuming country). In 1954, the cultural expenditure figure was 800,000,000 crowns, versus 4,888,000,000 crowns (2,700,000,000 on hard liquor) and in 1955, the last available reported year, the figure for cultural pursuits was 850,000,000 crowns, 5,750,000,000 crowns for beverage alcohol (3,100,000,000 for hard liquor).

Conservative estimates place the number of alcoholics in Czechoslovakia (one of the iron-curtain countries for which figures have been made available) at about 120,000 people, or roughly 2 per cent of the total population (versus 3 per cent of total population, or 5–6,000,000 alcoholics, in the United States). As in the United States, Czechs find that the association between alcoholism and broken marriage is very high.

The main impetus for alcoholism treatment endeavors in Czechoslovakia derives from a law passed in 1948. This law covers *all* measures directed toward protecting the health of the people from the consequences of alcoholism. The "fight against alcoholism" is mainly carried out by educational programs, by research into causes and complications of alcoholism, and their subsequent removal, and by treatment and supervision of people who injure their health by excessive use of alcohol. Further efforts against alcoholism include prohibiting the sale of alcohol to people under age eighteen, to intoxicated individuals, or to individuals whose work endangers their life or health or who are responsible for the physical safety of others (e.g. bus drivers and doctors). The main effect of the 1948 law is a program executed through various health, social, and political committees whereby alcoholism becomes a concern of all inhabitants, of all official bodies, and of all elected representatives. The Czechs have learned, as we are slowly learning in dealing with major health problems, that mobilization of total community resources is essential.

All efforts at prevention and treatment of alcoholism in Czechoslovakia are ultimately directed by the Ministry of Health. Most treatment takes place in out-patient clinics and is free of charge under the National Health Insurance program. These out-patient facilities are called anti-alcoholic clinics. With in-patient care afforded in psychiatric institutions, and custodial, long-term care at Lodijice, the Czech government has made provisions for an extensive program against alcoholism.

An innovation is the anti-alcoholic station, the first line of alcoholism prevention. Here, individuals are seen in acute states of intoxication which either endanger their health, their surroundings, or the public. Patients are brought to the anti-alcoholic station in an ambulance by the police, and they are put to bed and given any necessary treatment. When they become sober, they are released. For this "drying-out service" a charge of about thirty-five to fifty crowns is made to the individual for his transportation and treatment (apparently the only medical situation where a charge is made).

When discharged from the station, the individual has his name placed on the district list of the alcoholic center, and he must thereafter report for a lecture about alcoholism and its consequences (usually held on Sundays). The district doctor will also call upon him to evaluate whether or not he is an alcoholic. When a social problem is apparent, a social worker is called in to gather more information. When the district doctor makes a diagnosis of alcoholism, or if the individual shows up at an anti-alcoholic station a second time, the psychiatrist is called in and long-term therapy is begun.

Although most stations are open only at night, in large industrial towns they are open continuously. The stations are staffed principally by male nurses, and the psychiatrists on duty specialize in the problems of alcoholism. All stations are set up as annexes of medical facilities, so that the whole treatment program may be integrated. The anti-alcoholic station therefore functions primarily for early detection of alcohol problems and provides medical treatment for acute alcoholic states.

The second-line treatment facility of the alcoholism program is the anti-alcoholic clinic. The work of these clinics is to treat individuals who are diagnosed as alcoholic; i.e. who drink to excess causing disturbances of a medical or social nature. In the clinics, as well as giving treatment, the personnel is engaged in alcohol educational work and in mantaining files and a lookout for individuals who have been seen formerly in anti-alcoholic stations. Latest available figures reported that the average clinic serves a population of about 90,000 with an average annual case load of over 300 alcoholic patients. Only 10 per cent of the patient load is in attendance for treatment voluntarily, and the rest are undergoing treatment as a consequence of external pressures. The anti-alcoholic clinics are integrated from parts of psychiatric, neurological, or medical departments of the Institute of National Health.

A patient recommended for alcoholism treatment is asked to bring his spouse along for the first visit. If the interview shows that marital difficulties contribute to the drinking, the marital partner is also given treatment. Treatment for both alcoholic and mate consists of group therapy sessions together and also in separate groups. The major goal is to motivate the patient to seek treatment voluntarily and to avoid institutionalization. Therefore, anti-alcoholic clinics operate primarily to use available medical and psychiatric treatment methods to treat alcoholism on an out-patient basis, since treatment in institutions tends to take longer (anywhere from three months to one year).

When, therefore, the patient is diagnosed as alcoholic, he is first evaluated thoroughly. After evaluation he is given Antabuse, followed by an Antabuse-reaction experience. The Czech method of Antabuse administration is different from the usual practice in the United States in that the Czechs give Antabuse just on weekends, because they feel this is the most dangerous period for the alcoholic. An individual "booklet" is kept in the clinic on every patient, which includes details about Antabuse administration, drinking behavior, and any social problems that may exist which complicate the drinking. The social worker also investigates, in the patient's neighborhood, the behavior of the individual and his wife and any drinking that they may do. If in the alcoholic's booklet there are gaps regarding the taking of Antabuse, the following through on social obligations, or the incidences of drinking, the patient is institutionalized. If, on the other hand, in eight or nine months of clinic treatment there has not been a need for institutionalization, then the patient's active treatment is discontinued.

When institutional treatment is recommended, the patient is placed on a waiting list. During the waiting period, he attends group treatment sessions conducted by successfully treated patients. In other words, the patient is brought into a group setting similar to Alcoholics Anonymous, where people who have made successful adjustments to their alcohol problem are utilized in the treatment program.

In the department (Czech term for in-patient facility) of Apolinár as well as at Lodijice (the mansion and estate of a wealthy brewer whose property was confiscated under the Communist system and ironically turned into an anti-alcoholic institution), facilities for lengthy in-patient care are available.

The stated aim of the in-patient therapeutic approach is to systematize the various forms of treatment into a total approach. First the patient is isolated from alcohol and his activities put under continuous control. Physical and mental rehabilitation is instituted to teach him a "correct way of living and good habits." The program strives for producing an aversion to alcohol by active therapeutic methods while at the same time utilizing the patient's talents and work through self-government organization and occupational therapy. According to the Assistant Director of the nation's program it is directed toward attracting "... the attention of the patient from his own narrow, individual interests to the interests of a small community (roommates, family), a larger community (all patients in the department, people in the work place), and the whole community (society)."

The three-month treatment program includes both individual and group psychotherapy and work treatment. Individual psychotherapy means weekly interviews of twenty minutes' duration. Psychotherapy groups meet for one hour once a week with a doctor and once a week with either a social worker or a recovered patient. There are also groups for patients who have special problems associated with alcoholism, e.g. sexual difficulties while drinking or criminal acts while intoxicated. Group size varies betwen seven and twelve patients and points for attendance are awarded. Points are also given for work activities; for the patient's consistency in his social obligations; and for attending courses about the basic factors in alcoholism. If a particular group gains points, it receives special rewards (extra time off, awards) and competition between groups is encouraged. Points are awarded to the individual as well as to the group as a group. Therefore, the patients push one another to do better and get more points for the group. Information about alcohol is graded to the patient's mental and intellectual ability at all levels. If abstainers and wives come to a meeting, they get points and recognition. A patient who has abstained for three years can then get into a program assisting social workers and other patients. Abstainers form an Auxiliary Aid of Cured Patients and actually work in the clinic as part of the clinic personnel. Hospitalized patients take shifts at night helping out with intoxicated patients brought into the station, and this is important, because this work helps the alcoholic to see himself as he was in an alcoholic stupor.

Actors and artists who are alcoholic but who have abstained for long periods of time come to perform before other alcoholics, and this helps in the identification process which the Czechs feel is very useful in helping create new self-respect and maintaining it. A leading poet of Czechoslovakia, winner of a national prize and an abstainer for over five years, comes to read poetry before groups of alcoholics.

Patients sent to Lodijice work for the nearby co-operative farm, but the proceeds of their labors go to the hospital. Throughout hospitalization, the patient's family receives compensation just as it would have if he had been ill from any other medical condition. Regardless of how long he is institutionalized, work therapy, psychotherapy, and individual and group treatment continue. The Czechs believe that complete education about alcohol, scientifically and socially, helps in the treatment of the alcoholic.

After the first four weeks of institutionalization, patients are able to obtain passes for Saturday and Sunday. These leaves are designed to show the patient that he is able to remain abstinent outside the department's protective walls.

The Lodijice treatment center reports 50 per cent success, success being measured by abstinence from alcohol for one year. The patient who has maintained complete abstinence for one year after admission receives a diploma. After three years of abstinence, he gets increased recognition. He may even have rooms in a hospital named after him.

Follow-up of these patients is very close, with stress on continuing interest in him. Thus, the alcoholic is reassured that he can come to talk over problems even if he is not drinking, and this is often reiterated.

Anti-alcoholic propaganda efforts have increased in Czechoslovakia in the last four years, stressing that the alcoholic is not delinquent but ill. Despite extensive propaganda on the problems of alcoholism in Czechoslovakia, the most effective means of getting patients into treatment is by successfully treated patients telling another about the help they have received.

When alcoholics are picked up for drinking at work, the industry arranges for treatment, which permits early recognition and treatment. Teams of recovered patients in a factory setting are called in, along with a specially trained social worker, to help a person who has a problem of drinking in industry. In this way it is felt that recovered patients pay back the state for their treatment by their activities in helping other patients. If a man is in a milieu conducive to alcoholism the state may change his job and put him in a different situation, but this is rarely done.

In Czechoslovakia there are thirteen anti-alcoholic departments with a total capacity of 500 beds for the in-patient treatment of the alcoholic. These beds are mainly housed in psychiatric clinics or institutions. The individual medical departments throughout the country have their own specialists. If for some reason an alcoholic patient cannot come to the center, house calls are made. The main burden for the care of the alcoholic falls on the shoulders of the psychiatrists, and because they are in short supply, they rotate to different centers devoting certain hours to anti-alcoholic activity. Although some internists have expressed interest in alcoholism, the psychiatrists and specially trained social workers are mainstays of the program.

All in all, the Czechs are doing an excellent job, and some of their basic approaches and ideas are in agreement with our own feelings about helping the alcoholic. Their social system is more suitable to treating alcoholics than our own, since—in a controlled, Communistic government—one can exercise closer social controls over a patient and keep in closer touch with him than one can in a social system like ours. The fact that the government goes to the expense of paying the family during long hospitalization for alcoholism, as well as other medical conditions, is a broad social step forward.

The emphasis on various people who have successfully been helped with their alcoholism problem and who enjoy prominence in all levels of social life also is a sensible psychological means of strengthening identification and aiding the patient to develop self-respect. Then, too, the Czech program is a total program, in the sense that it attempts to deal with problems at intrapsychic, extrapsychic, and social levels.

The inadequate effort in Poland is in contrast to the comprehensive alcoholism program in Czechoslovakia. The Poles are experiencing great problems with alcohol excesses. These problems with alcohol have become uncontrollable since the end of the war, and although the Poles recognize alcoholism as a rampant public health problem, they apparently feel overwhelmed in dealing with it. Since the main goal of alcoholism treatment from the Polish viewpoint is hospitalization, they are able to handle only small numbers of patients. Not only are physical and professional facilities unavailable for the treatment of hordes of alcoholics, but a self-defeating attitude exists toward the entire problem. To the surviving Polish adult, as one phychiatrist put it, psychotherapy is the only remaining means of dealing with life, and the most readily available form of "psychotherapy" is drinking with one's friends and talking. In other words, according to these physicians, in order to deal with life as it existed before, during, and after the last war, one can only go out, get drunk, and talk. This has resulted in a social attitude of ambivalence not unlike that found in Irish drinking behavior. On one hand the Poles are unhappy that so much drinking and intoxication exist; on the other they accept this drinking pattern as an extremely important means of coping with their life. The result in Poland is a cultural value system which accepts the drinking of alcohol as a means of dealing with the vicissitudes of life. We feel that this attitude tends to increase the incidence of alcoholism.

Another major factor contributing to alcoholism problems in Poland was the drinking pattern during the Nazi occupation. Despite deprivation in many areas, drinking was common. The goal of Polish wartime drinking (not unlike the present-day drinking goals of American culture) was to reach an end point whereby one's tensions could be relieved, but not achieve such intoxication that one's ability to avoid detention by and difficulties with the Germans was impaired. This unpredictable hairline limit of drinking is now by-passed and often results in alcohol excesses.

A third important aspect of the impetus to alcoholism in Poland stems from social changes in Poland since the end of the war. There has been a strong movement from rural to urban areas. Urban existence is so different from rural existence in Poland that country people relocated in the city feel lost and lonely, without friends and familiar sights, and turn to alcohol as their only solace. To the Pole, alcohol is a friend.

For the rare alcoholic who is treated, drugs and psychotherapy are the treatments of choice. Psychotherapy to the Poles represents a form of re-education. By giving information about the cause, pathology, and course of the disease, the Poles feel they provide the means by which an individual may escape his dependence on alcohol. Drugs offered are Antabuse or Emetine, and an attempt to develop aversion to alcohol is always made. Along with drugs and psychotherapy, hospitalization for at least six months is required. The main purpose of hospitalization beyond drugs, work, etc., is to create an "alcoholic family situation" where aid is given by one alcoholic to another. Thus a therapeutic community is created which can extend itself into the outside community after the patients are discharged from the hospital. Hospitalization is accomplished either at the family's request, by governmental authorities, or by voluntary commitment. The alcoholic patient is considered and treated as a neurotic in Poland, and oftentimes receives subcoma doses of insulin (a fashionable therapy for neurosis in Poland).

Two months after the patient achieves abstinence, he is permitted occasional passes into town.

The medical and social attitude toward the alcoholic in Poland is that he is a sick individual. When hospitalized, he is given considerable autonomy and has contact with outsiders. There is no effort to isolate him or make him feel different. As with any illness, the Poles pay the patient's salary for his first three months of hospitalization and thereafter he is put on pension. Every effort is made to take care of his family during hospitalization, as well as to alleviate any possible anxiety the patient might have concerning his home situation during his treatment.

In summary, the Poles have an overwhelming problem with alcoholism, with insufficient facilities for treating the condition, and with cultural and psychological attitudes toward drinking which appear to lead to increased alcoholism rates.

In Russia, while the official policy is to deny the alcoholism problem, professionals have no hesitancy in stating that Russia has as much alcoholism as any other country although they are unwilling to estimate the size of their alcoholic population.

Treatment of alcoholics in the Soviet Union involves psycho-therapy (education against alcoholism), hypnotherapy (in which the mainstay is posthypnotic suggestion against taking a drink), and "reflex reaction" or aversion type treatment. In the latter, experience sessions of Emetine or apomorphine and alcohol are administered two or three times a week in the hope of creating "an aversion reflex." Although on occasion group sessions are held for aversion therapy, the Soviet practi-tioners prefer individual experiences, because they feel that an important aspect of treatment is the maintaining of contact between doctor and patient.

Another important component of the Soviet treatment of alcoholism is environmental manipulation. Environmental ma-nipulation is employed whenever the caretakers feel the pa-tient is living "in an alcoholic society." When this is the case, the alcoholic is placed in a different location (they have the means to change his society and prevent him from getting into further difficulties). The relocated alcoholic patient is asked to rid himself of old friends, and means are provided whereby he may meet new people. In treatment the image is constructed that the old friends with whom drinking is associated are the alcoholic's enemies and that the doctor and new friends are the means of conquering alcoholism.

Many Soviet psychiatrists specializing in alcoholism consider the chief etiological factor in alcoholism to be individual emo-tional disturbances, and believe that the tense, nervous person will become alcoholic sooner than other people. However, the general Soviet physician and psychiatrist, like many in the United States, consider the alcoholic a delinquent and not ill, and avoid treating alcoholism unless complications such as delirium tremens, alcoholic hallucinosis, polyneuritis, or Korsakoff's syndrome are present. Despite medical and social disapproval toward the alcoholic (the alcoholic and his family are denied certain benefits of the socialistic state while hospitalized, unlike other patients), the Soviet Government insists that all hospitals have facilities for the care of alcoholics, and these programs have increased governmental backing.

The main inconsistency about Soviet alcoholism endeavors is that, despite Soviet protestations in favor of conditioning factors in alcoholism, there is no systematized study (as far as we know) employing Pavlovian techniques of extinction of a conditioned response to alcohol usage.

In summary, we would say that in the Soviet Union the attitude toward the alcoholic tends to be moralistic and punitive, as in the United States. Although the Soviets do not achieve the sophistication, interest, and extent of Czechoslovakian efforts in alcoholism, their programs are more advanced than those in Poland.

What conclusions can we draw from our brief perusal of governmental alcoholism endeavors? First, that alcoholism is to a considerable extent a world-wide problem. Second, since alcoholism is truly a public health problem, the most effective action will be through total community involvement, with governments setting the lead. Throughout the world, governments are beginning efforts toward dealing with alcoholism, although with the exception of Sweden and Switzerland, this activity is recent. Though no nation can claim to have ultimate answers to alcoholism, certain effective attitudes exist. These are: consideration of the alcoholic as sick; use of a wide range of therapeutic techniques and programs; recognition of the need for environmental manipulation; emphasis on action programs (i.e. reaching out to patients); and concern with both prevention and early detection. The single major difference between European and American programs is European willingness to work with alcohol excesses as well as alcoholism.

7

Yale Center of Alcohol Studies

One of the most important endeavors to date in the field of alcoholism has been undertaken at Yale University. Yale has given the major impetus and respectability to modern scientific methods for dealing with alcoholism.

The Yale Center of Alcohol Studies and Laboratory of Applied Biodynamics is made up of four subdivisions: Laboratory of Applied Biodynamics (formerly the Laboratory of Applied Physiology); Summer School of Alcohol Studies; Documentation and Publications Division; and the Social Science and Applied Research Program.

Yale began to pay special attention to alcohol [4] in 1932, when the Laboratory of Applied Physiology (an autonomous unit of Yale created in 1919) instituted intensive studies of the physiology and metabolism of alcohol. As their research program developed, the complexities involved in alcohol problems became more apparent and the beginnings of a multidiscipline approach evolved. In addition, Dr. Howard Haggard, the director at that time, began to focus his laboratory's work on educational activities. He became active in popularizing varied aspects of medical science. Selden D. Bacon described the early years of the Center in an address at the Yale Summer School of Alcohol Studies: [2]

> ... these three points should be kept in mind if one is to gain a picture of the Center of Alcohol Studies—two driving brilliant personalities; a combination of scientific research with application to life-problem situations; and a function of education both within the formal educational institution and also in the broad area of informal and public education.

With a growing demand by the public for services, the Yale Center of Alcohol Studies was established. Financially the Center's undertaking was self-supporting.[2] Although Yale supplied a building and a token budget, financial support was derived primarily from the contributions of individuals and organizations. Contributions cannot have "strings attached," and the proportion of budget acceptable from certain sources was limited.[4]

March 1, 1944 saw the establishment of the Yale Plan Clinics in Hartford and New Haven, Connecticut.[3,5] Supported jointly by the Center and the Connecticut State Prison Association, the clinics' functions were to study, to determine appropriate therapy, and to make appropriate referral of alcoholic patients. As Jellinek[3] has described them, they were "two free Clinics for the guidance of inebriates." In a short time, however, the lack of adequate referral facilities led to a revision of functions, treatment being added to the clinics' program.[5] The established pattern for staffing the clinics consisted of part-time psychiatrists and internists, a psychologist, social workers, and secretaries. The critical role of the Yale Plan Clinics in the history of alcoholism programs is reflected in present out-patient clinic structure. Most present-day treatment programs still follow the principle of the multidiscipline treatment team located in the community. The appropriateness of this technique is further emphasized not only by the fact of its being imitated but also by the increased demands for such services. When Connecticut established its own outpatient alcoholism clinics, the Yale Plan Clinics were turned over to the state.

The National Council on Alcoholism, a national voluntary organization, was also started at Yale in 1944.[2] Since we shall devote a separate section to council activities, we shall not elaborate upon it here.

A major endeavor of the Yale Center was the Summer School of Alcohol Studies.[2] Established in 1943 under the leadership of Dr. Jellinek, a four-week course (six weeks the first year) was inaugurated. Reacting to the public's quest for information on alcoholism, the school began with 86 pupils, and student members have increased steadily, with as many as 300 in attendance. Forty-nine states and many foreign countries have been represented. By examining the make-up of the student body, one can see the changing interest toward alcoholism. Bacon describes the changes of interested groups as follows: [2] "The problems of alcohol, once admittedly the responsibility of but two or three groups, have come to be seriously recognized as an important and appropriate responsibility for all religious groups as well as for scientists; the medical and nursing professions; industrial groups; education; public health; for agencies of enforcement, adjudication and correction; for community and social agencies of many sorts."

The Yale Center's efforts in the field of documentation and publication have been very important.[6] The *Quarterly Journal of Studies on Alcohol*, founded by Dr. Howard W. Haggard in 1940, is easily the best periodical in the alcohol-alcoholism field. In this journal, articles appear regularly from many disciplines, running the gamut from biochemistry to psychiatry, sociology, and social work. In addition, abstracts and reviews of articles and books published throughout the world in any language are presented.

The Documentation and Publications Division of the Center reprints most of the significant *Journal* articles, prepares lay articles written by competent scientists, and supports the publication of books and monographs. In addition, educational posters are prepared, as well as brief reviews of new information on treatment for medical and allied professions.

Although Yale has made many contributions to the field of alcohol, it is our opinion that the Classified Abstract Archives of the Alcohol Literature will prove to be the most fruitful and meaningful. Already consisting of about ten thousand abstracts, the Archives are a unique collection about a single subject, and are increasingly used in the United States, Canada, and Europe.

Separate and apart from the Archives is the Master Bibliography of the Alcohol Literature, at present containing over 60,000 titles dealing with alcohol.[1] The Bibliography extends back to the earliest days of printing and includes many items not considered useful for archive abstracting. Both the Archives and Bibliography developed out of a co-operative venture between Yale and the now-extinct Research Council on Problems of Alcohol.

Along with the Archives and Bibliography, the Yale Center's library is the most complete, of its special type, in the world, offering photocopies and abstracts of its material to scholars and researchers. Yale, through its endeavor to systematize the existing knowledge and to keep it up to date, has created a foundation for fruitful research.

The Center of Alcohol Studies after long association with Yale is moving its activities to the State University at Rutgers, New Jersey. The Center's departure from Yale results from its diversified applied endeavors which run contrary to the recent purely academic policies of that university in this area.

To support the transfer to Rutgers, the National Institute of Mental Health has awarded a grant to the Center for moving and operational support. This move of the Center to new surroundings may provide a new impetus and vigor to its activities necessary to overcome the institutional hardening of the arteries from which it has recently suffered.

In conclusion, the important contribution of Yale to the field of alcoholism has been to bring respectable scientific efforts to a neglected condition: alcoholism.

8

The National Council on Alcoholism

A 1949 report to the Research Council on Problems of Alcohol [6] described the birth of the National Council on Alcoholism as follows: Mrs. Marty Mann, a recovered alcoholic, who is extremely well informed about alcoholism, had a series of discussions with Mrs. Grace Allen Bangs, then Director of the Club Service Bureau of the *New York Herald Tribune* about the problems of alcoholism. As a result of these discussions, Mrs. Bangs recognized that not only was she herself ignorant of the subject but that sound information about alcoholism was generally unavailable. As evidence of this, Mrs. Bangs stated that in her extensive professional career in dealing with women's clubs, she had never heard of an address delivered on alcoholism. Since she felt that there was a need to share unbiased informative material on the subject (especially to women who might be facing this problem), Mrs. Bangs urged Mrs. Mann to work with her, and together they evolved a program eventually called the National Committee for Education on Alcoholism.

Further impetus for the formation of NCA came out of

Mrs. Mann's personal experience in Alcoholics Anonymous. She says,[7] "NCA grew out of the needs of AA. NCA was designed to do those things for the alcoholic which AA could not, and did not wish to do." Mrs. Mann, recognizing the potential for a voluntary agency in alcoholism, worked out a tentative plan which she presented to a variety of people: Bill W. (co-founder of Alcoholics Anonymous), a stockbroker; Mrs. Bangs; and Dr. Ruth Fox, a psychiatrist. On Dr. Fox's suggestion, the revised plan was presented to Dr. E. M. Jellinek at the Yale Center of Alcohol Studies; and he, in response, came to New York and met with the planning group. He recommended, pending approval of Dr. Howard Haggard, that the plan be incorporated into Yale's program. Approval was given within two days and precipitated a meeting in May 1944 in New Haven at which the original articles of incorporation were drawn. Mrs. Mann was named the Executive Director and Vice President. Dr. Howard W. Haggard, Director of Yale University's Laboratory of Applied Physiology, became the President of the corporation; Dr. Selden D. Bacon, Assistant Professor of Sociology, Yale University, Secretary; and Mr. Edgar Lockwood, Vice President of the Guaranty Trust Company, Treasurer. Dr. Jellinek, Director of the Yale Summer School of Alcohol Studies, became the Chairman of the Board, and Professor Edward A. Baird, of Yale's alcoholism program, acted as legal counsel.

One other person and group also deserves recognition here.[8] From March through October 1944, Mr. Fred Hopkins, of the National Tuberculosis Association, not only acted as a consultant to Mrs. Mann but opened the Association's archives to her so that she could review the early history of the nation's first major voluntary health agency. The influence of this study can still be seen in the structure of the National Council on Alcoholism, for NCA is closely modeled on the National Tuberculosis Association,[8] whose original constitution and by-laws and their qualifications for local affiliation with the national organization were utilized.

Mrs. Mann spent much of the first summer at Yale attending the Summer School of Alcohol Studies, working closely with Dr. Haggard and Dr. Jellinek in the preparation of pertinent alcoholism literature. On October 2, 1944, the office of the National Committee for Education on Alcoholism, Inc., opened its doors at the New York Academy of Medicine Building. Press releases were sent out to all New York and national newspapers. Editorials and stories were written and as a consequence the response came "in flood proportions," [6] in the form of invitations to speak, inquiries about the committee and its services, and requests for help and literature. Clearly the need for the committee was manifest and Mrs. Bangs's predictions immediately were borne out. NCA's dual objective [2] "to arouse public opinion and to mobilize it for action on the problem of alcoholism" was well under way. The demand for council services continues today.

NCA then began a search for a formula, something which would translate the basic facts of alcoholism into easily understood and remembered phrases. This resulted in the well-known concepts or credo: [2] "Alcoholism is a disease and the alcoholic a sick person. The alcoholic can be helped and is worth helping. This is a public health problem and therefore a public responsibility."

In a personal communication Mrs. Mann says of these three concepts: [8] "It was and is our major goal to disseminate these facts as widely as possible, and to seek acceptance of them by using every means at our command."

We have here in operation one more illustration of that wonderful American phenomenon, the voluntary association. From NCA, local affiliates evolved. Also, the national and local committees are active in promoting conferences, lectures, and institutes to provide the means of disseminating alcoholism information. To professional, industrial, and lay groups, NCA stands ready to offer guidance with alcoholism problems, a gap too long unfilled by other interested alcoholism groups. By preparing and printing alcoholism literature, NCA serves to provide material, services, and editorial consultation to the public and professional press and attempts to act as a co-ordinator for these groups. Beyond these heavy tasks, it operates an in-service training program with Columbia University Teachers' College for workers in the field of alcoholism. Field services, including community planning, are provided at the local level. At the same time that NCA co-operates and works with other national health and welfare agencies, it also operates its own research program.

At the local level, the regional affiliates operate in a similar fashion to the parent organization in their own and adjoining communities. One special function carried out at the local branches—not ordinarily performed by NCA—is a referral source for individuals seeking help for themselves, family members, or friends. Treatment services are provided by some local affiliates.

Although we concentrate on the NCA, we do not intend to underestimate the importance of the local affiliates. The National Council's success, as with most national organizations, is directly dependent on its ability to communicate with and meet the needs of the individual which can only be accomplished at the local level.

Most major cities now have a local group. One example is the first local committee, the Boston Committee on Alcoholism, which had a major role in bringing about the Massachusetts State Alcoholism Program. Another, the Worcester County (Massachusetts) Council on Alcoholism was instrumental in establishing a state clinic on alcoholism, developing a city welfare halfway house for male alcoholics and a citizen-supported halfway house for women.

Now that its basic concepts (alcoholism is a disease, etc.) are becoming increasingly accepted, NCA has been able to focus on more sophisticated procedures. In a recent Annual Report,[4] NCA speaks of the need for an NCA affiliate in *every* major community in the nation. Along with these affiliates, community educational programs should be instituted to eliminate the stigma associated with alcoholism. Beyond this, NCA works for improved and expanded clinical facilities for treatment, and for support for scientific research in all phases of alcoholism.

The freedom of action afforded a voluntary health agency is important. Free from specific enabling legislation and from sharply defined program budgets of governmental agencies, the voluntary endeavor can be innovating, flexible, and broad in range, and this makes new experiments and new programs possible. If the voluntary agency is unsuccessful in its programs, it need only answer to itself. If successful, then tax-supported agencies can take over and support these programs without taking the risk of experimentation. The voluntary group then can become interested in other procedures and methods.

The major problem, as with most organizations, is fund raising. Local committees receive support from direct gifts, foundation grants, and from United Funds. NCA uses similar sources and in addition receives dues from affiliates (less than 3 per cent of NCA's total budget).[9] Actually, NCA is largely self-supporting, unlike many other national voluntary health movements.

NCA has not had an easy time, and the growth difficulties of the committee reflect the stigma attached to alcoholics and alcoholism. In 1945, five local affiliates had sprung into being, 11 in 1946, and 39 in 1948. Since 1951, the local American affiliates have fluctuated with 57 in 1951, a low of 40 in 1953, 46 in 1957, and a high of 59 in 1959.[1-4] In a fifteen-year period

(1945–60) of ten beginnings in Massachusetts communities only three affiliates survived. Although existing affiliates today are stronger, better supported, and offer more clearly delineated goals than before, growth is still slow and difficult. Contrast the above figures with the number of associations for retarded children. The National Association of Retarded Children is but ten years old and in Massachusetts jumped from seven local affiliates in 1952 to 31 in 1960.[5] Since the estimated number of alcoholics and retardates in the United States is roughly equal (four to five million), the contrasting rates of growth of these organizations are striking and revealing. Both movements began only recently. These late starts are probably due to the fact that alcoholism and mental retardation suffer from stigma, lack of public understanding, and professional disinterest. The differential rate of growth may be explained, as has been suggested, by the fact that organizations focused on youth tend to get more support than adult-oriented organizations. In addition, we believe that public anxiety about drinking and the still strong immoral connotation of alcoholism keep the public aloof.

In conclusion, we feel that the growth difficulties experienced by NCA emphasize the vital need for such an organization to enlighten the public about alcoholism, alleviate their anxiety and fear, and direct the alcoholic to treatment.

9

Alcoholics Anonymous

Now that we have viewed various government programs, we turn to the effort of the alcoholic coping with himself. Alcoholics Anonymous, or AA, as it is more commonly known, is a banding together of alcoholics to achieve sobriety. That it came into existence and flourished in North America has much meaning. However, before examining its significance let us try to understand some of its origins and structures.

Alcoholics Anonymous was founded by a doctor, Dr. Bob, and a stockbroker, Bill W., at a chance meeting in Akron, Ohio, on June 10, 1935. Bill W. had, through a mystical experience, stopped drinking and he wanted to share his sobriety.[1] Significantly, both founders had extensive contact with the Oxford Group Movement, participating actively in their respective homes of New York and Akron. The strong influence of the Oxonians survives and can be seen within the twelve steps of AA. Bill W. wrote,[1] "the early Alcoholics Anonymous got its ideas of self-examination, acknowledgement of character defects, restitution for harm done, and working with others straight from the Oxford groups."

During the earliest days of AA the co-founders were able to maintain allegiance to both their own group and to the Oxford Group Movement. The separation from the older movement

146

began in 1937, in New York, and a bit later in Akron. This was inevitable because their fundamental goals were sufficiently different to make success as a joint endeavor impossible. The Oxonians were broader in aim, attempting essentially to include all mankind. At the same time, the Oxford Group Movement used a "rather aggressive evangelism," and would not and could not "accept the principle of team guidance" for their personal lives. The need of the Oxonians to reach for the absolutes of purity, honesty, unselfishness, and love was too much to expect of the alcoholic waging his overwhelming battle with alcohol. Sobriety was a possibility. But to include the highest goals of the Christian ethic for personalities which had suffered from and had been subjected to some of the most detrimental forces of society seemed unrealistic. The final conflict between both groups involved the principle of anonymity. The alcoholic felt safe, secure, and comfortable surrounded anonymously by his similarly afflicted brothers, while the Oxonians thrived on the use of the names of prominent members.

In December 1934, Bill W., already a member of the Oxford Group Movement, was hospitalized at the Towns Hospital in New York, to begin withdrawal from alcohol. On the fourth day, deeply depressed and crying out for God, he experienced a spiritual moment. Bill W. writes,[2] "Suddenly the room lit up with a great white light . . . ecstasy . . . and then it burst upon me that I was a free man." This unusual experience he discussed with his physician and with a recovered alcoholic who was a member of the Oxford Group Movement. He was directed by them to the writings of William James, and was especially influenced by James's *Varieties of Religious Experience*. This reading crystallized the spiritual quality of Bill W.'s sober state, which rapidly became diffused throughout AA. Thus his experience became one of the sources of AA's reliance on spirituality. The influence of spirituality (not organized religion) has never left the movement and is constantly reinforced on the one hand by eleven of AA's twelve steps which refer to God directly or by implication, and on the other by the countless life histories that members relate in which the role of a "higher power" is influential in recovery.

We shall now look at AA membership. Fundamentally, there is no formal prerequisite for membership in AA other than an honest desire to stop drinking. Intoxicated and obstreperous members may be escorted from a meeting, with an invitation, however, to return when sober.

In the beginning, the growth of AA was extremely slow. Under Dr. Bob's influence, however, the Akron group solidified, and Bill W.'s efforts brought the same accomplishment in New York. Slowly the march began.[1] From June 1935, through November 1937, sobriety had been achieved by 40 alcoholics. By April 1939 the number had jumped to 100 and within a year, in early 1940, to 800. By the end of 1941, 8000 had found the respectable state of sobriety. With increasing strength the figures rolled in: by 1952 there were 150,000 and in 1960 the estimate had reached "more than 200,000." [10]

AA is based upon Twelve Steps and Twelve Traditions.[3] The intense, possibly overdramatized importance attributed to the Twelve Steps is described by co-founder Bill W. as follows: [1] "Unless each AA member follows to the best of his ability our suggested Twelve Steps of recovery, he almost certainly signs his own death warrant . . . we must obey certain principles, or we die." In spite of the strength of these words, Bill W. maintained that these steps were merely suggestions and that absolute belief in them was not a prerequisite for membership. They are as follows:

STEP ONE: "We admitted we were powerless over alcohol—that our lives had become unmanageable."

Step One makes a point which transcends all approaches to the treatment of the alcoholic: that the alcoholic, if he is to recover, can never drink again. The belief against ever drinking again has been better publicized and more effectively accepted by the citizen movement of AA than could ever have been achieved by any professional body.

In Step One, AA has laid stress on the necessity of the alcoholic's admitting his helplessness, which we interpret as "hitting bottom," before we can reach out for help. This "hitting bottom" we feel is individually and psychologically determined. It does not imply that the alcoholic must hit Skid Row. Hitting bottom for one may be losing an important, meaningful job; for another, the threat of family disintegration; for still another, the onset cf physical symptoms or social ostracism.

AA considers the remaining eleven steps dependent on the alcoholic's accepting Step One. For the alcoholic to succeed in his quest for sobriety he must believe in "the fatal nature of our situation."

STEP TWO: "Came to believe that a Power greater than ourselves could restore us to sanity."

To bridge Step One and Step Two is not easy for the alcoholic. For he is a human being and to resign himself fully to God is not easy. Even for the quasi-religious person it is not easy suddenly and freely to accept a principle of supernatural help he has always resisted partially. Even the staunch believer in God among the alcoholics finds difficulty in believing that God will perform the miracle of curing him of alcoholism.

As we study AA, a certain Spock-like flexibility of attitude becomes apparent. This is based on a sound principle. When one wishes to win the masses, to have the greatest universal appeal it is essential to be flexible and compromising, and to anticipate all possible reactions. This AA does and does well. The waverer is gently admonished to "take it easy," reminded that the program merely makes suggestions, and advised to maintain an open mind and remember that AA succeeds. By these reassurances, AA attempts to quell the doubt and insecurity that arise again and again in the mind of the alcoholic. Especially here, the plea is to believe that a greater power will be responsible for the restoration of sobriety. This plea is combined, however, with the subtle suggestion that it is acceptable to make AA itself the "higher power." In other words, if it is not possible for an individual to develop faith in a power greater than himself, he is advised to put his faith in his fellow AA members.

STEP THREE: "Made a decision to turn our will and our lives over to the care of God as we understood Him."

The first two steps are those of principle, requiring mere acceptance. However, Step Three and the remaining steps require positive action. The necessity for positive action is illustrated by the following quote: "In fact, the effectiveness of the whole AA program will rest upon how well and earnestly we have tried to come to a decision to turn our will and our lives over to the care of God as we understand Him." If the alcoholic striving for sobriety can turn over his will to AA ("a new-found Providence"), he will begin moving in an appropriate direction. Although AA is mindful that dependence can be dangerous in therapeutic relations, it is their experience that dependence on an AA group or on a higher "Power" has not produced any disastrous results.

Step Three emphasizes that the whole problem for the alcoholic has been the misuse of his will power, his refusal to bring it into agreement with the intent of God. This ever-present possibility of misuse of will power has led to the adoption of what is known as the AA prayer: "God grant me the serenity to accept the things I cannot change; courage to change the things I can, and wisdom to know the difference. Thy will, not mine, be done."

STEP FOUR: "Made a searching and fearless moral inventory of ourselves."

In this step can be seen the influence of psychiatry and religion. "By discovering what our emotional deformities are, we can move toward their correction" AA says; also "nearly every serious emotional problem can be seen as a case of a misdirected instinct." In other words, they claim the character defects of the alcoholic, emanating from the instincts gone astray, are the primary cause of his drinking and failure in life. These "serious character defects" are rationalized by the individual as being the result of excessive drinking, but AA states that perhaps his life was disturbed even without alcohol. To AA, fear, frustration, depression, a desire to "escape the guilt of passions and vainglory" are all underlying emotions associated with pathological drinking, resulting in an attempt at compensation via alibis, excuses, and self-justification. One AA author states, "It never occurred to us that we needed to change ourselves to meet conditions, whatever they were." Therefore, the alcoholic who undertakes the AA program must work very hard at ridding himself of his character defects. It is as though he were asked to tear out the "faulty foundation of his life" and begin anew. Significant character change is held out as a possibility for the determined member.

STEP FIVE: "Admitted to God, to ourselves, and to another human being, the exact nature of our wrongs."

In Step Five, AA begins to bring about the unification of the group. Although all AA's Twelve Steps crusade against natural desires ("they all deflate our egos"), one cannot live alone. There must be a general house cleaning according to AA, where the member should admit his defects to another human being. Without sharing problems, that is, merely describing drinking episodes without saying anything of the things "which really bother and burn us," the alcoholic cannot remain sober.

This mutual sharing of the confessional helps the member to feel that he belongs to the group, at the same time developing in him a sense of humility. This, it is felt, will produce realistic and honest responses, closeness to God, and a relation to other people.

STEP SIX: "Were entirely ready to have God remove all these defects of character."

With this step there is a reaffirmation of the possibility of alterations, which although not easy, can be accomplished by co-operation with God. The typical statement illustrating Step Six is as follows: "Sure I was beaten, absolutely licked. My own will power just wouldn't work on alcohol. Change of scene, the best efforts of family, friends, doctors, and clergymen got no place with my alcoholism. I simply couldn't stop drinking, and no human being could seem to do the job for me. But when I became willing to clean house and asked a higher Power, God, as I understand Him, to give me release, my obsession to drink vanished."

Although attainment may be difficult, the aim must be high. To reassure against the possibility of failure of goals and consequent unacceptable frustration, the AA member is constantly reminded that only Step One can be practiced with 100 per cent perfection, and that the other eleven steps are to serve as ideals.

STEP SEVEN: "Humbly asked Him to remove our shortcomings."

"Greater humility," one of the founding principles of AA, is always emphasized. "For without some degree of humility, no alcoholic can stay sober." With humility, the sober alcoholic can expect to find serenity, bringing strength from weakness. Humility is the guideline by which an alcoholic can begin to move out of himself "towards others and towards God."

In this step, further stress is laid upon de-emphasizing the self for the greater good of the group. Unification of the group can be anticipated and realized by such an emphasis.

STEP EIGHT: "Make a list of all persons we had harmed, and become willing to make amends to them all."

With Step Eight, the retribution cycle of AA is begun. Before one can learn to live anew, one must make an accurate survey of "the human wreckage one has left in one's wake." The ultimate goal of this step according to AA is to learn forgiveness, and this can only be accomplished by forgiving others. It is in this step that the guilt of the alcoholic is wittingly heightened because the emphasis is on one's drinking having aggravated the defects of others. Having raised the guilt feelings of the alcoholic, AA provides in the following steps means of expiation.

STEP NINE: "Made direct amends to such people whenever possible, except when to do so would injure them or others."

To alleviate the guilt raised by Step Eight, restitution is attempted. The member is cautioned, however, to use "good judgment, a careful sense of timing, courage, and prudence." This attempt at guilt alleviation, however, is recognized to be only superficial, and a more continuous source begins with the next step.

STEP TEN: "Continued to take personal inventory and when we were wrong promptly admitted it."

Step Ten begins to deal with eventual sobriety. The sober state may produce emotional hangovers associated with feelings of anger, fear, and frustration. To maintain emotional equilibrium, avoiding emotional "dry benders," the AA member must develop self-restraint, focusing on the ups and downs that everyone faces. Being dry does not suddenly resolve all the alcoholic's problems. Therefore, one must constantly be on guard, spotting faults daily, remembering that there is "a good and a bad side to us all."

With this action-oriented therapeutic step, AA takes on the quality of the self-help books of the 1950's.

> STEP ELEVEN: "Sought through prayer and meditation to improve our conscious contact with God as we understood Him, praying only for knowledge of His will for us and the power to carry that out."

By this step, a plea is made for support and a sense of security. Members are gently nudged back to the church of their choice with the reminder that prayer and meditation offer support to the mind and emotions, and that "the greatest reward of meditation and prayer is a sense of belonging that comes to us."

> STEP TWELVE: "Having had a spiritual awakening as the result of these steps, we tried to carry this message to alcoholics, and to practice these principles in all our affairs."

Here at Step Twelve the recovered alcoholic begins to help others, individually or in a group. With the aggressive casework approach, AA gives its member the opportunity to feel needed and useful once again. He can help others who will be dependent on him, and the only limits on his giving will be those drawn by himself. The following quotation best illustrates the potential of Step Twelve: "in well-matured AA's, we no longer strive to dominate or rule, we no longer seek favor and honor in order to be praised, we try to be humbly grateful."

Now that we have viewed the steps the AA member must take to achieve sobriety, let us look at the AA traditions which provide continuity.

TRADITION ONE: "Our common welfare should come first; personal recovery depends on AA unity."

From the very start, the need for a common welfare coming before all is stressed, and it is emphasized that by this unity "the most cherished quality our society has" comes into being.

TRADITION TWO: "For our group purpose there is but one ultimate authority—a loving God as He may express Himself in our group conscience. Our leaders are but trusted servants; they do not govern."

This tradition stresses an AA ideal: the discouragement of a hierarchy. Everyone is equal whether they be founders or members of the group. The leaders do not pressure their followers, but merely attempt to lead by example. We are reminded of George Orwell's statement in *Animal Farm* "All men are equal, some are more equal." AA lay themselves open to the hostility inevitably aroused when people constantly proclaim spiritual ideals they fail to live up to (even though their failure is human).

TRADITION THREE: "The only requirement for AA membership is a desire to stop drinking."

To become a member of AA, one must merely so declare himself. AA prides itself that it has no desire to exclude any individual. For a short time AA was looking for the "pure alcoholic," avoiding those with social complications, e.g. criminal records, mental illness, sexual deviations, etc. However, insight into the intolerance of this position was expressed dramatically by the following quote: "Who dared to be judge, jury, and executioner of his own sick brother?"

TRADITION FOUR: "Each group should be autonomous except in matters affecting other groups or AA as a whole."

The fourth tradition permits extensive liberty and freedom of action by individual groups limited only by the restriction of Tradition Six and the requirements of group survival.

TRADITION FIVE: "Each group has but one primary purpose—to carry its message to the alcoholic who still suffers."

Here as in Step Twelve, we have the idea that the keeping of "the precious gift of sobriety" cannot be maintained "unless we give it away." Here a uniqueness of ability to identify with and aid in the recovery of another alcoholic is stressed. To strengthen its universality of appeal and ease of application, emphasis is laid upon the fact that education, eloquence, or special skills are not required. The essential ingredient is having found the "key to sobriety." To AA, suffering and recovery are legacies which may easily be passed among alcoholics, one to the other. To focus on identification as superior to education or other attributes is a masterful psychological stroke.

TRADITION SIX: "An AA group ought never endorse, finance, or lend the AA name to any related facility or outside enterprise lest problems of money, property, and prestige divert us from our primary purpose."

This tradition evolves from sad experience by AA. Alcoholics Anonymous hospitals, educational programs, legislative intervention, were attempted, but only served to confuse the membership. Although some undertakings were successful, others bogged down and in time it was decided that the greater good could be served by avoiding endorsement of any enterprise.

TRADITION SEVEN: "Every AA group ought to be fully self-supporting, declining outside contributions."

This is a remarkable and wise decision. It not only establishes independence from outside forces, at the same time it also heightens dependence within AA itself.

TRADITION EIGHT: "Alcoholics Anonymous should remain forever nonprofessional, but our service centers may employ special workers."

AA contends, perhaps rightly, that money will not mix with spirituality. It further contends that money may well compromise the AA member, and attempts in using professionals in the Twelfth, or missionary, Step have always failed. The dogmatism and even necessary blindness of AA in its fight to maintain a special identity may be illustrated by this quotation: "Almost no recovery from alcoholism has ever been brought about by the world's best professionals, whether medical or religious."

It is possible for an AA group to employ a secretary for its center, since the secretary is not involved in actually doing Twelfth Step work. It is also permissible for AA members to work in the alcoholism field as long as they avoid advertising their AA membership.

TRADITION NINE: "AA, as such, ought never to be organized; but we may create service boards or committees directly responsible to those they serve."

It is possible for AA to take this unusual stand because in their opinion their operational philosophy is so basic and fundamental that members and groups must live by it or fail, thus obviating the need for rigid rules and regulations. Therefore, AA as a whole is not organized; no one can give directives or mete out punishment to another member; and, the avoidance of the dangers of wealth, prestige, and power is stressed. It is stressed again and again, that boards are created to serve AA, not to govern.

TRADITION TEN: "Alcoholics Anonymous has no opinion on outside issues; hence the AA name ought never be drawn into public controversy."

The survival and spread of AA is more important to the movement than the influence the group might have on any other cause. AA does not lose sight of the lessons to be learned from the Washingtonian Society of one hundred years ago. The Washingtonian Movement, like AA, was composed of alcoholics trying to help alcoholics and had a membership of over 100,000. In time the Washingtonians permitted politicians and reformers to use the society for their own purposes, e.g. slavery and temperance, and within a few years the movement lost its effectiveness in helping alcoholics.

> TRADITION ELEVEN: "Our public relations policy is based on attraction rather than promotion; we need always maintain personal anonymity at the level of press, radio, and films."

In order that the focus be on the principles and work of AA, attention is not directed to individual members. "Personal ambition has no place in AA." Although AA has been extremely successful in perpetuating its principle of anonymity, it has been less successful in separating promotion from attraction, perhaps because they are not clearly differentiated.

> TRADITION TWELVE: "Anonymity is the spiritual foundation of our traditions, ever reminding us to place principles before personalities."

Anonymity is useful because in sacrificing identity it heightens humility—a great safeguard to AA operations. Anonymity is not necessary, however, on a personal level or in small groups.

While the Twelve Steps and Twelve Traditions are the backbone of AA, the reader will wonder if such a large evangelical movement can have no institutional structure at all. Its leaders are "servants" without governing power. Yet AA is not an anarchy or the utopian, communistic order in which only the masses rule. They have their General Service Board made up of nonalcoholics (in the majority) and AA members. The Board assumes the responsibility for the integrity and service standards of AA's General Service Headquarters. In addition, there is the General Service Conference Charter. The Conference is not incorporated, nor is the Charter a legal instrument. Rather the Conference meets periodically to elect delegates from United States and Canadian groups and to perpetuate and guide AA in its world service. In New York, where the General Headquarters of AA is located, the linkage to the various groups throughout the world is maintained. Besides maintaining domestic and foreign group relations, General Headquarters fulfills various other duties.

AA speaks through its General Service Conference, General Service Board, Headquarters, and most effectively through its publications printed by the Alcoholics Anonymous Publishing Company. Besides books (*Alcoholics Anonymous*,[2] 1939, *The Twelve Steps and Twelve Traditions*,[3] 1953, and *Alcoholics Anonymous Comes of Age*,[1] 1957) the company publishes *AA Grapevine*, a monthly journal of a circulation of approximately 50,000. The *AA Grapevine*, well edited and well written, is a systematic and continuous effort on the part of AA to improve communication among its members and groups. In fact this perusal of Alcoholics Anonymous was developed directly from AA material and sources.

Now that we have looked at AA, what can we learn and understand of its significance and meaning? Seldon Bacon,[4] a sociologist, suggests that AA may be a resocialization process weaning the individual back into society. As Bacon interprets AA, it permits its members to go through a maturing process. This process begins when the member first comes into the program and is dependent on a sponsor. In time, with continued sobriety, he assumes more and more responsibility, and ultimately he himself becomes a sponsor. Finally, with more continuous AA involvement and activity with other alcoholics, the member may mature sufficiently to assume the responsibility of a leadership role in the group.

Trice [7] views AA's effectiveness as a result of the new self-concept it gives its members. This new self-concept evolves, according to Trice, when new members recognize that they have been sick and not necessarily bad, while at the same time they are developing new feelings of belonging. Feeling for the group is strengthened as the sharing of obligations, aims, and emotional problems progresses. To Trice, the more outgoing, sociable individuals, who can share emotionally with others, are most likely to be attracted to and succeed in AA. Trice points out that Step One "relieves the alcoholic of the need to demonstrate that he can drink like others"; Steps Two and Three "enable the alcoholic to realize that . . . he needs help from outside himself"; Step Five reduces anxiety by sharing and Step Eight helps to reduce guilt through restitution. He further contends [8] that successful AA members are motivated toward social acceptance and are anxious concerning rejection and separation.

Hanfmann [5] suggests briefly that successful AA members may be "those in whose life, for one reason or another, belongingness with a group of peers has been, from childhood on a significant or even the most significant relationship."

Lemert [6] also had some comments on Alcoholics Anonymous, based on his studies of West Coast Indians. He observed that non-reservation Indian members of AA were usually more acculturated and better educated than the reservation Indians, the latter interpreting AA as a further restraint on their drinking. Inability to accept AA was observed in those Indians who were hostile to whites. In addition, many Indians were unable to subordinate themselves to a power higher than themselves. Thus, cultural influences may affect acceptance of AA.

The very size of AA is socially significant. It is a reflection of the ostracism that always has plagued alcoholics. Morally shunned, punitively treated, the alcoholic's only hope for help lay in one person helping another. It is a sad commentary that even to this day the sick must lead the sick because of ignorance and bias. What we are suggesting is that because we failed the alcoholic, AA came into being. An invention does not occur when there is no necessity. We have stated before that AA has been the most effective mass approach to date. Their accomplishment is the result of a number of social and psychological mechanisms:

1. The focus on the symptom rather than the underlying problems which resulted in alcoholism. This focus fits rather well with the psychodynamic formulations of addictive drinking outlined in the chapter on etiology—namely, that alcoholism involves, among other things, object loss, especially of a mother figure during the earliest stage of psychosexual development. The symbolic and physiological replacement of this object loss is dealt with by substituting alcohol. AA in its uncritical accepting role, by its action on doing-for-the-other-alcoholic approach and especially by its heavy emphasis on spiritual conversion, produces a gratifying maternal reunion symbol like that formerly played by alcohol. As alcohol lubricates social intercourse, reducing cultural differences and personal inadequacies, so does AA. With alcohol it is the few drinks which fortify, with AA it is the suffering of a common calamity which creates the bond of equality. Physician, businessman, ditchdigger, the beautiful and the ugly, the rich and the poor, all are sufferers. This equality, besides satisfying the need to belong, alleviates the possibility of judgment or recrimination. For many, the surroundings of the anonymous mass are comforting and secure.

2. The mechanism of compulsion. We see this reflected in the strength of the AA member's compulsive, almost vengeful attention to the AA way of life, in his nightly attendance at

meetings, and in the fervor of his proselytizing. Here we see AA attempting to use this compulsion constructively to fulfill needs formerly met by alcohol.

3. The pointing of the road back to our middle-class way of life. We think that perhaps this is the essence of AA derived as it is from our dominant "Protestant Ethic" (emotional control, cleanliness, strength, and godliness). Drinking to loss of control is by these standards a sin, symbolizing failure and the basic weakness of the individual. Thus, the alcoholic must continue to drink or be confronted by the reality of the culturally defined Puritan image. AA on the other hand, offers redemption, permitting the wayward to admit his feelings and ultimately to turn his life over to God. We might expect to find that AA is not popular where cultural values are different, and in France this is true. Here, AA has had only limited acceptance.

4. We are struck by the sect or cult-like aspects of AA. This is true in terms of its history, structure, and the charisma surrounding its leader, Bill W. There is even a bible; the old testament of AA is the "Big Book" (*Alcoholics Anonymous*).[2] Its new testament is *The Twelve Steps and Twelve Traditions*.[3] Its Jehovah is Bill W., for it was he who developed the steps and traditions, wrote his own history; he is the main motivating force of AA. Bill W. aided others whose histories also comprise the "Big Book." We are not theologians and it is with some hesitance that we offer comments about the spiritual meaning of AA. Yet because the spiritual element is so critical in the dynamics of the organization, we suggest the following possible interpretations of AA. AA, as a social organization attempting to cope with a psychological problem, uses a unique combination of the sociological, the psychological, and the spiritual. The relationship with God is viewed as a living, dynamic one. God can be reached personally and will give help. The emphasis is on what God does. This view of God does not appear to be a highly intellectual understanding of spiritual means but

a more fundamental or emotional relationship. Thus as with many components of AA, the religion seems somewhat simple, but nevertheless it is appropriately developed in terms of the members' own emotional needs.

Before leaving this perusal of Alcoholics Anonymous, we wish to raise certain questions:

1. How accurate are the figures of AA's phenomenal growth? We know that each year the secretary of each individual AA group compiles the figures and forwards them, not the names, to the New York office. Since the secretaries are asked to include only regular members in their figures, the assumption is made that individuals are counted only once. But there can be many groups in just one city, and, with the mobility of AA members from group to group there may be a significant overestimate in the total of up to 20 per cent. Such a possible overlap in the figures does not, of course, negate prodigious growth.

Aside from numbers, one may seriously object to the criterion used—sobriety—as the sole measure of success. What about employment and marital status, or interaction with others? Have they improved or deteriorated further? Or, when is sobriety, sobriety? If a member has been dry for eleven months and drinks the week before the census, is he counted as recovered?

2. Will AA continue to grow? Most likely yes, but at a greatly reduced rate. We make this assumption because, as noted above, many alcoholics best served by AA are already involved. Also, AA's successes have promoted the interest of professionals in the alcoholic, thereby decreasing the number of candidates.

3. Why does it work with some patients and not with others? The ideas of Bacon, Trice, Hanfmann, and Lemert have already been cited. We believe AA works for patients whose social and psychological needs it can meet. However, the conscious turning toward God or emotional giving to others requires a certain sense of being a person, which many alcoholics do not

possess. Therefore, alcoholics who fail in AA should not feel that they are beyond the pale. They have just been asked to give when they had nothing to give.

4. Should AA change its procedures to bring in previous failures? The thought of change of method raises the specter of the Washingtonian Movement and its eventual failure.

5. If adaptation of procedures occurred, would this affect the group with whom AA is now so successful? In an interesting address to the 11th Annual Meeting of the North American Association of Alcoholism Programs in 1960, Bill W.[9] noted the need for flexibility in AA. He pointed out that AA was "beset with fears of survival" for many years, and that with developing maturity the AA "family was about to be weaned." Bill W. envisioned a much closer relationship in the future for AA with the professional community. We are uncertain as to whether this can be accomplished without diluting the necessary identity of the organization, which new AA members need so strongly. But if a closer relation can be effected and the identity sustained, then in this there would be great promise for the future.

6. Why AA's hostility toward other forms of rehabilitation? We believe this hostility exists to maintain AA's separate identity. Also, for the new member the suggestion of other approaches might undermine his tenuous faith in the spirituality of AA.

7. What will happen when the motivating force of Bill W. is no longer around? Is AA prepared to make the transition? The smooth transition of authority from a charismatic leader to an organization depends upon careful advance preparation. Bill W., an astute and wise man, recognizes the seriousness of this problem. He is attempting to plan for the future, and preserve AA by reducing his influence, permitting an orderly transfer of leadership to take place.

8. Is AA's focus alcoholism, alcoholics, or Alcoholics Anonymous? This important question reveals much by its answer.

AA is not interested in alcoholism as a medical problem. If it did have such an interest, it would be interested in etiology, research, and prevention. AA is not. On the other hand if it did have such an interest, AA might lose its therapeutic effectiveness.

The members maintain that they prefer to be involved with present-day, suffering alcoholics who are potential members than with theoretical formulations. In our opinion, AA is really not interested in alcoholics in general, but only as they relate to AA itself. By action and by rules, AA expresses more interest in strengthening and perpetuating Alcoholics Anonymous than in helping alcoholics. Many alcoholics cannot make the AA program for one reason or another. AA, if it were interested in alcoholics, would attempt to help these failures seek out other rehabilitative resources. In most cases they do not. At the same time, if AA were interested in alcoholics and not itself alone, it would not criticize AA members who use other treatment facilities. The pietism of AA may be necessary to many, but it strikes us as primarily a means of strengthening the group.

In conclusion, we feel that the major contribution of Alcoholics Anonymous has been not only in the rehabilitation of alcoholics, but also in the dramatization that alcoholics can be helped. By their efforts they have shown further that no one but the alcoholic himself was interested in dealing with his problem and that the community let him down. By virtue of their interest, they have made work with alcoholics legitimate.

10

Al-Anon Family Groups

Contrary to widespread belief, alcoholics do indeed have families, and whether or not the alcoholic lives alone, these families may influence the course of his alcoholism. All alcoholics do not live on Skid Row, friendless and forgotten. Most alcoholics seen in alcoholism clinics are married and live with their wife and children, and in general their marriage rate is not strikingly different from that of the general population for the same age range.[3] Alcoholics, however, have a higher incidence of marriage break-up than the rest of the general population. This indicates that alcoholism does have an impact on the family life and interpersonal relationships. Spouses, parents, children, and relatives are affected by the pathological drinker; naturally, the more intimate the relationship the more severe the effect.[1, 2] The recognition that the alcoholic himself is not the only one who needs help is manifested in the Al-Anon Movement.[4] Al-Anon evolved to meet the needs of the affected individuals.

Al-Anon is composed primarily of the spouses of alcoholics. Parents, relatives, children over twenty-one, and interested friends at times have also become members.

The idea of family groups is almost as old as that of Alcoholics Anonymous [4] and began when the wives of early AA members realized that they too had problems. These wives tried to deal with this need by attending AA meetings, by seeking church aid, or by turning to social agencies. Although these "usual" sources gave some help, a gap nevertheless remained. As a consequence, nonalcoholics began to meet at the same time that AA held its meetings. There was no established formal program. Yet the informal groups continued to grow.

This growth was not without opposition. Some AA members "frowned on the idea, feeling Family Groups could become gossip clubs or divert AA from its main purpose." [4] Similar opposition continues to exist among certain AA members and it is not difficult to imagine some spouses using the group as a means for controlling and punishing their alcoholic mates. Nevertheless the core idea was sound. Basic and mutual problems did exist among members of the alcoholic's family and as a consequence more groups sprang up around North America (in Chicago, Toronto, San Pedro, and Richmond). [4]

By 1949 AA's General Headquarters were receiving an increasing number of inquiries from nonalcoholics. Fifty groups (called Family Groups) requested listing in the AA Directory. Since AA felt this would be branching afield and might endanger their own organization, they refused. Consequently, in New York husbands and wives of AA members formed a committee which eventually became the Al-Anon Family Group Clearing House and in time was incorporated as the Al-Anon Family Group Headquarters, Inc. There is no formal relationship with AA. [4]

The movement grew rapidly. Fifty groups in 1951 expanded to 700 in 1955 and to 1308 in 1960. [4] We suggest that in another ten years, Al-Anon Groups and membership may easily outnumber Alcoholics Anonymous.

Despite the lack of formal ties with AA, Al-Anon has strong informal and spiritual ties to AA. Similarly, from small donations of its members it finances itself, and like AA has steps and traditions.[4]

Al-Anon asks its members these pertinent questions: [4]

1. Are you the wife, husband, relative or friend of a problem drinker who still *refuses* help?
2. Are you concerned with a member of AA who is still having trouble with alcohol?
3. Though the alcoholic member of your family may now be sober, do you still feel that your home life is insecure or difficult?
4. Do you understand fully how alcoholism and its consequences may have warped your own thinking and your own personality?
5. Do you know that you can find understanding, friendship and help in the Al-Anon Family Groups (a) regardless of whether the alcoholic member of your family has sobered up, or (b) whether he has made good in his business affairs, or (c) whether normal family relationships have been restored?
6. Do you know that your own ability to face every life problem serenely and with constructive attitudes can be a most important factor in helping your alcoholic partner to achieve a full and happy recovery from problem drinking?

To answer these questions, certain responses and behavior are stated.

First, the essential plea for unity; that "our common welfare should come first"; and from unity, personal progress for the greatest number can be accomplished. Second, that the single authority for group purposes is "a loving God as He may express Himself in our group conscience." The point is reemphasized as in AA, that leaders are but trusted servants who do not govern.[4]

For membership, the requirement is broad: a relative or friend with the problem of alcoholism. When the relatives and friends of alcoholics gather together for mutual aid, they may call themselves an Al-Anon Family Group provided that the group has no other affiliations. The groups are autonomous, except as they affect other Al-Anon Groups or AA.[4]

The singular purpose of Al-Anon Groups is to help families of alcoholics. This is achieved by the members themselves practicing the Twelve Steps of AA, by encouraging and understanding their afflicted alcoholic relatives, and by aiding the families of other alcoholics.[4]

Like AA, Al-Anon will not lend itself to any outside enterprise or purpose. Although it maintains its identity, Al-Anon co-operates with Alcoholics Anonymous. Like AA, Al-Anon is self-supporting, declining outside help; Twelfth Step work (helping nonalcoholics who need help) is nonprofessional; groups are never organized except as service boards; Al-Anon has no opinion on outside issues and cannot be drawn into public controversy. Public relations are accomplished via attraction rather than promotion; the anonymity principle is a reminder to place principles above personalities.[4] The reader can readily see in AA and Al-Anon the same tradition of focusing primary concern on understanding the alcoholic, which is extended in the case of Al-Anon to the alcoholic's family also.

In understanding the alcoholic, it is considered essential to understand that alcoholism is an illness and the alcoholic a sick person, that alcoholics can be helped and that pleas to will power, threats, and accusations are useless. The alcoholic's lack of drinking control is considered an obsession. The causes of alcoholism are seen to lie deep. Al-Anon writes, "Very often basic personality flaws can be traced back to the alcoholic's childhood," and therefore it is advised that the spouse or alcoholic is not to blame. Alcoholics as described by Al-Anon are "different," "perfectionistic," and "often lack emotional stability to face life's problems in a realistic manner." [4]

Al-Anon goes into further detail to understand the alcoholic. The alcoholic is described as an attractive and intelligent person who, when drinking, subordinates everything to his "craving for alcohol"; who lacks insight as to his disorder; who frequently does not want to recover; whose thinking is "warped and distorted"; and who, despite the facts, rejects the reality of his drinking. Al-Anon goes on to iterate that few alcoholics are beyond hope; they must admit that they cannot cope alone with the problem after they eventually "hit bottom" (mentally, emotionally, or physically).[4]

After considering the means of understanding the alcoholic, Al-Anon offers guidelines for understanding the indirectly afflicted, i.e. themselves. Some guidelines involve the understanding of their own emotional reaction to the alcoholic spouse, the possibility of self-righteousness and even retaliation. They recognize that the response to the alcoholic mate may be literally or figuratively getting "drunk ourselves," or looking for help for themselves. They confront the recognition that alcoholism "made us sick, too"; that their "emotional sobriety" is essential; that their thinking has become "twisted and warped"; cynical, negative, without faith in life, and without belief in the possibility of change in the spouse. As a consequence of the behavior of the alcoholic, family members can become arrogant and assume the alcoholic is always wrong and the nonalcoholic always right. The alcoholic submerges himself in self-pity and his positive features are ignored. Gradually, because the alcoholic is unpredictable, the mate must assume more and more responsibilities. With the alcoholic's recovery, it becomes difficult for the nonalcoholic to let the reins go. Al-Anon wisely advises that life, even after sobriety, does "not stay rosy," and that AA's Twelve Steps should be practiced by both the nonalcoholic and alcoholic. Al-Anon attempts to show the intertwined relations between alcoholic and family. It also raises the possibility that the nonalcoholic partner may resent time spent at AA meetings and the fact that AA has been able to help the alcoholic where the spouse has failed.[4]

Al-Anon has taken a broader view than AA about problems it cannot deal with. They have no qualms about suggesting other modes of help. They recognize that sex and marital problems will require assistance. "Affiliation with the Family Groups certainly offers no cure-all for the complex problems of marriage and sex as they are affected by alcoholism; and in severe cases, it is, of course, wise to seek the advice also of doctor, minister or marriage counsellor." [4]

The concern of Al-Anon with the effect of alcoholism on the children of alcoholics has been paramount. The manner of explaining AA and the reality that the parent is an alcoholic have led to the development around the country of a movement called Al-Ateen. This will, hopefully, provide information and aid to children of alcoholics.[4]

In summary, Al-Anon follows AA's structure but focuses on the partner of the alcoholic. The movement is a spiritually oriented effort to gain uncritical understanding of the alcoholic, and Al-Anon uses the "AA Prayer" at meetings. Their focus, like that of AA, is on helping themselves through helping others. It is striking that the number of Al-Anon members whose spouses have not yet begun to seek help is growing. Since most alcoholics have not yet sought help, this leads us to predict a more rapid growth of Al-Anon than AA. It is hoped that in time the influence of the nonalcoholics will cause more alcoholics to seek treatment. Al-Anon's influence will also grow because of the apparent diminishing of hostility toward Al-Anon by AA members and the gradual and increased support of Al-Anon by the members of AA and the organized social and health agencies of the community.

IV

The Concept of Alcoholism Prevention

In the difficult area of alcoholism prevention, medicine and society have tended to throw up their hands and to give up prematurely. Here we shall discuss methods of preventing alcoholism not only when a tendency toward it is recognized early but also when the alcoholic is late in his disease. Our frame of reference will be primary, secondary, and tertiary prevention. Primary prevention is the use of social, chemical, or biological procedures to prevent the onset of alcoholism. Secondary prevention consists of early intervention in excessive, pathological drinking by medical and/or social means to prevent the major consequences of alcoholism. Tertiary prevention involves rehabilitative efforts for the chronic alcoholic in order to avoid further complications of the illness and prevent the spread of its influence to other members of the alcoholic's environment.

11

Primary Prevention

Following the public health tradition, we shall approach primary prevention from the point of view of agent, host, and environment. Although the host and environment factors are interwoven in the etiology of alcoholism, the agent, alcohol, stands out as a constant. By first examining the agent, in the context of the observations drawn in our chapter on etiology, we shall see possible approaches to primary prevention of alcoholism.

Can we manipulate the supply and availability of the agent, alcohol, in such a way as to prevent alcoholism from occurring? Of the possible ways to control alcohol's availability we shall discuss three: forbid the sale and/or use of alcohol by legal or social measures; limit legally the sale and/or use to certain people at certain times and in certain places; alter the chemical composition of alcohol so that so-called "habit-forming properties" are removed.

Forbidding the sale of alcohol is a technique well over a hundred years old in the United States. It is a familiar one, since the Prohibition Amendment (18th) is still recent history. Before the 1840's, as noted by McCarthy and Douglass,[19] "legis-

175

lative action concerned with the alcoholic beverage industry was purely regulatory in character and not repressive." But in 1844 the Oregon Territory adopted a constitution which was the first to carry a prohibition provision. Specific state prohibition laws date from 1851, when Maine first enacted such legislation. Although by 1855, thirteen out of thirty-one states had "dry" statutes, by 1863 this first social experiment in alcohol control had lost much of its momentum.

A second wave of state prohibition legislation developed after 1880 when eight states passed such laws.[19] Although fewer states were involved in this phase of the prohibition reform movement, the tide nevertheless was stronger and more persistent. After 1904 most of these eight states had repealed their state legislation. World War I once again turned public interest to prohibition, this time national public interest. By means of tremendous persistence, energy, and effort on the part of prohibitionists, twenty-five states by 1917 had gone "dry," and at the time of enactment of the Eighteenth Amendment in 1919, the number had increased to thirty-three. Similarly Russia, Finland, and Iceland had enacted national prohibition laws between 1915 and 1917.

Prohibition's drive came from temperance groups led by the Anti-Saloon League of America. Although they concentrated on state and eventual national prohibition, they succeeded in having enacted, prior to the passage of the 18th Amendment, other national legislation. McCarthy and Douglass [19] note some of their successful efforts: "exclusion of alcoholic beverages from Army Posts; prohibition of their sale in Federal buildings; prohibition of their transportation through the U.S. mails; prohibition of their sale to Indians; the Webb-Kenyon Act, which made it illegal to ship liquor into dry states; prohibition bills for Alaska and Hawaii; exclusion of advertisements from the U.S. mails; and wartime prohibition in World War I."

Despite all the efforts of the prohibitionists in the United

States, they failed to abolish effectively, by legal action, the use of alcohol. Their failure is reflected in the Twenty-first Amendment repealing the Eighteenth Amendment. There is no doubt that the proponents of prohibition were sincere and serious, and in theory their approach sounds reasonable, but for practical reasons it was doomed to failure. Alcohol is too popular and can be made too easily for legislation to remove it from use and misuse. It is like the automobile—despite its obvious drawbacks it serves too many useful and varied purposes to be abandoned. As Jellinek [12] notes, "Legal measures have generally not taken into account the origins of the use of alcohol, the functions which society attributes to it, the social factors which reinforce it and which tend to keep it within bounds."

We do not suggest that the failure of national prohibition was total. It was a failure in prohibiting the use of alcohol, but it provided many lessons. For we learned, as McCarthy [18] tells us, that "This is a piecemeal approach to a complete problem in a complex social structure." He further states: "Control of intoxication will emerge only after acceptance of responsibility by the society in which the condition originates. The development of a system of social controls is a job of social engineering. It will not be achieved by well-meaning pressure groups."

Straus and Bacon [30] suggest that the conflict concerning what should or should not be done regarding alcoholism may well have been more socially destructive than the basic problem of alcoholism itself. Even definition of the problem is unclear. Many of those who agree that drinking is a problem do not believe that abstinence should be enforced by law. Organized religion, a powerful social force concerned with alcohol usage, has been divided on this issue church by church, denomination by denomination, sect by sect. Subgroups within specific church bodies develop varying attitudes toward alcohol based upon variables of social class, ethnic division, education, and income. Many individuals do not follow formal church policy on the matter of alcohol, and some go so far as to campaign openly against their church's stand, feeling that it is either too rigid or not strong enough.

Confusion about defining and approaching alcohol problems is not confined to religious organizations alone. As Straus and Bacon [30] state: "The problem is seen in sanitary codes, zoning regulations, traffic laws, educational requirements, welfare and penal legislation, medical administration, supervision of federal wards, maritime jurisdictions, military activities, veterans' affairs, even budgets for diplomats reflect the conflict."

Do the failure of prohibition, the lack of definition of the problem, and the confusion as to method preclude legal measures as the means of preventing alcoholism? The answer is *no* as long as the legal approach is recognized as only one part of a total program of prevention. There are legal measures other than prohibition which might control and retard the development of alcoholism: excessive taxes on all alcoholic beverages; limits on retail sales outlets; requirement that food must be purchased at the time alcohol is bought; variations in taxes (i.e. higher taxes on distilled spirits than on beer and wine, assuming that spirits cause more drunkenness); state-operated liquor stores (thus removing or controlling competition); controls on advertising; and a rationing system, and so forth.

Historically, there are precedents for legal manipulation of alcohol, although the goal in most of these cases was to raise income. In England in 1690 there was passed "An Act for the Encouraging of the Distillation of Brandy and Spirits from Corn." The bill was strikingly successful; output doubled in twenty-five years; it was eleven times greater within forty years.[24] The United States in 1789 at the opening session of its first Congress passed a tariff bill on spirits.[19] More recently,

Sweden repealed its alcohol rationing system, and the greater freedom of purchase brought a striking increase in alcohol consumption which is now beginning to level off.

Clearly, governments can influence, in either direction, the amounts of alcohol consumed. The major question is whether government action affects the amount consumed by alcoholics as well as that consumed by social drinkers. We believe that legal controls are more likely to affect the social drinker than the alcoholic. But we do feel that such measures are more subtle and less challenging to drinkers—social as well as pathological—than prohibition measures. Hence, opportunities for developing unhealthy attitudes are reduced.

Another possible method of controlling the agent, alcohol, would be to alter its chemical composition to remove the so-called "habit-forming" properties. These are usually said to be the substances which act as depressants on the central nervous system. As noted earlier, these depressants reduce inhibitions, and the entire release pattern follows. But this inhibitory release, to varying degrees, is the goal of both social and pathological drinkers. Conceivably the removal of tension-reducing properties could be accomplished, but we are certain this maneuver would fail, for man would surely return to manufacturing the old beverage. After all, it is this depressant quality that accounts for the enduring popularity of alcohol.

Although we consider impractical the removal of alcohol's tension release factor, it may be practical to manipulate chemically the other components of alcohol. These, called congeners, are ingredients other than ethyl alcohol and water in beverage alcohol. We do not suggest that such chemical manipulation will reduce the rate of or prevent alcoholism, but we do feel that there are other gains to be derived from such manipulation which may alter features of our drinking behavior.

The study of congeners is not new, although relatively little interest, popular or scientific, has been shown in the subject.

In a systematic review in 1943, Haggard, Greenberg, and Cohen [11] noted that Joffroy and Serveaux had first studied the subject of congeners in 1895.

Congeners are made up of volatile and nonvolatile components. The volatile part derives primarily from the grain, and secondarily from the fermentation and aging process. The nonvolatile fraction consists of many materials, notably tannins drawn from the wood during the process of aging. Essentially, the longer a whiskey is barreled the higher will be its percentage of congeners. Furthermore, the blended whiskeys contain significantly fewer total congeners by weight than cognac and straight and bonded whiskeys. Therefore, cognac, bonded liquor, and aged whiskey, the more costly, sought-after beverages, are higher in congener content than the cheaper, younger, blended whiskeys. None of the congeners is present in beverage alcohol in large amounts; most exist only in trace amounts, the total rarely exceeding 0.5 per cent of the beverage by weight.

The total number of congeners is estimated [20] in the several hundreds. Snell [28] isolated seven major congeners for analysis: fusel oil, total acids (acetic acid), esters (ethyl acetate), aldehydes (acetaldehyde), furfural, tannins, and total solids. Other observers [3] have found that vodka contains only one-tenth the amount of congeners found in rum and whiskey.

We do not know all the effects of congeners, but color, flavor, and bouquet of whiskey are all affected. Since few drinkers use raw straight grain alcohol, we can only conclude that taste and aroma are important factors in the choice of beverage.

Beyond color and aroma, what other effects do congeners have? In a general way, and there are exceptions, a high incidence of congeners provides a somewhat toxic beverage. This is not surprising since many of the congeners are highly poisonous substances (fusel oil, furfural, tannins). The toxic effects of congeners are exaggerated by the slowing down of the rate of metabolism by alcohol, which thereby enhances undesirable side effects of congeners. Although Haggard and his group [11] have suggested that there may exist some yet unidentified congeners which affect liver function in a physiologically desirable way, most contemporary investigators agree that beverages with a high congener content, when contrasted with those of a low content, affect *adversely* the rate of alcohol's disappearance from the body. This therefore means a slower rate of recovery from intoxication, more severe hangover effects, diminished motor response, poorer judgment, and decrease of learned skills.

We assume that most people drink alcoholic beverages for the relaxant effect. Since we feel that people will not give up the social mechanism of drinking, it would help if they could at least recover their equilibrium and skills as quickly as possible after drinking. Congeners act against this desirable goal. As McKennis and Hagg [20] stated, "The physiologic studies already cited demonstrate that control of congeners, as achieved through manufacturing and blending techniques which regulate their type and quantity, can lead to either an increase or decrease in toxic effects. For the consumer, the latter is certainly more desirable." Since congener content can be materially influenced by altering the distillation and aging process (as has been done with vodka-type whiskey by a filtering process over heavy charcoal), we feel that every effort should be expended by research in the alcohol industry for their removal.

How does manipulation of congeners concern alcoholics? The only suggestion in the literature comes from Damrau and Liddy,[5] who feel that "vodka [a low congener beverage] does not appeal to alcoholics and does not provide the complete psychological satisfaction which they demand." Our own experience does not support this contention. Our patients do not sip or flavor their drinks; they drink for the effect. Although whiskey may be the preferred beverage (as it is for 80 per cent of American drinkers, social and immoderate),[10] alcoholics will not refuse alternate beverages if whiskey is unavailable. Further, alcoholics in their attempts to control their drinking frequently switch brands and types of beverage.

What we suggest from the point of view of primary prevention is this: Major evidence indicates that congeners have toxic effects; therefore it behooves the alcohol beverage industry to make a strong effort to cope with this problem. They could use the filtration method they already employ for the removal of congeners in vodka production. In order to maintain the smell, taste, and appearance of the different types of beverages, nontoxic flavoring, coloring, and aromatic substances could be substituted. It may well be that the social drinker in his infinite subconscious wisdom has already switched to the increased use of those beverages with relatively low congener content, vodka and dry gins.

When we look at cultures in our agent-host-environment triad, other methods of prevention come into view. Around alcohol a constellation of attitudes, feelings, and ideas exists in any person's environment even before his first drink. Unhealthy attitudes strongly influence the development of alcoholism. Cultures which preach prohibition are likely to create unhealthy attitudes about drinking which contribute to alcoholism (for example, the Mormons). Therefore let us review cultures where alcohol has been used in a healthy way to see which features are significant in prevention.

We saw that the Aleuts [2] used alcohol in an integrative way, allowing for relaxation of inhibitions without moral condemnation. As a consequence, like the Salish,[15] the Aleuts are apparently without guilt feelings or ambivalence concerning the use of alcohol. The Mohave,[7] who also used alcohol integratively, have low levels of anxiety about drinking. Group drinking where all share in the supply develops healthy attitudes as evidenced by Aleut, Salish, Mohave, and Ecuadorian Indian [25] cultures.

Where alcohol is introduced to children in a ritualistic, controlled setting, such as in Coconuco, Mestizo, Zarzal,[26] or Jewish cultures, alcoholism is on the whole rare. Generally, when drinking is associated with an expression of profound religious sentiment, healthier attitudes tend to evolve.

One of the more important cultural attitudes from a socially preventive view is the approach which supplies consistent definitions of alcohol use. The low alcoholism rates of South Colombian Indians, where general attitudes toward drinking are relatively consistent and defined, are examples. Ecuadorian Indians, in a culture where males are instructed not to remain continuously drunk, drink only on special occasions. They are taught that alcohol is good, helping strength, life, and blood; they rarely have alcoholism. The same is true in the Mestizo [27] culture, where there is suspicion and disapproval of the solitary drinker and approval of group drinking. Drinking is permissive and positive without an abstinent movement and without apparent guilt. The Andean Indian [16] resists alcoholism by defining drinking and integrating it with social customs, e.g. beer is considered health-giving, any social situation is appropriate for the use of alcohol, and drinking should be a group activity.

In studying the low rate of Jewish alcoholism, certain social attitudes seemed pertinent. The Jewish view that drinking is socially practical and religiously communicative and symbolic helps prevent addictive alcoholism, according to Glad.[9] According to Rosenman,[23] alcohol for the Jew is a gift of God and must be used as such. The ritual introduction of alcohol to the Jewish child in which family, religion, God, and alcohol are all associated is the factor to which Bales [1] gives greatest weight for the low incidence of Jewish alcoholism. Kant [13] emphasizes that because Jews are a minority group and fear censure, they have throughout their literature described Gentiles as drunkards, and sobriety as a Jewish virtue. Although focusing on different cultural configurations, all these observers stress healthy attitudes surrounding alcohol usage among the Jews.

What do we learn about preventive attitudes toward drinking from this quick review? Preliterate and contemporary societies both offer models for drinking practices which permit varied and even heavy alcohol usage and at the same time seem to lead away from pathological drinking: group drinking (versus solitary drinking); drinking in a consistent and defined pattern; ritual drinking; traditional drinking with meals; introduction to alcohol at a young age within one or more of these patterns.

It is important that alcohol not be defined as a magical substance, able to meet all needs. If this image does develop, alcohol is likely to be fitted into an emotional system as a defense or symptom mechanism.

Drinking to drunkenness, if it occurs, should be in a safe setting, at an occasion at which alcohol use is sanctioned. The group drinking behavior of preliterate cultures seems to be a protective device even when drinking to drunkenness results. The preliterate societies' usage of alcohol to enhance social relations and conviviality rather than to meet life's problems results in little ambivalence or guilt.

If we are to learn from the experience of others, we must see that the teaching of a proper use of alcohol is not only preventive but also does not provoke more potentially socially destructive methods of dealing with drink. We must also keep in mind Bales's [1] suggestion that cultures must provide mechanisms to meet inner tensions. If we do not have alcohol, something else will be necessary. As we consider the development of healthy and preventive cultural attitudes, we are increasingly aware of the dangers of arbitrary total prohibition. In the absence of any culturally meaningful substitute for alcohol's tension-reducing function, drinking in a prohibition era will continue and ambivalence and guilt will increase. One thing is clear: admonitions never to drink, particularly in the complex societies of today, frequently bring about the opposite results.

Ullman [33] has developed a clear-cut hypothesis: "In any group or society in which the drinking customs, values, and sanctions—together with the attitudes of all segments of the group or society—are well established, known to and agreed upon by all, and are consistent with the rest of the culture, the rate of alcoholism will be low."

Knupfer [14] has suggested that "We might learn something from the attitude that control measures should concentrate on the possible dangerous results of drunkenness rather than on drunkenness itself. For example, it is conceivable that a custom might arise in our society which would dictate that when people go out to drink at festive occasions they would make special transportation arrangements so as not to drive an automobile while intoxicated."

It is of interest to note that not only are there ethnic differences in alcoholism rates but also occupational and social class differences. For example, salesmen, bartenders, woodsmen, and construction workers all have high rates of alcoholism. Even more interesting than this group variation is the question of leadership in these groups. We believe that the foreman who is an alcoholic or heavy drinker may well have considerable influence on the drinking patterns of those workers under him. It is therefore important as a preventive technique to reach such supervisory personnel.

In conclusion, our review of healthy cultural attitudes suggests that social manipulation is a method of prevention. One widespread technique is alcohol education. It would seem clear that methods of alcohol education should vary to meet the needs of various age groups; but before we consider alcohol education in the schools, let us review the history of the alcohol education movement.

The temperance movement of 1870–1900 drew the public

schools into the first wave of legally required education regarding alcohol and narcotics usage. Some of these laws specified the grades to be taught and the number of hours or pages to be devoted to the subject. As with the second wave in the 1920's, the goal was total abstinence and the elimination of the alcohol beverage industry. The third wave (1945 to present) is being motivated by alcoholism treatment programs and alcoholism prevention endeavors of governmental public health movements. New Hampshire School Committee members are still liable to fines if the state alcohol education requirements are not completely fulfilled in the curriculum. Many of these laws have been revised, but all states still have them, although they vary considerably in content.

One historical note: A physiology and hygiene textbook [31] of 1885 concluded its chapter on alcohol information by describing it as a powerful drug which causes narcosis, an enfeebled constitution in offspring, and a substantial proportion of crime and pauperism. The author of this text cited possible medical complications of alcohol usage: Bright's disease, softening of the brain, stomach ulcers, indigestion, arteriosclerosis, and blindness. Here we have an example of an attempt to give objective (though incorrect) information about alcohol use.

Demone [6] in a presentation to a group of teachers stated:

I would like to suggest that you are also in an appropriate position to bring about more objective attitudes toward alcohol. If we can agree that people have attitudes which we can identify and manipulate, it is reasonable to suppose that anyone with an extended and intimate relationship with young people can help them. This means that a chance for young people to talk, look and think about alcohol in a healthy and rational way can be of assistance to them. They should be allowed to look at alcohol, at the reasons people drink and do not drink, because eventually they are going to have to make their own decisions. You can assist them to make sensible ones, as you do in other health and social problem areas.

In a similar conference, Pasciutti [22] emphasized that the curiosity of children about the effects of alcohol manifests itself early and in many ways. They ask many questions about why people drink, why people stagger, why some people act strangely after drinking. If his emphasis is correct, then one simple function of alcohol education is to give factual information. Children deserve and should receive unvarnished facts and objective answers.

Many other nations are engaged in alcohol education. Germany,[8] Hungary,[29] Sweden,[32] Great Britain,[34] Uruguay,[4] and Brazil [21] are all active. Dresel,[8] a German, writes firmly: "The government must require all public teaching forces to educate the youth in the proper view on alcoholism." Sombor,[29] a Hungarian, similarly states: "The early education of growing youth is important."

The role of the school in alcohol education is best summed up by McCarthy [17] who states:

The school has the responsibility to make available scientific data, and such data are becoming available. It has a responsibility to reduce the atmosphere of emotionalism which surrounds much of this material. It has a responsibility to encourage young people to develop insight into their feelings about themselves and others, and the role that alcohol may play in reducing sensitivity to standards of behavior which are consistent with their own family and group.

When this is compared with the 1885 textbook cited earlier, where the focus was on the physiological effects of alcohol, the reader can see how the pendulum has swung in a broader arc. The need for focusing on goals which are meaningful and possible to the people being educated is stressed by a World Health Organization publication on health education: [35] "Education must be scientifically sound and built on current attitudes and understandings of the people to be educated."

One pitfall to be avoided is that of expecting too much of

school alcohol education programs. Although these programs can help, the home, the church, and the peer group influences ultimately will be more important. School programs cannot alter an inadequate socialization process, although they might counteract some of its influence. Students will certainly bring to the classroom a series of different attitudes toward alcohol, but this should not deter the teacher. There are no clear definitions, no clear solutions, and instruction about alcohol and associated attitudes and practices can provide a good introduction to the complexities of society in general.

Are the goals of alcohol educators realistic? Can our schools really help to prevent alcoholism? Since attitudes toward alcohol are a critical variable in the etiology of alcoholism, the question is tenuous. We suggest, however, that alcohol education must be taught before the first drinking experience. The effectiveness of education is sharply reduced once alcohol has been sampled. We further suggest that past endeavors to create a fear of alcohol and its effect probably did more harm than good. If education could do away with instilling fear and guilt about alcohol, this would be a major positive step.

What about mental hygiene? Now that we have talked about manipulation of the environment through education, we shall discuss manipulation by mental health techniques.

In our chapter on etiology we noted that many alcoholics have psychological problems in common; these problems are accentuated by the alcoholism but they clearly were present before the onset of alcoholism, before even the first drinking experience. We believe that if the individual and our society achieved improved mental health, the system-addiction phenomena known as alcoholism could probably be prevented.

Necessary to mental health is the development early in life of sound emotional relations, which results in a flexible adaptable personality having the capacity to withstand emotional and physical trauma. Necessary to a healthy attitude toward alcohol is a socio-cultural milieu which fosters group identity in drinking behavior as well as the ritual and symbolic use of alcohol as a food and as an aid in social process. Negative attitudes must be avoided.

Solving psychological problems is never simple. Although parents have been blamed for causing maladapted personalities, it is unwise to assume that their role is the sole determining factor. Too many interpersonal and environmental circumstances come into play during the course of an individual's development to make the parents alone responsible. Prenatal influences also produce a personality bedrock that we cannot influence and control.

The ideal of a perfect being in a perfect society is questionable from a philosophical, moral, and ethical point of view. Perhaps such a goal might produce behavior even more socially and physically deadly than alcoholism. If we assume, however, that society will remain essentially emotional rather than perfect and robotlike, it seems that cultural problems will always exist. This certainly does not mean that a search for a realistic compromise between extremes is to be put aside. There must be a continuing search for means of developing more flexible and more adaptable character structures. Societies, by their very nature, do not accommodate socially destructive behavior. However, when an anti-social activity is blocked, new outlets for the tensions which result in the anti-social behavior must be found. Too often the principles of homeostasis and equilibrium, essential to the functioning of man and society, are ignored. This alleviates one problem but at the same time creates a new one. For example, one should not create a situation of leisure time without providing healthy means of utilizing and understanding it. If alcoholism is the result of disturbed emotional, physio-chemical, and socio-cultural factors, one cannot take away alcohol and not provide a substitute.

The next step along the road of prevention and treatment is

an understanding that the concept of cure is inapplicable to alcoholism. Theoretically, to effect cure one should be able to reinstate the organism to the conditions that existed prior to the onset of the pathological state. Thus, to cure alcoholics, they should by treatment be restored to a state in which their drinking could fall within the norms of social imbibing. This is, at present, impossible. Regardless of the mode and success of treatment, true alcoholics cannot drink socially. If the intertwined psychological, physiological, and social factors we described are causative, then cure is unlikely. Treatment for cure's sake would require techniques for altering genetic, psychological, and physiological systems as well as social attitudes relating to the etiology of alcoholism. These techniques would have to operate at the level of earliest influence. To our knowledge such techniques do not exist. Psychological treatment can touch only portions of personality aberrations; physiological treatments affect only part of the disturbed response patterns; social attitudes can be altered only in part. When the recovered alcoholic drinks, the effectiveness of recently learned emotional and behavioral responses diminishes, again bringing to the surface infantile, primitive conflicts and the basically unhealthy alcohol attitudes. In time the recovered alcoholic responds to alcohol by a reawakening and strengthening of his former deprived feelings with a patho-physiological relapse that results in regression to alcoholism.

A realistic alternative is to locate children with evidence of inadequate coping mechanisms. Then by individual or group treatment of parent and child we can attempt to develop a more flexible and adequate personality structure.

We illustrate the possibility of preventive intervention by an actual case history of a boy who we predict will become an alcoholic, although he has yet to have his first drink. A fourteen-year-old male delinquent from an Irish-American, upper-lower-class, broken family was interviewed in an on-going study of alcohol and delinquency. Unstable, strongly attached to his mother, articulate, and bright, he answered the interviewer's questions without too much discomfort until the interviewer began to query him as to his use of alcohol. He punched the arm of his chair, denied that he had ever drunk, although he granted that his gang did, and spoke of alcohol usage as evil and sinful. As the interviewer changed the subject, he again relaxed until he was asked about his father. Again the same vehemence and emotion were noted; he hated his father, he was "no good." His father, who had deserted the family, was an alcoholic.

This boy we believe has many of the ingredients necessary for alcoholism: emotional instability with strong feelings against the use of alcohol, an appropriate alcoholic role model, and strong cultural pressures to drink.

The possible genetic factors affecting the development of alcoholism may eventually be handled through new techniques to affect the fetus *in utero* or by means of natural selection. What these genetic factors are and how they could be altered we do not yet know.

In conclusion, we emphasize that the prevention of alcoholism is a multifactored problem. There are no simple answers. The philosophies of single cause and single effect hinder progress in understanding alcoholism. The interrelationship of precipitating and contributory factors suggests that the best approach is simultaneous work in all relevant disciplines in the fields of research, treatment, and prevention. A spirit of scientific inquiry is the necessary criterion for success. Progress at best will be slow and steady. Our initial goal is to reduce the rate at which alcoholism is occurring.

12

Secondary Prevention

The reader will remember that in the preceding chapter, secondary prevention was defined as "... early intervention in excessive, pathological drinking by medical and/or social means to prevent the major consequences of alcoholism." In order to understand secondary prevention, a knowledge of the so-called early signs or symptoms and effective intervention techniques is essential. In discussing early detection, we shall focus therefore on the "phases" Jellinek [8] formulated in 1946 after he had administered a questionnaire to AA members. During the next five years, Jellinek further administered an expanded questionnaire to more than 2000 alcoholics,[10] and his findings were published by the World Health Organization (WHO) Expert Committee on Mental Health, Alcoholism Subcommittee,[9, 23] in 1952. Jellinek, however, was not the first to note different stages of pathological drinking, for clinicians previously had observed that a "constellation of symptoms" was useful for the diagnosis of alcoholism. For example, Haun [6] in 1941 stressed the following signs of alcoholism: Sprees or daily excesses; eye-openers; quantitative excesses; failure to stop drinking when discretion indicates; and mental changes as a consequence of imbibing.

The WHO Subcommittee Report sets forth two categories of alcoholics: "alcohol addicts" and "habitual symptomatic excessive drinkers." We shall concentrate on the alcohol addict, the patient most commonly seen in AA groups and in alcoholism clinics. Phasic differences between the two categories we shall describe later. The specific percentage of alcoholics that each category forms is unknown.

According to the WHO report, the beginning of pathological drinking is socially motivated, and tension relief is critical in the early stages of alcoholism development. In time the drinking, including relief drinking, of the alcoholic, becomes more frequent than the drinking of those about him, but does not necessarily result in intoxication. Although the drinking of the pre-alcoholic is already different from that of his associates, it is not conspicuous. This early stage lasts from several months to two years and is designated as the *pre-alcoholic phase*.

With Ullman,[22] we believe that the difference is actually much sharper between the drinking of the social drinker and the potential alcoholic, even at this stage. In the first place, from the first drink the response to alcohol and its significance are much greater for the alcoholic than for the nonalcoholic. Furthermore, some alcoholics show a pathological drinking behavior almost from their first drink and at a very early age. One patient reported that with her first drink she knew she was an alcoholic and almost immediately began using alcohol in an unhealthy way. Another patient (cited in Chapter 3) had her first drink, a home brew, when eight, and even then returned again and again to the supply until it was gone and she was severely intoxicated. Her pattern of drinking thereafter rarely deviated from her early experience until she began treatment.

MacKay[13] reports in a similar vein on the clinical observations of twenty youthful drinkers, aged 13–18, who were clearly alcoholic despite their youth. All these adolescents retained a vivid recollection of their first drink. They could recall the brand name, the time of day the drink was consumed, and the companions with whom it was experienced. The first drink caused them to feel "high" or actually drunk, and they reported hangovers, blackouts, frequent excessive drinking bouts (as often as several times a week), and intoxication.

The second major phase is described in the WHO report as the *prodromal phase*. This phase is distinguished from the pre-alcoholic by the sudden onset of "blackouts" (temporary amnesia). Blackouts are either followed or preceded by drinking behavior which suggests that alcohol has become a "drug" to the individual and not a beverage. Drinking becomes surreptitious; there is great preoccupation with alcohol; drinks are gulped down; and there are well-developed guilt feelings about drinking behavior. Although the blackouts continue, marked, overt, and frequent intoxication does not occur. This prodromal period may last from six months to four or five years, and the WHO report states that "as in the prodromal phrase rationalizations of the drinking behavior are not strong and there is some insight as well as fear of possible consequences, it is feasible to intercept incipient alcohol addiction at this stage."

The next phase is the *crucial phase*. Here, loss of control over drinking occurs and the alcoholic often drinks to a serious state of drunkenness. At this stage once drinking has begun, the ability to control the amount consumed is lost; only the decision whether or not to take the first drink remains. The interesting question arises as to why an individual will take that first drink again and again while he still retains elements of control. To the WHO report the answer is that the addict fears he has lost his will power, i.e. his ability to control his drinking. "To master his will becomes a matter of the greatest importance to him." As a consequence, the individual continues to test himself. Although the WHO does not go on to interpret this observation, we believe that the urge to show "will power" is in part socially motivated, and that the social engineering approach described in primary prevention is a possible vehicle for developing a more realistic social attitude here. If society could allow some inadequacy of personality as appropriate behavior, the challenge would be reduced and the alcoholic could find social understanding of his problems. Loss of will power is not the most serious failing of a man. With more realistic standards the alcoholic might more readily recognize that a pathological state exists, and be less apt to "rationalize his drinking behavior" (alcoholic alibis) when loss of control occurs. These rationalizations are essential for his own self-esteem because, at this stage, his environment has recognized and condemned his unhealthy union with alcohol.

Beyond the stage of loss of control, the WHO notes that social pressures mount. Grandiose and aggressive behavior become more common. If the alcoholic cannot find fault with himself or his drinking, the burden of guilt must lie elsewhere. However, since these attitudes and feelings are not clearly distinguished, persistent remorse also develops, so that the alcoholic has an ambivalent attitude toward himself. He makes attempts to change. He goes "on the wagon" (voluntary total abstinence). He changes the "pattern of his drinking"; he decides to drink a different beverage at a different place at a different time.

The pressure builds up. As a consequence of the alcoholic's aggressive behavior, he feels mounting inner turmoil, and the strain begins to take its toll. He begins to "drop friends and quit jobs." Perhaps, in fact, friends and employers have dropped him or are preparing to do so, but with his extreme sensitivity to possible rejection, he will often anticipate their moves and soften the rejection by instigating the action. Thus, he develops his trend to greater isolation with more and more energy being directed inward and his "behavior becomes alcohol centered."

Now his major concern is not controlling drinking to avoid its interfering with job and interpersonal relations, but the reverse. How can activities be controlled so that they do not interfere with drinking? Rapidly thereafter there comes a "loss of outside interests," a "re-interpretation of interpersonal relations," and "marked self-pity." "Geographic escape" is now a possibility.

If the family is still intact, the wife and children begin to seek outside solace and activities, with a sharp break in family habits. This only serves to increase the "unreasonable resentments" of the alcoholic. Assurance of alcohol supply becomes paramount, nutritional needs suffer, and a first hospitalization for alcoholism may occur now. Accompanying these developments are diminished sexual drive and hostility toward the wife, manifesting itself in "alcoholic jealousy." At the end of the crucial phase, alcohol has become a life-giving drug and there is an intense need for it.

Ushering in the *chronic phase* is the final disintegration, the loss of the struggle to retain an ever-lessening social status. The capacity to support a family financially, the ability to avoid intoxication during the day, and the independence from a morning drink all markedly diminish. Prolonged intoxications, "benders," "marked ethical deterioration," and "impairment of thinking" may occur rapidly. In 10 per cent of Jellinek's group, alcoholic psychosis developed. In striving for redeemed status and morale, the alcoholic drinks with "persons far below his social level," and some even experiment with toxic agents—for example, bay rum or rubbing alcohol—when their supply of beverage alcohol is depleted. Mendelson and his group [15] have described a "superalcoholic" who prefers the severely toxic substances to alcohol itself.

At this late stage of alcohol addiction, a number of changes may take place. There may develop a "loss of alcohol tolerance," that is, considerably less alcohol than formerly brings about intoxication and stupor. As anxieties increase and tremors are more constant, the ability to perform simple manual tasks is reduced (psychomotor inhibition) and the alcoholic feels a "need" to take alcohol as a medication. With drinking taking on an obsessive character, ambivalence heightens and rationalization weakens, and "vague religious desires develop" (60 per cent of the sample). Once the denial system of the alcoholic fails, his emotional and social defeat is complete. As we shall discuss in the next chapter, therapeutic intervention even at this stage is appropriate and often effective.

When and why the alcoholic seeks treatment are important considerations. There may be an external or internal coercive force resulting in the motivation for treatment. This coercive force has been described as the "alcoholic hitting bottom." Hitting bottom, however, is a response running through a continuum from the alcoholic who "hits skid row" and develops a cirrhotic liver to the alcoholic who seeks treatment because his children have lost respect for him. Alcoholics may only seek treatment when threatened with the loss of some positive relationship which is so meaningful that some action becomes necessary to save it. What constitutes "hitting bottom" for one person may be quite different for another.

What about the nonaddictive alcoholic, referred to earlier, who was not included in the alcoholics Jellinek studied and the phases he described? The WHO suggests that nonaddictive alcoholics do not go through such clear-cut phases as do addicted alcoholics. The sharpest distinction between the groups is that nonaddictive alcoholics do not suffer loss of control. This observation should not suggest that the phasic pattern of the nonaddict stops prior to the crucial stage. Rationalizations, problems with family, friends, and employer may also occur with the nonaddict. Some tend toward isolation, requiring hospitalization; they may develop alcoholic psychoses as well as other symptoms of the crucial phase. But this group of alcoholics usually stops short of the chronic phase because of the retention of a measure of control.

How do these phases, first described in 1951, apply today? Two studies tend to duplicate the original Jellinek study, and in general their data support the original findings.

Trice and Wahl [21] found that some phase symptoms tend to cluster—a group of symptoms occur roughly at the same time. They note that although Jellinek prefaces both of his reports with warnings that not all alcohol addicts follow the same sequence in the development of their addiction, he leaves the impression in both of his reports of a relatively smooth transition and progression, symptom by symptom. In contrast, they found a clustering of symptoms. Trice and Wahl's "findings showed that if the concept of a disease process in alcoholism is valid, only the earliest or the most advanced stages of the process are reliably indicated by the symptoms studied herein."

Jackson,[7] asking different questions, presents some empirical data which test Jellinek's hypothesis regarding drinking and related behavior of alcoholics. Dr. Jackson administered to all her subjects, as part of her research program, the Jellinek Drinking History Questionnaire modified by reclassification of the initial phases into three major divisions: (1) Solitary and sociable drinking; (2) Belligerent and nonbelligerent drinking; (3) Periodic, steady, and changing drinking. The solitary drinker avoids social interaction while drinking, even though he may be physically surrounded by people. In contrast, the sociable drinker wants to interact with people continuously while drinking. For him, solitary drinking is a last resort and develops only after efforts to find drinking companions have failed. The desire for company exists whether he is drunk or sober. In Dr. Jackson's study 60 per cent were solitary and 40 per cent sociable.

Some sharp behavioral differences were found between the two groups. The solitary drinker is less likely to appear at work while intoxicated, losing his job by default. Although the job loss rate is the same for solitary and sociable, the solitary drinker's drinking extent is less well known to his employer than that of the sociable. Furthermore, the solitary drinker's drinking behavior is disruptive to intrafamily relations and the family finds difficulty in convincing relatives and friends of his alcohol problem. As a result, the solitary drinker's family has a fragmented relationship with the surrounding community. The sociable drinker's family, on the other hand, because of community awareness and its consequent support, tends to band together against the alcoholic.

As with the solitary and sociable drinking group, Jackson's samples fully illustrated her other two categories of belligerent and nonbelligerent and periodic, steady, and changing drinking. In her sample, 43 per cent were belligerent and 57 per cent nonbelligerent. As might be expected, the social consequences of belligerent drinking are heightened and sharpened: the family collapses more rapidly; more social and emotional disorganization are suffered. The belligerent alcoholic is more quickly rejected by family, friends, and community than the nonbelligerent. For the family an overriding fear of violence exists even after many years' separation from the alcoholic. The family of the belligerent alcoholic, in contrast to the family of the nonbelligerent, is more ready to see the alcoholic as having a psychiatric problem rather than merely having a drinking difficulty.

The final classification of Jackson's study concerns patterns of drinking: periodic, steady, and changing. By periodic drinking, she means alternating patterns of excessive on one hand, abstinence or moderation on the other. By steady drinking is meant a pattern "characterized by a gradual increase in frequency until it is a daily habit." Changing drinking is characteristic of those alcoholics who switch patterns, steady to periodic and vice versa.

As with the belligerent, nonbelligerent patterns, there are some obvious and expected differences. The periodic drinker, and often his family, finds it easier to rationalize his drinking behavior than does the steady. Crises, although acute, are intermittent. As with the family of the nonbelligerent alcoholic, the family of the periodic alcoholic does not receive immediate community support. Too often, suggestions that perhaps the family or some other social situation is responsible for the latest binge are offered. Here, again, the caretaker (e.g. policeman, doctor, public health nurse, or clergyman) must be firm and explicit with all concerned or the problem will be prolonged. For the steady alcoholic, crises are inclined to be continuous and elongated with steadily increasing intensity. With these patients, family, friends, and employers are more accepting of therapeutic intervention than are those of the periodic class. The alcoholic who switches patterns apparently shows more rapid disorganization, socially and emotionally, than those who find a stabilized drinking pattern. From Jackson's study, there is the suggestion that this group had serious conflicts in their attitudes toward drinking which made the breakdown more rapid. Jackson reported no material on therapeutic effectiveness in reaching these "changing" alcoholics.

Wahl and Trice, and Jackson, point out the need for flexibility in utilizing these phase guidelines. For they are only limit markers to be quickly discarded when confronted with the facts of the variable responses of alcoholics and alcoholism. If these categories become rigid descriptive laws for understanding alcoholics they will defeat the purpose for which they were developed.

Straus and Bacon [19] examined the potential pathological drinker in their college study. In trying to select that group of college-student drinkers who might possess the ingredients to become problem drinkers, "to differentiate between incidental problem drinking and that which may be repetitive and patterned," they devised a "social complications scale." This technique, known as Guttman [4] Scaling after its innovator, relates one series of items to another series of items; a positive response in one group implies a positive response in the other. Straus and Bacon used four items to study the social complications associated with drinking; formal punishment or discipline for drinking (most meaningful item); drinking leading to an accident or injury; loss of friends or damaged friendships attributable to drink; failure in academic or social obligations because of drinking, the lowest point on a social complication scale. The value of this study is not ascertainable at present, because follow-up data are not yet available. However, this scaling technique offers a possible vehicle for locating potential pathological drinkers since the technique is based exclusively on behavioral phenomena, where observed phenomena are more easily measured than subjective. Straus and Bacon correlated the social complications with family income, religion, and levels of anxiety about drinking. Separately, the material suggests that some students drink differently from their associates. Together, a high degree of correlation was found between various warning signs and such factors as the frequency and quantity of drinking, the psychological importance of drinking, and the incidence of complications resulting from drinking.

Straus and Bacon suggest, and we agree, that some tools essential to detecting incipient alcoholism already exist. They think that the anxiety which some students experience in relation to their drinking may provide the lever by which "constructive counseling" may be offered to prevent pathological drinking.

Who works at secondary prevention, and how? Voluntary health associations—cancer and heart groups, for instance—alert the public to the early symptoms of the conditions they fight. Although they sometimes scare individuals, these organizations suggest to people and families that they should be aware of the symptoms and seek medical advice when necessary. Alcoholism agencies use the same principles and techniques. As long as the public, and indirectly the patient, is not persuaded that alcoholism is an illness and the alcoholic a sick person, early intervention is impeded. Clinical experience suggests that family members recognize signs of pathological drinking in their loved ones early, but, because of social stigma and other psychological reasons, prefer to ignore what they see. Of course, the ultimate action must wait for acceptance by the alcoholic of his need for help. That some measure of success in the acceptance of alcoholism as an illness has been accomplished is suggested by the gradual age reduction of individuals attending clinics and AA groups.

Another type of community group action in secondary prevention lies in industrial alcoholism programs. In 1946, Spears [18] wrote a vigorous report about industrial alcoholism and urged action by management and employees. Two years later, Norris,[16] of Eastman Kodak, wrote of a treatment program for alcoholics in that company. He recommended understanding by management, education of supervisory and personnel employees, and referral to local AA groups of workers with problems.

At present many of North America's largest and most successful firms have instituted detection and treatment programs for alcoholics. Their results have been gratifying in achieving motivation for early treatment of alcoholic employees, as they often allow the employees to maintain their jobs while undergoing treatment.

What are some of the common signs by which industry is able to locate an alcoholic employee? From his studies of alcoholism in industry, Maxwell [14] lists forty-four possible signals. The most frequently cited are: hangovers on the job; increased nervousness and jitteriness; edgy or irritable disposition; putting things off; red or bleary eyes; less even, more spasmodic work pace; sensitiveness to opinions about drinking; hand tremors; avoiding boss or associates; neglecting details formerly attended to; indignation when drinking is mentioned.

Last but not least, the education of the caretaking community constitutes a vital area of secondary prevention. Physicians, clergy, social workers, and public health nurses can spot alcoholics in the early stages, and by their authority and status intervene quickly and actively. Unfortunately, the formal education of the medical profession has been lacking in the area of alcoholism. No individual is a better "secondary preventer" than the family physician. Yet the ignorant moral attitudes of the lay public toward alcoholism still strongly manifest themselves in many physicians, blinding them to early recognition and treatment of this condition.

13

Tertiary Prevention

In tertiary prevention we include the components most often found in discussions of treatment. We regard treatment as a phase of prevention for a number of reasons. When treatment of alcoholism is effected, serious physical complications may be obviated or arrested. On the social level, whenever the recovered alcoholic is returned to usefulness and productivity, he is no longer a drain on and a problem for community resources. Furthermore, the negative influence any alcoholic may exert upon the environment during his illness is considerable, as is evidenced by the high incidence of pathological drinkers in the family histories of alcoholics. Prevention occurs at any point at which the downward progression of the individual is delayed, halted, or reversed. Therefore, we believe that by treating the alcoholic—even late in his condition—one brings about influences of prevention at the family and community level.

Early in the life of the Clinic for Alcoholism at the Massachusetts General Hospital, the drinking of a mother of a large family was brought under control. This patient's propensity for frequent hospitalization and her ability to mobilize the community resources on her behalf had been so great that after only one year of successful treatment, the savings of the hospital and the community were equal to the entire clinic's budget for that year. In addition, the behavioral difficulties of the patient's children began to diminish.

The common thread in treatment is the relation of the patient with another person. By relation we mean a positive feeling for, a trust in something or somebody. Whether it be clinic, group, physician, psychiatrist, social worker, drug, hospital, or AA member, there must be some positive tie between the patient and the treatment mode. The sooner this positive relation occurs, the greater the potential for success.

Two broad approaches will be considered in this chapter: physiological and psychological. A major form of physiological therapy is conditioned reflex therapy. This mode of treatment is an attempt to create a distaste for alcohol by developing a reflex association between alcohol and vomiting. A noxious stimulus such as Emetine or apomorphine is given with the beverage. The hypothesis is that repeated association of alcohol and illness induced under appropriate conditions can produce a conditioned response with the drinking of alcohol.

Although there are many modifications in the conditioned reflex method, Lemere and Voegtlin [30] emphasize that the alcoholic beverage must be drunk slightly before the onset of the drug-induced nausea and vomiting to effect true conditioning. Drinking alcohol after nausea and vomiting have begun apparently nullifies the treatment. Conditioning sessions lasting 30 to 60 minutes are given on alternate days for a total of four to six treatments. Reinforcement to the aversion by one or two reconditioning experiences is given any time the patient develops a desire to drink. Routinely, at the end of six months and again the year after the original treatment, reconditioning treatments are administered.

Lemere and Voegtlin [30] in their evaluation of the aversion form of treatment state that this treatment is of value mainly for the "better-circumstanced" alcoholic patient. Only occasionally does the "indigent, inadequate, psychopathic or extremely neurotic" patient respond to the conditioned reflex treatment according to these authors. They further feel that there is an automatic selection in favor of the patient prepared to undergo the treatment voluntarily and pay the substantial fee. Most adherents of conditioned reflex therapy suggest that other types of treatment should be combined with the aversion approach.

Wallerstein [47] in his evaluation of alcoholism treatment methods felt that conditioned reflex therapy was not strikingly effective and that its best results are achieved with depressed patients; the "punishing aspect helps to alleviate guilt and externalize aggressive charge." Wallerstein suggests that paranoid, anti-social, and hostile passive-aggressive patients do not do well with aversion therapy. He emphasizes that for all patients the conditioned response should be offered only as partial treatment.

Kant,[27] Carver,[12] and Carlson [11] criticize the method, describing it as symptomatic and not dealing with the underlying factors. In Kant's terms, alcoholism as a psychological defense is ignored. Carver focuses upon the punitive and disgust factors in the treatment and feels that this approach may vitiate permanent readjustment. Carlson also emphasizes the necessity for careful selection of patients and stresses the need for additional therapeutic measures, for otherwise, he says, without psychotherapy especially, and when used indiscriminately, conditioned reflex treatment gives successful results in as low as 15 per cent of the cases.

This form of therapy, although some have reported as high as 51 per cent success for it (Voegtlin),[45] is apparently for the more integrated personality who finds pathological drinking a problem. In spite of reported successes, aversion therapy is not widely used in the United States at present although it enjoys wide popularity in some eastern European nations.

Our personal experience with conditioned reflex therapy has been limited. If alcoholism is a learned or conditioned response, it would seem that aversion therapy should be a completely effective form of treatment. That this has not proved to be the case refutes, we feel, the learned response definition. We speculate, however, that aversion therapy with its inherent punitive component can alleviate guilt for some patients, so that they can give up alcohol, or experience a punishing episode for relief—drinking and getting sick. This speculation is based on clinical experience where other psychiatric patients who suffer excessive guilt and must punish themselves, as do alcoholics, are relieved of their guilt and depression for awhile after undergoing an extremely painful event.

Dent [17] in England reports using apomorphine in low dosage to avoid clinical nausea and vomiting and in spite of avoiding aversion reactions, still reports this to be an effective drug in alcoholism.

Benzedrine and amphetamine enjoy varying popularity in the treatment of alcoholics. The rationale for their use is their effectiveness in combating depression and general malaise. These stimulants were considered helpful in getting the patient over his initial feelings of hopelessness and hostility, thereby facilitating rapport with the therapist. Bloomberg [8] hypothesized that since addicts were accustomed to solving problems by ingesting something, and since Benzedrine tends to smooth out mood swings and provides the patient with some stability, the drug will be effective in alcoholism treatment. One major danger is that patients with addiction may substitute one dangerous drug for another.

Insulin was formerly used as a mood elevator and appetite increaser for the alcoholic. Like Benzedrine and amphetamine, insulin was useful primarily before the appearance of the ataractic drugs.

Neveu [33] in Paris used Pentothal in his narcoanalysis of alcoholics. Neveu's impression was that the pharmacological action of Pentothal is similar to that of alcohol and permits the patient to tolerate analysis and, in time, reality. We wonder if this is a valuable method. Other barbiturates and sedatives have been suggested for treating the alcoholic but have not been helpful because of their own addictive potential.

As noted earlier, several authors have postulated that alcoholics suffer adrenal cortical insufficiency. Most other studies report adrenal function in alcoholics not significantly different from normals.[34, 45] More recently, Kissin and his group [28] report that although alcoholics may have diminished adrenal cortex function, this is secondary to liver damage. Consequently, because of the postulated insufficiency of the adrenal cortex, adrenocorticotropic hormone (ACTH) and adrenocortical extract (ACE) have been used in the treatment of alcoholism. Smith [39] first used ACTH and ACE in the acute phases of alcoholism and reported that they were effective in quickly alleviating the withdrawal symptoms of the alcoholic. Smith further stated that ACTH was effective in abolishing addictive behavior. Voegtlin [45] reported his findings on adrenal steroid and ACTH therapy of alcoholics and concluded that although subjective improvement occurred in one way or another in all patients, the improvement was not uniform in degree or direction. He therefore believed that "adrenal therapy will prove to be of little specific value in the treatment of alcoholism except as an adjunct to other existing methods of treatment."

Tintera and Lovell [43] offered a "stress" hypothesis for using adrenal therapy. Their formulation is that hypoadrenocorticism, developing as a response to stress, may be aggravated by the excessive use of alcohol. They further hypothesize that hypoadrenocorticism results in hypoglycemia and a consequent "craving for alcohol." It is to counter these effects that adrenal compounds are utilized. It is the opinion of these authors that some one adrenal steroid will eventually prove to be specific in the therapy of alcoholism.

The appearance of the ataractic drugs on the medical scene has been significant. The number of patients in mental hospitals has gone down, the need for restraints has been reduced, electro-shock and insulin units have lost much of their importance, psychiatrists have new adjuncts, and the public has another new way of dealing with their lives. The tranquilizer has not only helped the general population and the psychiatrist, it has also been useful in aiding the hapless alcoholic.

The ataractic drugs, according to Feldman,[18] decrease the physical and mental symptoms of the alcoholic—anxiety, tremor, restlessness, and hyperirritability. By their use, Feldman feels a better therapeutic relation can be effected. The tranquilizers are available to help the patient over difficult periods in his psychotherapy and in achieving abstinence.

Kissin [29] suggests that since the alcoholic manifests his psychological disturbance physiologically, alcohol will reduce both his physiological and psychological tensions. Because the tranquilizers act similarly to alcohol in dealing with these tension states, they can be used in the treatment of the acute withdrawal state and in rehabilitation efforts.

Cummins and Friend [16] at the Peter Bent Brigham Hospital used a combination of chlorpromazine and disulfiram in the initial contact with alcoholics. Additional doses were given for the next two days. Chlorpromazine, according to these authors, was not only effective in the suppression of vomiting of the disulfiram-alcohol reaction, but prevented post-alcoholic psychomotor agitation. Some patients who received the tranquilizer without disulfiram did not do as well and continued to drink with only partial alleviation of their agitation.

This combined use of tranquilizer and disulfiram leads us to a discussion of this important drug—disulfiram. Introduced as a new wonder drug from Denmark, disulfiram—trade name, Antabuse—entered the scene with great promise. Although the fanfare has diminished, Antabuse still occupies a prominent role in the treatment of alcoholism.

Very simply, people who are taking disulfiram have an abnormal reaction to alcohol. Without the presence of alcohol, Antabuse is a relatively inert substance with only occasional side effects. However, 5 to 10 minutes after the ingestion of alcohol, the individual taking Antabuse develops a sensation of heat in the face accompanied by intense, lobster-red flushing. This redness involves the face, sclerae, upper limbs, and chest. Further complicating the plight of the Antabuse-reactor is a slight constriction in the neck, and an irritation of throat and trachea, resulting in coughing. The greatest intensity is reached approximately 30 minutes after ingesting alcohol.

If a large amount of alcohol has been taken, nausea may begin 30 to 60 minutes after the symptoms have begun. Intense flushing may be replaced by pallor. Commonly, the pallor will be associated with a considerable fall in blood pressure, and the nausea may develop into vomiting. Most disagreeable to the patient is the feeling of uneasiness that develops.

Beyond the symptoms noted above, other bizarre symptoms may occur. These may be feelings of warmth, dizziness, head pressure, blurred vision, occipital headache, palpitations, air hunger, chest pain, tightness in the throat, numbness of hands and feet, and sleepiness. Most patients who have had an "experience session" with alcohol and Antabuse, or who have tried to "drink through" Antabuse, usually must "sleep it off" for a few hours following the reaction.

The advent of disulfiram resulted in a flood of articles on its use. Glud,[21] who helped introduce Antabuse to the United States, stressed that it is no cure for alcohol addiction and should only be used as an adjunct to treatment.

Gelbman and Epstein [20] related the response of patients to Antabuse to their personality problems. For example, they contend that patients who have alcoholism as their "only" major problem will respond to Antabuse without psychotherapy. Antabuse, emotional support, and guidance suffice for those patients who have had an initial period of anxiety before starting the drug. Patients who react with anxiety and who find it difficult to continue drug therapy are best treated by Antabuse and psychotherapy. Finally, Gelbman and Epstein suggest that "deeper psychotherapy" without Antabuse is necessary for patients who are totally unable to carry on sobriety for any protracted period of time.

Carver [12] also iterates Antabuse's function as "a useful ancillary" but not as a substitute for general and psychological methods in the treatment of addiction. He feels that the drug cannot rectify defects of personality structure of which alcoholism is a symptom. Carver stresses that although disulfiram may halt excessive drinking, the underlying neurotic tendencies, their alcohol outlet denied, may seek out other possibly more objectionable outlets.

Gottesfeld et al.[22] reported the development of psychotic episodes in their series of patients treated with disulfiram. They suggested that the use of the drug was successful where patient selectivity was made according to psychiatric suitability, "including a demonstrated ability to utilize psychotherapy." According to the authors, disulfiram is indicated for alcoholic patients without organized paranoid reactions who have the ability to form good interpersonal relationships; who have had a sustained psychotherapeutic relationship; who believe that with the drug they will be able to abstain; or who have had a fairly stable vocational history.

Jacobsen [26] emphasized that in using Antabuse the most dangerous period is the third or fourth month after the start of treatment. Overconfidence of the patient and therapist usually will lead to a relapse. The author suggests a team of doctors, social workers, and group therapy as the necessary complement of Antabuse treatment.

Usdin et al.[44] suggested that there may be psychological as well as pharmacological components to the usefulness of disulfiram. They viewed the drug as having the meaning to the patient "of a powerful superego agent incorporated from the doctor, which may be internalized with effective ego-strengthening value or rejected and used as a focus for rebellion." Usdin suggested that the drug's effectiveness was related to a warm feeling being developed and maintained between doctor and patient.

Antabuse was given in conjunction with group therapy by Greenbaum.[24] He felt the drug prevents impulsive drinking by the patient, providing an alcohol substitute by reducing the patient's anxiety about his inability to remain sober. According to Greenbaum, disulfiram permits the alcoholic, when he is emotionally upset, to manipulate his environment by dramatically discontinuing his Antabuse instead of getting drunk.

Wallerstein [47] thought that Antabuse was effective by substituting "good" drug for "bad" alcohol. This resulted in an external nonpunitive control. He also suggests that the "compulsive" patient will do better with Antabuse therapy than some other kind of alcoholic.

A newer and similar medication called Temposil (citrated calcium carbimide)[2] has recently been introduced by workers at the Alcoholism Research Foundation, Toronto. Although not as widely evaluated as Antabuse, in being less toxic, it shows promise.

In summary, we feel that disulfiram has assumed a useful place in the toolbox of the alcoholism worker. The drug will not cure, but it will help give the patient a proper measure of control over impulsive drinking. In our opinion, use of Antabuse and Temposil should be only in conjunction with other therapeutic endeavors.

Other forms of physiological treatment, not now enjoying much use, are (1) elevation of the blood sugar level in patients who suffer chronic or sporadic hypoglycemia thought to produce excessive drinking. Treatment consists of glucose and insulin by injection and sugar by mouth. (2) Spinal drainage to reduce intracranial pressure. (Craving for alcohol has been attributed to increased spinal fluid pressure.) (3) Electroshock, insulin coma, and serotherapy (an injection of horse serum to deal with addiction as an allergic phenomenon). Treatment results have been indifferent.

In turning from physiological to psychological treatment of alcoholism it seems pertinent to refer briefly to the role of the general hospital (versus the specialized) since it is becoming increasingly popular in this field and has been recommended by the WHO, Walcott and Strauss,[46] Wenger,[48] Prout,[35] Gottsegen,[23] and Brunner-Orne.[10] We feel that the general hospital, with its resources to handle the multiple needs and complications of alcoholism, is an excellent place to begin rehabilitation of the alcoholic. If a rehabilitative clinic exists as part of the general hospital, it will provide continuity and support for long-range treatment. With a team approach and the essential facilities of the general hospital available to alcoholics, an optimum setting is created to handle the many problems that arise before, during, and even after treatment.

Psychological methods have included a broad range of approaches, from compulsory, punitive methods (jails and penal colonies), through prolonged institutionalization, religious conversions, and pastoral counseling, to social work, hypnosis, and psychotherapy. Our main focus and experience lie in the area of psychotherapy. In this context, we shall also discuss psychiatric social work. Before proceeding, a brief word about pastoral counseling, classical social work, and hypnosis is in order.

The success of intelligent pastoral counseling has demonstrated that it can be a useful therapeutic tool in the management of alcoholism. By virtue of his intimacy with the family, the counselor can recognize abnormal concern with alcohol and aid the alcoholic in procuring early treatment for his condition.

Social work has been an extremely valuable aid in alcoholism. The classical form of social work has been most effective in the team setup of alcoholism treatment facilities where psychotherapist and social worker combine to assist the patient and his or her spouse. The worker offers advice and help in securing employment and correcting faulty home environment, and helps smooth out domestic and other incompatibilities. The case-work activities of the psychiatric social worker in the psychotherapy of alcoholics are discussed later in connection with that treatment.

Hypnosis has enjoyed varying levels of acceptance and popularity in the treatment of alcoholism. This treatment has usually consisted of hypnotic suggestions against drinking followed by some conditioning routine. Group hypnotherapy has been used by Wallerstein,[47] who reports this form of therapy useful in the passive-dependent personality. He believes that the ability to form a dependent relation with the therapist is essential for successful treatment, and we agree.

Bachet[3] suggests it is possible to create conditioned reflexes of nausea by hypnosis. In time, the reflexes disappear. However, he finds that in some patients, the hypnosis alters the effect of alcohol; patients become intoxicated more quickly and are anxious and depressed following the drinking episode. In some patients, Bachet merely strives to achieve "hypnorelaxation" as an aid in resisting a return to alcohol.

In dealing with psychotherapy, be it individual or group,

the problem of definition arises. The term psychotherapy has been used to include almost every manner of interpersonal contact, so that it has lost its meaning. Uncounted articles have been written about psychotherapy of alcoholism. We shall attempt to review some pertinent articles on the psychotherapeutic approach and then supply our own formulation.

Bales,[5] a sociologist, has suggested social therapy for a social disorder alcoholism—psychotherapy in its broadest sense. Bales's formula is that an interruption of the habitual social patterns of the alcoholic will bring relief. He suggests that a reintegration of the individual with his social group is needed along with a gratification of his psychic needs. Resocialization is best accomplished by means of a group endeavor, wherein the alcoholic can develop shared experience, "talk the same language," obtain recognition, and be accepted as an individual in spite of his alcoholism. Bales contends that with incorporation as a member of the group and the strengthening of identity, the alcoholic's craving for alcohol will disappear. This concept is in part the strength of AA.

Gottesfeld [22] focused on the transference situation in the psychotherapy of the pathological drinker. He suggests that the patient's motivation is enhanced by explaining to him that the results of treatment will be worth the means and that a cordial and receptive approach will prevail throughout therapy. With rapport established, Gottesfeld feels that the motivation for treatment is strengthened. He emphasizes that it is important for the patient to accept the therapist on an "equal level" if treatment is to be successful.

Tiebout [41] accuses psychiatrists, correctly we believe, of focusing on the underlying problems in early treatment and "side-stepping the drinking as a mere symptom . . . forgetting that a symptom may assume disease proportions." By focusing initially on the drinking, the psychotherapist can then confront the patient with the reality situation and in time, with control of the symptom (drinking), the underlying conflicts may be dealt with.

Treatment and psychotherapy in several stages are developed by Bell.[6] The first stage consists of abrupt alcohol withdrawal, the administration of vitamin B complex, the glucose and insulin for a subcoma reaction. This stage is followed by medical and psychological evaluation. The third effort involves twenty-two lectures and films designed to make the patient understand the nature of his disease. Psychological aids, including group instruction in relaxation, and social aids in working with the family, are instituted simultaneously with an educational program. (We have noted this same approach in the Czech program.)

Chambers [14] underlines the basic emotional immaturity and passivity of the alcoholic in suggesting that the psychotherapist attempt to lead his patient into an active role in the treatment. The therapist must, according to Chambers, continually confront the alcoholic with his typical rationalizations. Chambers believes that group psychotherapy "precludes the rapport which has been shown to be so necessary."

Sinclair [38] believes that the physician's attitude is all important: friendly, nonmoralistic, attempting to build up a close dependent relationship between patient and therapist to help the alcoholic understand himself. Attention must be paid to the personality make-up rather than to the alcoholism itself, maintains Sinclair. Along with psychotherapy, he advocates education of the family and manipulation of the patient's social setting.

Shea [37] sides with Tiebout, contending that the relief of psychic pain is *not* the key to sobriety and therefore it is important to combat the symptom of drinking as a symptom regardless of the underlying problems. He believes that the psychotherapy of alcoholism should be directed toward substituting one obsession for another, i.e. the obsession to be sober in place of the obsession to be intoxicated. Therefore, Shea's approach would make "nonalcoholism" the obsessive issue with the patient, emphasizing complete sobriety and satisfaction with limited goals.

Directive group therapy is advocated by Brunner-Orne,[9] who views alcoholism as a distorted method of adjustment whereby personality development comes to a standstill and regression occurs. If the alcoholic is deprived of alcohol, he is forced to deal with his anxiety, and when given therapeutic support he will gradually acquire more adequate defense mechanisms. She also contends that once alcoholism is established, it loses much of its connection with the original conflict and becomes "functionally autonomous." Treatment is directed toward withdrawing alcohol and providing the alcoholic with substitutive emotional satisfaction. In Brunner-Orne's group setting, utilizing the wards of the general hospital, the therapist introduces topics for group discussion and keeps them "goal-oriented." A series of topics has been developed such as "why must we stop drinking," "how may we substitute something for what alcohol does for us," etc. The group's orientation is "work" rather than therapy, seeking a solution for all members. Although the technique is not modeled after individual therapeutic lines, Dr. Brunner-Orne feels the total effect is therapeutic, providing substitutive emotional satisfactions and decreasing the feeling of social isolation.

In North Carolina, Forizs [19] used brief, intensive group psychotherapy for alcoholics. Groups of 40 to 45 patients were subjected to discussions following the stimulus provided from special films on mental health and alcoholism. The therapist attempted to assist patients to mobilize early emotional experiences through an identification with characters in the films and thereby attain insight into the conditions of their own lives which contributed to their alcoholism. During these group sessions, acting out emotional responses formerly reserved for drunken behavior was encouraged.

Armstrong and Gibbins [1] maintain that the group method of treatment for alcoholics provides certain distinct advantages over individual therapy by lessening the patient's need to reject authority as symbolized by the therapist. Further, group activities reduce anxiety resulting from transference situations, allowing a permissive sharing of experience with others similarly afflicted. The authors contend that a group is capable of self-management through the emergence of a central, stabilized core. The physician is seen by the group not as an authoritarian figure but as a representative of a part of the ego-ideal of the patients, symbolizing for them many factors involved in their goals.

The hostility of caretakers is taken into account by Selzer.[36] He reviews many subtle ways in which the hostility of the therapist may be expressed toward the patient. Selzer says, "The constant admonitions not to drink are other examples of hostility. It would be more helpful, instead, to discuss reasons why the patient feels that he must drink." According to Selzer, the therapist's hostility must be explored by him and dissipated to create a good therapeutic milieu.

Tiebout's [42] article in which he contends that the alcoholic must surrender before he can be treated has evoked much interest among alcoholism workers. We question this concept, believing that fundamentally alcoholics have already lost all their self-respect and self-esteem. The concept of giving up one's ego and surrendering one's self to another force tends to perpetuate the loss of self-esteem and loss of self-respect increasing the helplessness and dependency of the alcoholic. As a consequence, the alcoholic is deprived of the opportunity to delineate an identity, which perhaps explains why AA, which asks for surrender to another force, has to rely upon constant reinforcement to maintain its successful results. We believe, wherever possible, that the patient should be helped to grow up.

Myerson [32] states as a general rule of therapy: "acceptance but no condonation; protection but with encouragement toward as much independence as possible; a struggle to break through the complicated and self-induced sense of isolation, with the recapture of lost values; and improvement of physical condition." Alcoholics who are parents, adds Myerson, influence their children by their behavior, and by treating the parents we may prevent future alcoholism in the children.

We define psychotherapy as a structured emotional experience resulting from an intimate relation between two or more people where a trained person helps the patient or patients to achieve emotional understanding.

For purposes of psychotherapy and training, in the Alcohol Clinic of Massachusetts General Hospital we have classified alcoholics into two broad categories as noted earlier: the reactive alcoholic and the addicted alcoholic. While these categories have limitations, they help to define the problem for therapeutic purposes. Let us review them.

Psychiatric evaluation usually reveals marked differences between reactive and addictive alcoholics. Reactive alcoholics tend to use alcohol to excess when temporarily overwhelmed by some external stress. Retrospective examination of their life patterns reveals that they have in general made reasonable adjustments to life. They have been able to support their family and have been responsible to their obligations. Goals have been achieved in educational pursuits, their occupational history is relatively stable, and they have been participating members of a social order. A psychiatric and social perusal would reveal reasonable progression toward realistic goals. Drinking bouts for reactive alcoholics are usually associated with observable external situations. An episode of excessive drinking has a determinable onset, runs a course consistent with great tension release, and frequently terminates through a direct effort of control exercised by the individual. The difficulty is that some reactive alcoholics become so involved in their drinking that regression to behavior approximating the addicted alcoholic occurs, blurring differentiation. The psychotherapy for reactive alcoholics is the use of psychotherapeutic techniques employed in neurotic disorders, i.e. difficulties in relationships, retaliation, testing-out, etc., the problems in the treatment of the addicted alcoholic, do not operate to the same extent here. Treatment for the reactive alcoholic is a comparatively simple procedure.

The addictive alcoholic is another story. Gross disturbances of the pre-alcoholic personality are clearly revealed in the life history of the addict. Disturbed interpersonal relations are in evidence early. Adjustment in family and in school are seen in extremes of controlled or uncontrolled behavior. Educational goals seldom have been reached, and if accomplished, with unwarranted difficulty. Occupational instability is the rule. Although the marriage rate of alcoholics approximates nonalcoholics, marital disintegration is greater among addictive alcoholics. No definite point is apparent in the addictive alcoholic when loss of control over drinking occurs. The onset of drinking episodes is unrelated to observable external stress and seems to have neither rhyme nor reason. For the addict the drinking bouts will usually continue until sickness or stupor intervenes. Most striking in the history of the addicted alcoholic is a life pattern of self-destructive behavior, and a drinking history with a marked, self-destructive component. For these addicted alcoholics, the psychotherapeutic techniques must be very flexible, and the therapeutic challenge is very great.

As we noted earlier in the chapter on etiology, one aspect of the alcoholic's problem relates to the deprivation of a significant emotional relationship during the early years of life. Without the warm, giving, emotionally positive relationship with another figure during the early period of development, the alcoholic strives to adapt to life by satisfaction of a main, devastating, unconscious wish: a passive dependent reunion with a symbolic all-giving mother figure. The absence of an important mother figure early in life is responsible for the all-pervading, ever-present depression found in the alcoholic. It is in trying to cope with the depression that the alcoholic develops his main mental mechanism: denial. Denial is the main means by which alcoholics deal with life. They deny their feelings of inferiority, lack of self-respect, and dependence on alcohol. Alcohol becomes for addicts a simple, easy method of achieving control over feelings of fear, helplessness and deprivation, by symbolic substitution of an object they feel they can control.

Object loss sustained during early life ultimately produces primitive, excessive demands which are insatiable; interpersonal relations fail and are interpreted as a rejection by the addict. Ancient feelings of original loss and rejection in childhood are reawakened. The pain, depression, and loss of self-esteem emanating from supposed rejection is so traumatic that an all-consuming intense rage develops, like the murderous ferocity of a deprived infant. Rather than destroy another, the alcoholic turns his anger inward and consumes it in alcohol. As some alcoholics have even verbalized, there is greater social acceptance of intoxication than murder.

This fixation at the infantile level of psychosexual development may explain why the alcoholic is never satiated. Developing mature relationships, one loves without destroying that which is loved. "In mature love, the instinctual wish is gratified but the object is preserved." [13] On the other hand, at the infantile level of behavior, all objects are taken into the mouth. In this way, the infant expresses all feelings toward people and objects by making them part of himself, and at the same time, destroying them. In other words, "In the oral stage, the instinctual wishes are gratified by incorporation and the love object is destroyed." [13] Since to the alcoholic alcohol is an object of love, an object he feels he can trust and control, each drink gives him gratification. Of course, as it gratifies him, at the same moment it has been destroyed. Hence, he must strive to replace the destroyed object. Therefore, for the alcoholic to gratify himself with alcohol, pills, or people, there is always an inherent danger that the source of gratification will be destroyed in the process. Before the alcoholic drinks, he has to have some assurance that more alcohol is available. With pills and people the emotional need is the same. This can be illustrated.

Many alcoholics will describe how the sight of a diminishing supply in a bottle will panic them, and how they must purchase another supply before they can drain the first. The need for some alcoholics to hide their bottles—even when no one is attempting to interfere with their source of supply—is further evidence of their fear of a break of a relationship. When alcoholics have been in a therapeutic situation, and the therapist is slated to go on a trip or a vacation, alcoholics become fearful. Examination of this fear reveals that it is not simply the anguish of a dependent person over a separation, but that the alcoholic patients are certain that they will never see the therapist again—he will be surely killed or destroyed. This is because the alcoholic is convinced that anything or anybody with whom he has a meaningful contact must disappear or be destroyed. As we have written,[13] "the continued consumption of alcohol is a symbolic acting out of the oral (infantile) conflict; satisfaction of the instinctual wish is achieved by means of the destruction of a love object which must continually be replaced."

Some aspects of the psychodynamic formulation of the alcoholic have been reviewed because an understanding of these factors is essential in any psychotherapeutic approach. Failures in therapy are usually due to failure in understanding. Too often psychotherapists approach alcoholics with the same techniques suitable for treating neurotics. The passive, nondirective therapist waits in vain to help most alcoholics, for by his very lack of action he telegraphs his lack of understanding of their basic needs and problems. Beyond a rigid therapeutic approach, many psychotherapists come to grief in failing to recognize the individual weaknesses and strengths of the particular patient, preferring to carry into therapy the stereotype of *The Alcoholic*. Unhampered by such a stereotype, the therapist could set realistic goals for each patient consistent with his potential. A further lack of understanding of many psychotherapists treating alcoholics is their failure to deal with the excessive drinking. Alcohol provides, among other things, a psychological defense. Psychotherapy in its broadest sense is an emotional experience as well as an intellectual one. If the patient has a barrier, i.e. alcohol, to establishing emotional and intellectual contact, therapeutic efforts are blunted. For this major reason, the psychotherapist must acknowledge alcohol as a barrier to establishing the treatment relationship. The way this relationship is developed should be consistent with the realities of the situation and the state of the patient. We do not suggest that unless the alcoholic immediately stops drinking, treatment will be terminated. This is unrealistic. What we do suggest is that a confrontation with this step be considered early and maintained as an early goal, being consistently reinforced at each interview.

What should the therapist do? First, he should not try to be anything he is not. The alcoholic—like the child—is especially sensitive to the true attitudes and feelings of his caretakers. He cannot be fooled. The treater of alcoholics must constantly examine his own reactions and feelings. All responses within himself—even a hostile one—should be shared immediately with the patient. This will serve a number of purposes: it will eliminate the alcoholic's tendency to distort the feelings and responses he senses; a feeling of trust and relationships cannot help but develop; a feeling of sharing and comforting will be communicated to the patient, because the feeling of others' perfection and his relative unworthiness will be mitigated. Most important, this method strongly and continually confronts the alcoholic with reality.

Certain qualities in the therapist are fundamental. Trying new tactics and approaches is essential. Stereotyped, rigid, or passive methods are generally to be avoided. This is especially true early in the therapy. Later on, when the firm bonds of a therapeutic understanding and relationship are in evidence, a more formal structuring may be gradually developed. Although the therapist should be warm, kind, and interested, he must at the same time set and maintain reality-oriented limits. While there should be no tendency to moralize or behave punitively, therapists who offer too little control are expressing hostility just as much as those who overcontrol, and this will quickly be noted by the patient.

Many therapists do not succeed with the alcoholic because they do not put their theoretical understanding into practice. They will agree that the alcoholic is suffering a disorder of early personality development and then they will be surprised when the patient does not respond to their words. Because the alcoholic suffers from early deprivation, it is not what one says to the patient, but what one really feels and does that will determine the outcome of therapy. This especially holds for the early therapeutic relationship. Alcoholism, as a preverbal disorder, must be treated by action—by "doing" for and with the patient. Alcoholics, emotionally primitive and deprived, want to be treated, and want to grow. Yet all their emotional life experience warns and threatens them against entering into relations where rejection is the inevitable outcome.

In order to provide the "giving" necessary in early therapy, first of all a therapeutic locale must be available to the psychotherapist which will enable him to provide hospital and medical care when the reality needs of the patient require physical treatment. An early opportunity for concrete giving is often provided by the need for prescriptions and medication when the patient needs evidence of tangible support. Conversely, the therapist who understands the progress of the therapy should be able to refuse certain requests, pointing out to the patient the rationale for such action. Here the gift is in the form of needed control.

For example, a patient had been relating the ease with which certain pharmacists provided him with quantities of barbiturates. In working out the patient's feelings toward the druggists, it was revealed that whereas consciously the patient had looked at these pharmacists as friends who cared for and were interested in him, the underlying reaction was quite different. The deeper feeling was that these barbiturate dispensers were "leeches, trying to make money out of the suffering of others." More important, the patient eventually recognized that these pharmacists under the veil of kindness were in reality pushing the patient toward loss of control and regressive behavior by satisfying his demands.

When a few months later the patient requested barbiturates from the therapist because he "couldn't stand it without them," the doctor responded by refusing. The patient became angry and said that he would be taken care of by his druggist "friends." The response of the psychotherapist was that of course the patient could procure the medication elsewhere, but since his role was to help the patient, the physician was not going to fall into the trap of providing him with a substance that had a deleterious effect on him. "I want to help you," said the doctor, "and because of that I'll not do anything which we both know does you great harm." The patient continued to press for the medication for several interviews thereafter but did not tap his drugstore sources. As he progressed in treatment he no longer made his unrealistic demands.

We cannot forget that just as a parent expresses love and

concern for the child by exercising reasonable restraints, so does the psychotherapist express interest and understanding of the alcoholic when he sets reality limits. We reiterate that excessive permissiveness is but an expression of hostility—of not caring, of not being interested. The attitude of tolerant acceptance with consistent limits is both healthy and reassuring. Constancy and absolute honesty, acknowledging errors and feelings as they arise, provide the only course of action in relating to the alcoholic.

We stress these points because they are critical in the therapy of alcoholics for the following reasons. In all therapeutic situations dealing with primitive problems, a positive relationship is of prime importance. Without this firm bond between therapist and alcoholic no exploratory approach can ever hope to succeed. This bond may take several interviews or several years to develop, but in the therapy of alcoholics, it cannot be bypassed. When the relation appears to be firm, alcoholics will test it again and again. They will test it subtly and frequently. The therapist must always be alert to these testing-out activities in order to interpret their significance to the patient. It behooves the therapist to ensure his bond with the patient by offering him help no matter how often he resorts to alcohol. Relapses, missed appointments, and acting out of conflicts are part of the therapeutic difficulties of maintaining a relationship and treating alcoholics. Unless one is prepared to understand the meaning of this behavior and work with it, one should not treat alcoholics. There is much frustration and there are many temporary failures; but if the underlying aim of the therapist is to help the patient and not gratify himself alone by therapeutic successes, the treater of alcoholics will be able to handle treatment disturbances effectively. The therapist who must dominate his patients to compensate for his own insecurity and the one whose motivation is to be loved by all will rarely deal successfully with the addictive alcoholic.

Besides testing, there is another meaning to relapses, missed appointments, and acting out which challenges the therapist: the expression of hostility. Since the addictive alcoholic is fundamentally afraid and angry (because of the deprivation he has experienced and continues to feel all about him), his behavior is unconsciously designed to arouse negative feelings and to invite retaliation. Hostility and retaliation must be constantly guarded against by all treatment personnel. In this context we note once more that excessive permissiveness of "being nice" to the patient can be an expression of counter-hostility. An absence of controls by the therapist is poorly tolerated by, and threatening to, the patient who is overwhelmed by hostility. To the patient, the absence of controls indicates a lack of understanding of the basic problem, intensifying the identification of loss of control with loss of contact with reality. Loss of contact with reality can only increase personality disintegration for the alcoholic. Anxiety in the therapist is often interpreted by the patient as evidence of insecurity and uncertainty of control.

Denial, a major mental mechanism of the alcoholic, must be dealt with as soon and as often as it becomes recognizable in the treatment setting, since the recognition of denial allows the patient to be more aware of his problems and his role in their causation. Too often therapists do not "call a spade a spade," and inadvertently strengthen a patient's denial. Wherever in the therapy or activity of the alcoholic the therapist recognizes denial, he must guard against his own denial mechanisms. This may occur by the therapist refusing to diagnose his cases as "alcoholics" or failing to label his efforts as involving "alcoholism." If therapists themselves are not anxious about the diagnosis, the patient will, correspondingly, be better able to be confronted with the real problem.

Once a satisfactory relationship has been successfully developed, the therapist must gradually wean the alcoholic from his dependent needs to a recognition and acceptance of reality factors. More and more the patient must assume responsibility. Once the drinking is controlled, the therapist must avoid the tendency to continue the outgrown protective attitude. Patients at this stage of therapy must be encouraged to carry out tasks, make decisions, and—consistent with their abilities—to meet and deal with reality in a mature manner. As the patient's independent activities increase, the therapist must with greater care guard against situations which will encourage emotional reactions associated with the patient's original rejection. Such situations include the therapist's missing or canceling appointments without adequate warning to the patient, his tardiness, making promises and not keeping them, and his telling the patient untruths. Such events tend to be interpreted as rejection, leading to a catastrophic setback in the progress of therapy and to renewed acting out.

Although the therapist must be an active, continually supporting substitute for the alcohol, he cannot help but become aware of a third challenge, the insatiable demands of alcoholic patients. Few human beings can long endure alone the pressures, hostility, and acting out of conflicts of alcoholics. For this reason, the locale of treatment should be such that the therapeutic responsibilities can be shared. Preferably, a hospital (as indicated earlier) and most especially a clinic setting is indicated. In this way, social workers and psychologists as well as other ancillary medical aids can be available when necessary and can offer supportive treatment and case work. For example, the all-important social worker should be available to help with financial, family, and social pressures which commonly arise to complicate and interfere with treatment. Also, by sharing the treatment activities with the psychiatric social worker, the psychiatrist often can take advantage of the resulting diminished intensity of the transference relationship. That is, the wholesale depositing of former relationship experiences will not have to be carried by the therapist alone. Furthermore, intense transference problems—too often unrecognized by psychotherapists—frequently cause the patient to flee a therapy which they otherwise desire.

Essential medical facilities, which are readily available in a hospital setting, can prevent the patient from utilizing physical symptoms and demands for medical treatment as a weapon against the therapist. The division of labor with the team approach makes it possible to separate physiological needs, socio-environmental demands, and underlying emotional upheavals. As a consequence, the task of the therapist becomes more manageable and the possibility for arousal of his counterhostility through a sense of inadequacy to meet multiple demands is minimized. Finally, the patient is also more readily confronted with reality.

The effectiveness or the failure of the course of psychotherapy may be influenced, unfortunately, before the therapist has ever met the patient. Since the initial contact is not usually made by the therapist but by a secretary, a social worker, or a house officer in an emergency ward, initial rejection is a constant hazard. Here, at the first contact, the therapeutic battle may be won or lost. Permitting the patient to be treated as a second-class citizen who must wait around, or handling him gruffly and with little interest, or forcing him to deal with a whole string of clinic personnel in order to enter into psychiatric treatment are major examples of initial contact rejection. Also, merely pushing some medication at the patient and discharging him outright hinder the establishment of a proper therapeutic relationship. Since the patient already comes to the first contact with a great store of experienced and imagined rejection, maltreatment or fragmentation of contact at the first encounter can so cripple his attitude toward the treatment facility that the psychotherapist just does not have a chance. During the course of therapy too many patients have reported how the attitudes occasioned from the first contact significantly influenced their subsequent relationships.

Too often failures in therapy of the alcoholic are attributed to the patient or to the method of treatment, when, in reality, familial and environmental factors are in operation to perpetuate the alcoholism. For example, the emotional problems of a nonalcoholic spouse can be effectively camouflaged by the excessive drinking and antisocial behavior of an alcoholic marital partner. Despite conscious protestations to the contrary, unconscious needs of denial of the nonalcoholic's own difficulties are fulfilled. With the threat of successful treatment of the alcoholic, emotional turmoil seems to spring up in the nonalcoholic mate, increasing the stress on the patient. Some partners will even push a drink upon a tenuously sober spouse under the guise of easing the patient's suffering. Frequently, when treatment is successfully effected despite these strong environmental pressures, the nonalcoholic partner will rapidly develop behavioral and emotional difficulties, sometimes even a marked increase in drinking activity. More and more the therapist of alcoholics must look beyond the patient and attempt to involve significant members of the alcoholic's family.

Baldwin [4] felt that a successful case-work relationship (i.e. by a social worker) with the wife of an alcoholic depended upon the wife's ability to have activities outside the home and at the same time to be devoted to her children. Baldwin states that since usually both marital partners are neurotic, it is necessary to work with both.

Cork [15] used the group setting to aid the wives in the release of tension. By sharing experiences with others in similar difficulties, and by evolving a warm, mutually supporting group relationship, the wives gained in self-understanding. This, the author feels, helped the participants themselves, their alcoholic husbands, and their children.

Bensoussan [7] hypothesizes that the retarded affect, immaturity, instability, anxiety, insecurity, and weak ego of the alcoholic, developed from a relationship with an inadequate mother, emerge in marriage. The marital partner is usually a woman who is domineering, frigid, and dedicated to preserving those social and moral values the alcoholic is bent on destroying. According to Bensoussan, the wife will react to the drinking of the alcoholic husband with violent passion and little insight to his or her own motivations. His drinking is a repetitive demonstration of the failure of her devotion as well as a source of frustration, since her weak mate "escapes from her into drink." The author suggests psychotherapy with both individuals as essential but recognizes the difficulties of getting the wives to co-operate.

Macdonald [31] reports that out of a series of eighteen wives of alcoholics studied, eleven developed a mental disorder severe enough to require hospitalization after improvement in their husband's illness. As a "prophylactic" measure, Macdonald instituted group sessions for the wives, the results of which he reports to be disappointing. He attributes the failure to failures in technique, structuring, and approach, but especially to the unwillingness of the wives to recognize the possibility that they might have problems.

A report by Strayer [40] of successful treatment of a client and spouse by the same worker illustrates the unorthodox approaches which can be employed when necessity demands. He stresses further the need for the treatment of both individuals.

Igersheimer [25] formed a group of nonalcoholic wives of alcoholics for the announced purpose of considering whether some of the thoughts and feelings of the wives might aggravate their husbands' drinking problems and add to the family chaos. Using psychoanalytic concepts, the leader was an "active listener," and within eight sessions a group-centered, therapy-oriented group crystallized and worked efficiently. It was the author's impression that as a consequence of attitude changes and a more realistic self-appraisal, these wives came to behave in a way which benefited their husbands and children.

A last word about the psychotherapy of alcoholics—be realistic about setting goals. For some patients a supportive relationship and the provision of external aid in control over drinking are all that can be provided. Others may require partial custodial care and more continuous support. For many others, however, an intensive, exploratory, uncovering psychotherapeutic approach with resolution of the transference may be necessary. Whatever the goals, they must be consistent with the abilities, capacities, and desires of the patient, and not set to please the therapist, family, or community.

Our impression is that formulations about psychotherapy are best taught by the case-history experience. For this reason, we shall describe some psychotherapy case-history experiences to enable the reader to see theory and principle in action. But first we shall discuss our methods of prevention.

14

Our Methods of Prevention

For primary prevention to operate, we need consistent attitudes about the use and nonuse of alcohol.

In social settings where the use of alcohol is approved, we must maintain positive attitudes toward drinking. Alcohol should not be singled out for special significance and defined as a magical substance to meet all needs and all problems. Preferably, alcohol should be integrated into social customs, particularly in eating and in group activities. For instance, the use of wine at family meals is one way of developing drinking models which are clear-cut and consistent with group practice. For those who drink, the introduction to alcohol should be made in a normal, comfortable setting, by loved ones; it should not be fitted into a system to demonstrate masculinity; it should be used to enhance social relations, not to meet life's problems.

In social settings where alcohol use is disapproved, we must not be arbitrary in our admonitions not to drink. Alcohol should not be set up in the family as the motivation for rebellion. If the adolescent wishes to revolt (and most American youngsters do) he will most often turn to whatever is forbidden—in this case, alcohol. When the parent wishes to have his child avoid the use of alcohol, he should examine the reasons for this decision with the child. If the children are allowed to participate in the examination and are not merely passive recipients of outside decisions, any final agreement will increase their sense of responsibility.

Society's role in alcoholism prevention is significant. Discussions about drinking should focus on the possible consequences of drunkenness and not on the drunkenness itself. Teachers should be prepared to discuss alcohol use and nonuse in objective, unemotional terms and should attempt to reduce the emotional content associated with drinking. All instruction to be most effective should be given *prior* to the first drinking experience. Social attitudes should not force alcohol on an individual, and nonalcoholic alternatives should always be available and legitimized. The attitude must never prevail that the individual who does not drink is a "sissy" or antisocial.

Beyond these attitudinal approaches, early case finding of personalities likely to turn to alcohol as a coping mechanism for their problem should be instituted. This would involve children and young adults who by psychiatric evaluation have been emotionally deprived, who show grave adjustment difficulties in relations within family, school, and work, and who are known to have alcoholism in their families. Of course, since we feel that these early case-finding endeavors should operate before the first drinking experience, they could exist as part of any mental-illness prevention program.

Although there is no simple answer to primary prevention in alcoholism, the total involvement of the community and support of society is essential.

Failing prevention of alcoholism or use of adequate case-finding methods before the first drinking experience, the next effective technique is to identify alcoholics early in their drinking. In order to accomplish this, we must first make alcoholism a socially acceptable form of illness, in order to allow patients the opportunity to seek help just as soon as they recognize that there is something "different" about their drinking. Although we are opposed to public campaigns focused around symptoms of excessive drinking, we feel that family physicians, doctors in industry, personnel in general hospitals, social workers, public health nurses, ministers, and the police should receive training in the detection of alcoholism. These caretakers are in an excellent position for early case finding in alcoholism. Therefore, they should have more specialized facilities for study, experimentation, and treatment of alcoholism.

We believe that if the preventive approaches we have suggested were implemented, the incidence and threat of alcoholism would be drastically reduced.

Case Histories

Marty

On occasion, the physician of alcoholics has a patient who by exerting tremendous self-control has interrupted his drinking. As a consequence of this enforced abstinence, physiological and psychological symptoms frequently develop which tend to threaten the patient's control. These symptoms complicate the patient's difficulties. He must counteract his longing for alcohol and at the same time deal with the new and frightening symptoms which threaten him. We are, of course, not considering here the alcoholic faced with the physiological response to sudden alcohol withdrawal but rather the patient who develops so-called psychosomatic symptoms when the underlying conflict begins to exert its pressure on him and he refuses to respond to it by his previous defense of alcoholic intoxication.

PROBLEM:

Marty is a 25-year-old married mechanic who was referred to an alcoholism clinic by a physician who had recently placed him on Antabuse. He had gone to the physician for help because he realized that to continue to drink was certain to lead to complete social and physical disintegration. The patient's opinion was that his drinking had become uncontrollable shortly after his marriage and in some way was related to his getting angry. Before his present period of abstinence he had often tried unsuccessfully to stop drinking.

MEDICAL DATA:

Marty had had the usual childhood diseases without complications. Following his marriage, he had steadily gained weight until he weighed 250 pounds. Just before discontinuing his drinking, he had gone on a diet and reduced his weight to 158 pounds. During this period of weight-reduction and abstinence, however, he had developed severe headaches and hypertension with a blood pressure reading of 210 mm. systolic and 125 mm. diastolic. During the course of his psychotherapy he developed a nonspecific prostatitis which was treated successfully.

FAMILY BACKGROUND:

The patient's family consists of his wife, their four children, and his mother-in-law; they live in a Detroit suburb, of upper-middle-class means. The patient's father died when Marty was three months old and his mother remarried when he was seven. He was an only child.

The patient's father was a highly talented, successful man of twenty-five at the time of his death. He had excelled scholastically and athletically in school and college. He was the only son of doting parents; his only sibling was a younger sister. He drank heavily and frequently and expended much of his leisure time in the pursuit of women.

The patient's mother is an attractive, aggressive woman in her mid-forties who lives in Iowa. Brought up in poor surroundings by a strong mother and a passive father, she had one younger sister. She received a high-school education and was considered socially inferior by her first husband's family, who violently opposed the marriage. Following the death of the patient's father she worked as a secretary and was courted by many men until her second marriage. She is prone to easy mood swings and has a severe temper. She tends to be "very bossy," and during her infrequent visits to the home of the patient, quarrels often develop.

The patient's wife is three years his senior and is a very successful businesswoman, managing her own business. She is the only daughter in her family of four. Two of her three brothers serve in the priesthood, and the family adheres strictly to Roman Catholicism. The patient married his wife only after he learned that she was pregnant. Despite the fact that she has four young children, she has continued to work since her marriage and has always earned more money than her husband. The children are cared for by her mother, whose role is that of housekeeper, since she has little actual contact with either the patient or his wife. Marty's wife was not very hopeful about the possibilities of his psychiatric treatment and avoided contact with the clinic. She is reported to be popular with many friends, but her efforts to bring her friends and husband together were unsuccessful because of his hostility toward them.

TREATMENT:

The patient has been seen for 102 interviews. A few minutes before he was to arrive for his initial interview, his wife called to say that he had gone away for an indefinite rest, and the clinic was not to try to find him. When he arrived a few minutes later, he explained that he had spent the night in a local hospital. Developing palpitations, he became afraid that his heart was going to stop and so he checked into a hospital. During the interview he did not seem overly concerned about his heart, but was quite tense, sitting on the edge of his chair expectantly, and constantly asking questions for reassurance. He made a pleasant appearance and was a rather intelligent person. At certain times he had a curiously fixed nervous smile. His severe drinking history went back six years, to the time he was released from the Navy and had married. The drinking rapidly progressed until he was suffering from blackouts and would stay continuously drunk for days to weeks at a time. He had been hospitalized twice for delirium tremens and had only recently stopped drinking with the aid of Antabuse. Accompanying the fear that he would drink was his concern over his high blood pressure, his palpitations, and his inability to have any feelings toward his wife and children. He was well read in the psychological field and expressed a keen desire for treatment.

The early interviews were devoted to the patient's disclosing his concern over his "loss of control" in his dealing with women. Although he had had occasional extramarital episodes since his marriage, following the cessation of his drinking he had become increasingly promiscuous, having sexual relations with other women three to five times per week, at the same time maintaining an active sexual life with his wife. He was at a loss to understand this need within himself, because his sexual life with his wife was very satisfactory. He noted also that after escapades with certain women, symptoms of anxiety were sure to follow. When the therapist prodded him about his sexual activity, in time it became apparent that the common denominator to his sexual activity and anxiety attacks was relations with women who had children—in other words, mothers. This was not readily apparent to the patient, and as a matter of technique it was considered too early in treatment to pursue further. In the course of exploring the patient's need to have intercourse so frequently, the therapist gently asked what he was trying to prove. His response was striking. "You mean I'm trying to prove I'm a man?" he said. "I don't have to" and with this he stood up, flexed his muscles, and said, "Look how strong I am." The therapist remained silent and the patient's next association related to homosexual activity during his military service. He recounted how on occasions, when intoxicated, he had permitted homosexuals to perform fellatio. He quickly rationalized this activity to the therapist saying, "There were not many women around, I needed the money, and anyhow, I was doing them a favor." The therapist immediately challenged the rationalization by pointing out that the experience only occurred when he was intoxicated. The therapist also pointed out that the patient could not express anger except when intoxicated and that when this occurred he was usually involved in violent quarrels. It was further pointed out that his promiscuity had been heightened when his drinking had been brought under control.

In succeeding interviews, it became apparent that not only did the patient suffer acute anxiety attacks following relations with women who were mothers, but that they also occurred when he was thrown into an intimate situation with men. Because of the anxiety symptoms, the patient desired to return to alcohol, since he had never been aware of any anxiety attacks while drinking. This was true despite the fact he had associated closely with all sorts of men in bars. His discussion of men in bars in time led him to talk about his dead father. With a great deal of feeling and resentment, he described how he had always been compared so unfavorably by everyone with his father. The scorn of people was so great, the patient contended, that he left high school at the end of the second year rather than compete with his father's scholastic record. He rather gleefully pointed out, though, that his father and he shared two weaknesses: alcohol and women. He seemed pleased with himself when he informed the therapist that he had learned that his father had died in an automobile accident, while drunk, returning from an extramarital affair.

Discussions involving his mother were also of a highly sexualized nature. He recalled that as a young child he had shared his mother's bed and remembered how he was comforted by the warmth of her body when he was frightened. Only in bed did he spend time with his mother, since she worked during the day and spent her spare time with her many suitors. At age 7, after his mother remarried, he was displaced to a cot outside the door of her room and admonished never to enter it without first knocking. Feeling resentful toward his stepfather, he never became close to him, although the patient often admitted being treated fairly by him. During treatment the patient went to visit his mother, who decided to drive the 1300 miles back home with him. His anxiety was so intense at being alone with his mother that he drove 25 hours without stopping to avoid having to spend a night alone with her. He explained he was not afraid of his own feelings, but of what his mother might do. The recounting of his emotions concerning his mother was followed by an upsetting dream. In the dream, a young girl, in whom he had been interested as a youngster, was surrounded by a group of girls. He watched her for some time waiting for her to be alone, to speak to her. Finally he waited no longer and went through the group saying to her, "Have you got any children?" She began to cry and stared at him in a strange way. The patient awoke from this dream depressed. When he was shown that this dream symbolized the rejection that he had suffered at the hands of his mother, which he in turn was repeating in his marital situation, his depression lessened.

In time the patient began to focus on his feelings involving death and funerals. He reported a time when he had been present at an automobile accident with severely mutilated bodies: a woman with her head cut off, and a man ripped to bits. He emphasized that horribly mutilated sights did not disturb him but he could not stand the sight of a body in a casket. Having collapsed at the bier of a dead friend, he had vowed never to go to another funeral and had kept his vow. It was after this episode, according to the patient, that he had developed "his death feeling." This feeling he described as a sensation whereby he was convinced that he was going to die. Further associations led back to the dead friend. The material revealed that this dead friend had started Marty in his profession. The friend had "fathered" him along, imparting his knowledge to the patient until Marty was quite proficient. In time the patient learned that the only obstacle to proceeding up the ladder of promotion was his mentor. He recalled vividly his wishes of that time that in some way his friend would disappear and leave him a clear field. Some time thereafter the friend suddenly developed heart symptoms, which he described to the patient (which were identical to the patient's eventual heart symptoms), and within a few days was dead. It was at this funeral that the patient had developed so many of his anxieties and had made his vow. The correlation was then made to the patient between the wishes to have the friend out of the way and the hostile feelings he had previously expressed toward his father. After a number of interviews of working out these feelings, his anxiety attacks, heart symptoms, and "death feeling" completely disappeared. The anxiety attacks alone have from time to time returned.

As therapy progressed the patient was able to express his anger at appropriate times without resorting to alcohol. His sexual acting out greatly diminished and he was able to relate in a healthy way to his wife and children. Examination by an internist revealed a normal blood pressure reading fluctuating between 120 over 80 to 140 over 90. The patient on his own motivation decided to complete high school and go on to college, which he succeeded in doing. At the last follow-up he had not touched alcohol for six years and was achieving good grades at college.

DISCUSSION:

In treatment the patient was able to establish, apparently for the first time, a healthy relationship with a nonthreatening male figure. He was able to work out his intense hostility toward women and realize that much of his feeling was based on fantasy. The therapist was one who could control when necessary, not judge, in spite of the emotions involved, and could not be destroyed in a re-enactment of the Oedipal situation.

Dynamically, this patient illustrates early deprivation in the loss of his father. The fact that his paternal family always held the dead father up to him as an unattainable goal lessened his opportunity to develop fully his identity as a man. Only with alcohol and women could he compete with his father. The seductive attitude of the mother only aroused and heightened feelings he could not understand. His marriage to an older woman, his anxiety attacks when he had sexual relations with "mothers," emphasized the underlying Oedipal conflict. He tended to re-enact the history of both his father and mother and had to deal with hostility which terrified him (e.g. if I wish someone dead they will die). Only by gradually working out his problems in intensive psychotherapy could he resolve his transference problem and proceed along the lines of his capabilities, from which he had previously departed. The correlation of his emotional state to his hypertension is an extremely interesting finding and illustrates the interrelation of psychological and physiological findings.

This case history emphasizes the type of woman an alcoholic tends to marry. Marty's wife was able and strong with a high tolerance to frustration. While he needed the strong woman, she needed the weak man. At first such a marriage effects a balance of emotional needs but, in time, the alcoholic tends to regress, destroying this subtle equilibrium. For this reason, many of these marriages are doomed to failure. Marty also illustrates the so-called homosexual problem of the alcoholic, seeking to be loved at all costs and having no specific sexual identity due to early deprivation and the resulting oral fixation.

Paul

PROBLEM:

Paul has used alcohol for twenty years without serious consequences or inability to stop when he so desired. For the preceding eight years, however, there had been a significant change in his drinking habit. Whereas Paul formerly drank whiskey and beer in the company of others, in recent years he has drunk sherry in the solitude of his home. Although he consumed two pints of sherry every evening, he managed to attend to his work. He came into treatment at age 44 because he "just didn't feel well."

MEDICAL DATA:

His physical health has been good without acute or chronic illness of any sort. In 1953, however, there was a suicidal attempt with carbon monoxide gas in the town dump while he was drinking, which necessitated state hospitalization. From there he saw a private psychiatrist for a short time, but he discontinued the treatment for financial reasons.

FAMILY BACKGROUND:

The patient's mother is living and enjoys good health. Paul has always been cool and distant toward his mother. Although he never could turn to her with his problems, he consistently denied any hostile feelings toward her. Rather, he admiringly says, "She's quite a gal, just as all the women in my life are." As an example of the prowess of his mother, Paul "proudly" describes how his mother took charge of the family after his father's death, went to school to become a dietician, and then served her local community successfully and competently. His mother is now retired, and he is unable to accept any favors from her unless he has been drinking.

With his father, Paul felt much closer. For example, he could freely and easily turn to his father with his problems. His father was his inspiration for continuing his education; and a most pleasant memory was the time that father and he fixed up a room as a joint study, and Paul calls it "sharing a room." According to Paul, he and his father "had a lovely time together." When the patient was sixteen, his close relationship with his father was suddenly ruptured. The father became severely ill and required mental hospitalization. The father's diagnosis was manic-depressive psychosis and this was of a sufficient intensity that he was hospitalized for seven years until his death, when Paul was twenty-three. Although Paul remembers his father's becoming ill, he cannot remember his death. As a matter of fact, Paul contends that he never knew what was wrong with his father. Not once during his father's hospitalization did he visit him; he did not ask to go to see him; he did not talk to his mother about him. The patient has never been able to explain to himself why he reacted so, since he had been so close to his father, missed him so, and resented being unable to see him. The entire seven-year period is described by the patient as hazy. Repeated efforts to return to these episodes result in varied stories. At times Paul says that he wanted to see his father or ask about him but was afraid to do so; at other times he says that he understood the situation and since he could do nothing to alter it, he had no desire to be more closely connected with it. The reader can quickly see the conflict and confusion that existed here.

The only sibling was a brother, six years younger. Paul has never been close to his brother and experiences difficulty in communicating with him. In retrospect, he has the feeling that he may have been jealous of his brother but can give no confirmatory data on this.

Paul married at age 29 a woman he describes as able and intelligent. He is, however, ambivalent in his feelings about her. On one hand he is proud of her intelligence and ability but on the other annoyed with her "perfectionistic" striving. He is certain that his intellectual prowess is equivalent to his wife's although he lacks her education. He reports that he is able to perform at his best whenever his wife is not around. Since the birth of their first child, Paul's wife has been without sexual interest, which frustrates him and makes him angry. Her ability to speak readily and convince him that he is wrong is another source of annoyance in their relationship. He resents her being "smarter," "the better talker," and "so good." To him she is the tower of strength in the family and he is unable to compete with her. If confronted with the possibility that he may bear a deep resentment toward his wife, he retreats and takes the position that his wife has never nagged about his drinking. As a matter of fact, she does not seem to get upset when he does drink. Although she does not forbid or actually stop him from doing anything, his knowledge that she disapproves tends to halt him. He has called his wife "Sam," an abbreviation of her maiden name, from the first week of their acquaintance, since he did not like her given name of Valerie. Her pet name, "Sam," was given to his son at his birth as a name after his wife. On one occasion he summed up his marital situation by saying, "I do not want to be a kingpin in my family; my wife is that—what I want is to be a happy cog."

Paul has never been close to his son, and reports a good deal of friction and competition. He resents his son's not listening to and respecting him but denies actual hostility, although it is obvious by his speech that marked hostility exists. His daughter, on the other hand, is a source of pride, and he feels closer to her. He has often commented on the fact that all women in his family (mother, wife, and daughter) have been both intelligent and capable.

According to the patient his life had been quite satisfactory until his father's illness. After that, "Things went upside down," and with the head and center of the house gone, home no longer seemed home. With his mother assuming control of the family, his enthusiasm and incentive disappeared. He completed one year of preparatory school, but did not go to college. This he attributes to a loss of inspiration which he formerly derived from his father. He now works as a factory employee in a position of little responsibility, below his intellectual capacity.

TREATMENT:

Before his last course of treatment, the patient had joined Alcoholics Anonymous and abstained from alcohol for two years. When he again began to drink, he decided AA was not for him and gave it up as unnecessary. His most recent course of treatment involved psychotherapy and Antabuse. Just as Paul was ambivalent about many relationships, he was ambivalent about total abstinence. His manner in therapy has been one of extremes: patronizing, hostile, affable, and pleasant. He is acutely attuned to the psychiatrist's reactions, and shows great satisfaction whenever things are going well, but expects reproach whenever things are going poorly. There has been considerable working out of the emotions relating to his capable mother and capable wife. His reactions to his father's illness and death were carefully developed and worked out. A major effort was directed against the conflict of his desire for self-determination and the need to please others.

During the first six months of psychotherapy, he continued to drink intermittently. Thereafter, there was a marked change toward abstinence with only rare drinking episodes. To Antabuse he had an interesting psychological reaction which emphasized his ambivalence. On one hand, he wanted something to help him stop drinking, on the other, he wanted control over the agent itself. Thus he insisted on taking Antabuse only if he could arrange his own dosage schedule. When on one occasion his therapist suggested that he must continue on Antabuse, the patient discontinued the drug and began to drink. When the significance of this act was interpreted to him, he resumed taking his drug and discontinued drinking. From this time, he did not drink.

His therapy focused on his seeing women as rather formidable figures against whom a man must protect his individuality. Women were strong and capable; men weak. As his ambivalent relationship to women was worked out in therapy, he was able to assume an assertive role with his wife. She in turn was taken into treatment by a social worker at this time to help her manage her new role in the family. In general he handled his day-to-day situations more realistically than before and was enjoying life. The frequency of appointments was stretched to one visit per month from once a week, and six months later, by mutual agreement, treatment was discontinued. Paul managed to remain abstinent and returned only once to see his psychiatrist when difficulty at work caused him to become drunk. He resumed his Antabuse, discussed the precipitating factors leading to his drinking, and has remained sober since. He calls his doctor from time to time on the phone to report that he is not drinking and all is going well.

DISCUSSION:

In reviewing the dynamics in this patient's history, a significant area involves his parental relationships. His father was a source of companionship and love, while he was not close with his mother. When his father became sick and was hospitalized, the patient felt deserted and rejected. He had been let down by his idealized father, and his hostility toward his father was evidenced by his lack of interest in the father after his illness. His mother became the dominant, forbidding figure in the family after his father's departure, as though by ridding herself of her husband, she became prominent and strong in the family constellation. The patient's haziness and blocking out of memories of his father's mental illness, collapse and death, and his mother's stepping into the father's role underline the severity of emotional trauma he sustained in his late teens. The fright and threat he felt following these episodes in his life are illustrated by his behavior later on. His concept of men was that they were capable of collapse and disintegration, whereas women were strong and dominant. As a consequence, this conceptualization has interfered with his own image of himself, giving rise to problems in his competition with both men and women. He is afraid to be close to his own son for fear that the same thing will happen to him as happened to his own father. Also, by assuming an occupational role much beneath his capabilities he was refusing to compete with men. He is unable to assume a masculine role in relation to strong women because he unconsciously feels women have the power to protect or destroy men.

Paul hides his angry feelings under a mask of great affability and tries to avoid argument and competition with both men and women. Not only are angry feelings hidden, but feelings and symptoms of emotional upset or depression are denied. Depression must be covered up "because other people will react adversely to emotional upsets." At a deeper level, depressive symptoms would be especially threatening to the patient because of his father's psychotic depression. His desire to please or displease was related to winning approval or disapproval "like a good or bad boy." Attempts at control as well as the prevention of too passive a situation developing were manifested by his need to manage his own medication. For Paul, his drinking served two prime purposes: (1) as an antidepressant medication protecting him from a fate similar to that of his father and (2) as an assertion of his masculinity and independence in the face of threatening women.

In conclusion, this patient illustrates how, emotionally, a patient can separate male and female figures into categories of strength and weakness, dominance and passivity. Women are to be respected, admired, and feared. Men are fragile, tend to disintegrate, and must fight for their masculinity. Both these identifications have passed through the patient's emotional life for three generations: his mother, wife, and daughter; his father, himself, and his son.

Therapeutically, this patient illustrates that with ventilation, interpretation, and identification a serious drinking problem can be brought under control. The identification with the doctor who was masculine, who did not disintegrate, and who did not reject the patient was extremely useful. Of course, the fact that this patient's traumatic emotional experiences happened relatively late in his psychosexual development (after many years of seemingly healthy contact), meant that the alcohol problem he developed was less severe than those seen in more deprived patients. It is also important to recognize that the wife's problem relating to her own sexual identity also required solution to aid Paul's treatment.

Barbara

PROBLEM:

Barbara suffers chronic alcoholism which began in late adolescence. Her drinking was of a destructive type and she was unable to stop until she reached a point where illness supervened. Barbara never bothered to eat while drinking, and often when intoxicated would become attached to some man in the immediate vicinity. One such attachment resulted in a liaison perpetuated for four or five months resulting in pregnancy and the birth of a son born out of wedlock. Barbara came for treatment at age 27 because she was afraid she was losing her mind.

MEDICAL DATA:

Despite the patient's heavy drinking and lack of food, there is no significant physical illness and she enjoys good health.

FAMILY BACKGROUND:

Barbara's mother suffered from a manic-depressive psychosis which necessitated a number of mental hospital admissions. She died from a stroke when the patient was 17.

The father was described by the patient as a "Lothario" type: a very good-looking fellow who had a number of affairs with women who lived nearby. Barbara was always considered his favorite child.

The patient has one younger brother and two older sisters who are married and have families. Her relationship with her siblings is not good. She envies her sisters for their marriages and is in turn shunned by them because of her past behavior. Barbara's rejection of their "stuffiness and middle-class morality" does little to foster affection between them.

She lives with her illegitimate son, aged five. Although she was promised support by the child's father, he has been reluctant to help, and Barbara and he are no longer in contact. The boy, Jerry, is a problem child in school mainly because of his outbursts of aggressive behavior which make it impossible for him to socialize with children his own age without getting into mischief.

Barbara was raised in the Italian section of New Haven, Connecticut, and has extremely vivid memories of her childhood. Some of these memories are so vivid that they approach what might be called imaginary hallucinations—the content is not pleasant. The family life was violent. Her mother, in the throes of developing an overt manic-depressive psychosis, had frequent outbursts during Barbara's infancy and early years. Her mother also openly and strongly resented her husband's interest in Barabara, and Barabara remembers actually wanting to do away with her mother and marry her father. The patient also recalls a number of times when her mother would chase her into a closet and lock her there; when she would be pursued by mother with knife in hand; when she was threatened with expulsion from the household; when she was raped by a baby sitter or raped by her uncle. Barbara also recounted a number of times when she was caught in an alley by some boys and abused. Her memory of her first actual kiss was complicated by the fear that this would cause pregnancy, and she reports having developed some of the signs of pregnancy at that time. Since these fears of pregnancy occurred at the onset of her adolescence, the family had her examined by a child psychologist, who is reported to have merely admonished her to obey her mother and father. Barbara even into her teens knew of her strong attachment to her father and was quite aware that she was searching for a man who resembled him.

Barbara's pathological drinking seemed to begin around the time her mother died. Because she recalled having wished often for her mother's demise, she felt very guilty about it. During therapy she would alternate between fearfulness in remembering her horrible death wishes for her mother and furious rage when she remembered the ferocity of her mother's accusations and assaults. Once the drinking began, however, it continued unabated until she became pregnant and was deserted by her suitor. He was much older than she, married and with children. Barbara actually had expected him to leave his wife and marry her, something which he made plain he would not do when he learned of her pregnancy. When he left her, she became enraged. Nevertheless because the illegitimate pregnancy assuaged her guilt, she was able to pull herself together and stopped drinking even before coming into treatment.

The patient lives in a housing project with her son and is supported by welfare. Most of her time is consumed in housekeeping, caring for her son, attending bingo games, and desperately searching for someone to marry. Her potential for marriage is not very good. Most of the places she picks to find companionship are barrooms. Although she does not drink and is able to tolerate the sight of others drinking, her contacts seem to be with men who want her only for sexual pleasure. When she began coming for treatment, her manner and especially her dress would indicate to men immediately upon seeing her that she was available for sexual purposes. Since her therapy her dress has been modified.

TREATMENT:

Follow-up by both psychiatrist and social worker has been part of the patient's treatment. This approach was necessary for a number of reasons. Barbara's need for intense relationships was best handled by a "split" in treatment ties. Also, there were many reality problems involving finances, care for the son, etc., which required the help of an experienced social worker. Then, too, since she had intensely sexualized every contact with a male, having a woman in the picture tended to protect the patient against becoming too involved with her psychiatrist and fleeing treatment.

Barbara's response to her therapeutic hour has not varied. She will come in and begin to talk about something which has happened to her since her last visit. Frequently, these will relate to either feelings of panic in which she complains of an intense sensation that she is smothering, or perhaps a burst of anger at her son or at one of her sisters. From this introduction, there then issues forth a steady shower of associations which go back to her earliest years. The flood of associations reaches its climax when she remembers a particularly vivid scene of being locked up in a closet, of being raped by someone, or of realizing her intense desire to kill her younger brother of whom she was intensely jealous. On achieving one of these points, the patient will literally scream out and then gradually become calmer. If the interview, however, is not brought to a close, she begins to build up associations again and could easily continue for hours. Although volatile and intelligent, the patient can be easily controlled by the therapist. When the orgastic pattern of the interviews was pointed out to her young therapist by his supervisor, Barbara was helped to discuss more realistic topics. Barbara at first was reluctant to deal with reality questions, because she enjoyed wallowing in her fantasies of the past. Her therapist was certain that much of her material was fantasy deliberately colored by her fine imagination. Not only was she intelligent, she also enjoyed reading Freud, in popularized form, which complicated what she had to say. The fear of smothering, however, was related directly to her fear of being punished for some of her hostile acts against her mother. Always in the background was the constant, seductive tendency of her father toward her of which she was fully aware.

Finally Barbara was able to focus on reality problems. She could even talk about men, how to approach them, and what caused them to become sexually interested in her. Immediately it became apparent that she was terribly naïve in these areas. Her only means of establishing contact with a male was to put herself in a role whereby she was the passive object of his active desire. By her dress and by her manner, she flirted with men. Only when they were at the point of expecting intercourse would she call a halt. Having led them up the "garden path and then suddenly shutting the gate," Barbara found men to be angry, hostile, and rejecting. Their rejection caused her to become sadder and more desperate. Whenever a man would promise her that he would call, she would often wait days for the phone to ring, which it never did. Since her therapy, however, the patient no longer finds herself with difficult sexual situations facing her, and she has been sober for over four years.

DISCUSSION:

Much of the patient's material has been colored by her reading of psychiatric literature. From the data, however, it is possible to ascertain that this patient suffered early deprivation as a consequence of her mother's psychosis. The deprivation was further compounded by the overt hostility expressed by the mother toward the patient. Involvement with a seductive father in a household where sexuality was highly charged partially produced the emotional patterning in this patient. Her only means of relating to men was through sex, and because of her fear of her mother, she treated women as she treated her mother, by avoidance.

With a history of extreme pathology in her environment, this patient has shown a great deal of strength. Since treatment Barbara is managing more and more of her affairs, caring better for her son, and relating to people in a less seductive way. The relationship with the psychiatrist—a man—permitted her to experience contact with a male without it culminating in sexual activity or rejection.

The social worker has been very important here. She has managed contacts with welfare departments, arranged proper school facilities, helped Barbara clarify budget and financial problems, and has been generally available to the patient. Most important Barbara was able to relate to a woman who was unthreatening and stable. This permitted the patient to see that not all women were uncontrolled, violent, and psychotic, as was her mother.

This case illustrates the effectiveness of dual relationships in the psychotherapy of a severe alcoholic problem. It also serves to emphasize how treatment of this patient is also a preventive therapeutic encounter as it pertains to the emotional development of her illegitimate son. If effective intervention did not take place, it is likely that her son, Jerry, would perpetuate into the third generation the pathology of the first.

Harry

PROBLEM:

Harry's alcoholism has been obvious since he was age 23. At that time, he had just married a "nagging" wife, and was so unhappily married that within a short time the marriage was annulled. Since then he has suffered the effects of his uncontrolled drinking spurts, some of which necessitated hospitalization. His alcoholism has cost him several jobs as a college teacher, newspaper editor, and magazine editor. His motivation at age 43 for treatment was his fear that he might shortly develop a cirrhotic liver.

MEDICAL DATA:

Although Harry has been hospitalized for alcoholism, there has been no evidence of delirium tremens or liver damage. A diagnosis of duodenal ulcer was made in 1954, but the condition has not influenced the patient's activities in later years.

FAMILY BACKGROUND:

Harry felt he had a very close relationship with his mother after he turned 8, but before this period there was not much communication between them. His mother managed an office until illness forced her to leave work, and she moved to the country to raise dogs to sell. She died one year before Harry came into treatment.

His father, on the other hand, never worked. Having inherited much money when quite young, the father devoted his energy and interest to liquor, morphine, and gambling. It was reported to the patient by his mother that the father had been impotent for most of the marriage and was undesirous of other children. Because Harry's father was said to have tuberculosis, the patient was raised by foster families until he was age 8, while his parents lived in hotels in order that the father not be diagnosed as tubercular and ordered to a sanatorium. Finally, the mother insisted that his father undergo an extensive examination, and he was found to be free of disease. The family unit was then reconstituted. Although the parents rarely argued, Harry felt that no deep feelings really existed between him. The father died when the patient was 23, of an unknown cause, since his wife refused permission for an autopsy.

Two years after his father died, Harry's mother remarried, and she and her new husband ran a dog-breeding business together. Harry felt they were happy and well suited to one another and enjoyed an excellent relationship. Ten days after his mother died, Harry's stepfather became deeply depressed and committed suicide.

Harry's earliest years were spent, as already noted, in foster homes. All he recalls about these foster homes is that whenever his parents visited him and left him a gift or a toy, the foster parents would take it away and give it to their own children. Harry attended local schools, received his college degree and attended graduate school in Wisconsin, failing in receiving his Ph.D. degree in English only because of his drinking. His many academic jobs were terminated as a direct consequence of his alcoholism.

TREATMENT:

Harry was seen only for a period of several months. He had been in psychiatric treatment with another therapist, and when the doctor was forced to discontinue therapy because he was leaving the area, Harry became resentful at being put "too much on my own," and went out and became intoxicated. Following this bout, his anxiety about cirrhosis led him back into treatment. An intelligent, able, and well-groomed individual, Harry attended each therapeutic session with his heavy briefcase. Verbalizing easily, the patient tended to intellectualize rather than feel. His briefcase was used as a means of pointing out to the therapist the challenge and responsibilities the patient faced daily.

At the first interview, Antabuse was discussed but he decided against it. When he did some drinking after the first interview, he began the second by requesting Antabuse. The content of his interview sessions centered on his wife, his children, and his feelings about becoming an author. He also required some emotional help with feelings involved in divorcing his second wife (after fifteen years of marriage), and marrying the divorcee with whom he had been living for several months. The responsible position he had achieved as the head of a scientific library was also a source of concern, as well as his feelings of rejection by his previous psychotherapist. Treatment consisted of a clarification of some of the reality problems and a mobilization of the feelings of rejection emanating from the sudden departure of his previous psychiatrist.

DISCUSSION:

Although our information about this patient is incomplete, it would seem the early, fairly protracted separation from his parents and his identification with his unstable, bright alcoholic father were predisposing factors in part for his alcoholism. Although he had high standards of achievement, his intense feelings of inadequacy and his ambivalent self-esteem caused him to fail always just as he reached the end point of success (two broken marriages and many lost positions illustrate this). A combination of mixed feelings of pride and guilt tended to make him flee situations where his potential could develop. His strong, ambivalent hostile-dependent relationship to female contemporaries is apparently related to his mother's onetime rejection and early deprivation of him and their subsequent close relationship.

His problem with alcohol manifested itself early when Harry was faced with two major responsibilities: his first marriage and earning his doctorate. In Harry's history, a significant figure in the environment, the father, used alcohol to deal with the stresses of life. Although Harry entered treatment presumably because of a fear of cirrhosis, his decision actually followed the death of his mother and stepfather. The feelings of these losses were reawakened by the sudden loss of his psychotherapist.

The patient illustrates how alcoholism can fit into the self-destructive drives of an individual with a high potential and cause him to function at the just-below-par level so that ultimate achievement never occurs. Treatment has been beneficial to this patient by clarifying and delineating the reality problems and by mobilizing some of the hostile feelings emanating from earlier and repeated rejections.

Will

PROBLEM:

Will has a history of chronic, severely destructive drinking dating back into adolescence and continuing until the time of his admission for treatment.

MEDICAL DATA:

Will's health has been fairly good except for cirrhosis of the liver. There is also a history of delirium tremens. However, since the onset of his present treatment, his liver has been under good control.

FAMILY BACKGROUND:

Little is known about the patient's mother, father, or siblings. Will was an illegitimate child who was adopted a few days after his birth by a childless couple. His adoptive father was a professor of theology in the Midwest, and the patient has offered no information about his adoptive mother.

Will has been married twice and is, he believes, the father of a child born out of wedlock. His first wife was a café owner in New Orleans, and during the course of their marriage both were frequently unfaithful. After three years of marriage, the relationship was dissolved. However, after the patient returned to the East, his former wife followed him there and worked as a cashier in a local restaurant. His present and second marriage is to a chronic alcoholic. She has cirrhosis so serious that the doctors do not expect her to survive long. She becomes sober only when Will is drunk, and he becomes sober only when she becomes drunk.

His theologian father raised the patient strictly according to the tenets of the Episcopal Church. Although Will attended high school, he failed to graduate and attributed his failure to his lack of interest. His thoughts and fantasies turned more readily to an adventurous life, and at age 17 he joined the Merchant Marine. He spent time in China, traveled on road gangs, and joined bridge-building teams in South America. Most of the time, however, he spent aboard ship drinking heavily. Because voyages were so long, there was usually sufficient time for sobering up before reaching land, and consequently he did not get into serious difficulty. During World War II, he served as a radio operator on board ship and sailed all the major oceans of the world. Once the war ended and job opportunities aboard ships lessened, his drinking became far more intense, ending with a number of hospitalizations for delirium tremens. A suicidal attempt led to a state hospital admission after he had left the sea.

TREATMENT:

The patient had never had continuous contact with a psychiatrist prior to coming into treatment at an alcoholism clinic. He quickly developed a relationship with a young, male psychiatrist who offered him friendship and emotional support. Much of the first year of treatment involved establishing a therapeutic relationship and the discussion centered around marriage. Very soon after establishing himself in the clinic, Will stopped drinking and insisted on taking Antabuse. His therapy has not proceeded along classical psychiatric lines. Psychiatrist and patient talked about many things: sometimes mutual experiences, oftentimes about the sea, horse racing, women, politics, philosophy, religion, and sometimes the patient's wife. She is a constant source of trouble for him. This trouble consists not only of her drinking, but also of her promiscuity, which she uses as a means to obtain money for whiskey. Now and then, the patient would find actual evidence that a man had been in his bed while he was at work. Although he responded to such evidence with anger and occasional physical attacks, at no time did he give vent to his full violence. Apparently he kept himself in check because he, himself, enjoyed the favors of a number of women, all of whom were alcoholics.

One complication of his treatment was his response to Antabuse: impotence. This impotence took many forms ranging from premature ejaculation to inability to have an erection. Finding his sexual performance below par, he became depressed. This serious blow to his ego (he had always prided himself on his sexual prowess) caused him to try harder and harder to perform sexually. When he found after many attempts during the course of a month that nothing he did seemed to improve his sexual performance, he went on a "bender." This drinking bout was severe enough to land him at the general hospital where the clinic was located. Unfortunately his therapist was on vacation, and Will was so abusive and nasty to the admitting physician that he was turned away and ended up at another hospital. Since he had identified the first hospital with the source of support, encouragement, and friendship he had been receiving in the alcohol clinic, his rejection resulted in a rupture of his relationship with the psychiatrist. The psychiatrist, learning of his hospitalization, reached out for the patient, visiting him at the nearby hospital and listening to his angry words about his treatment at the clinic hospital.

The psychiatrist's interest reawakened a desire in the patient to continue treatment. In time, with elaboration and classification of the sexual conflict, the impotence diminished. The doctor pointed out to the patient that with increased age, performance falls off some and that perhaps the patient had set his original standards of sexual capacity too high. When Will realized that he had previously failed to acknowledge the fact that age did have some influence on sexuality, he felt better. His wife's behavior, however, did not improve. Continuously drinking, isolated within the home, the wife remained intoxicated from morning until night. The psychiatrist tried often through the patient to motivate the wife to seek treatment for her alcoholism. Only once did she come to see the psychiatrist, but she was so drunk and seductive that a treatment relationship was impossible without damaging the contact with the husband. She rejected all treatment plans offered her.

Will has kept the same job for two years. There has been only one drinking bout lately. This occurred when Will and some fellow employees picked up some girls after work and checked into a hotel with them. Attempting sexual intercourse, the patient found himself once again impotent. He reacted by a three-day drinking bout severe enough to necessitate hospitalization. Since that single episode there have been no further difficulties.

DISCUSSION:

The therapy of this patient has not been directed toward uncovering deep, unconscious material. Will's drinking problem became obvious early. Associated with alcoholism, Will has suffered a series of failures. He was born out of wedlock, failed to complete high school, had two unsuccessful marriages, sired no legitimate children; and finally, when he entered treatment he experienced a new failure: impotence. These failures were coupled with problems of heightened latent homosexuality, which was demonstrated by his attachment to male activities; e.g. Merchant Marine, construction gangs, etc. Interestingly, Will's best adjustment has been made in these situations. Will's drinking behavior seems to be in part a revolt against the middle-class standards of his adoptive parents, which is also reinforced by his inability to talk about them. Much pertinent material about his early life or his relationship to his parents, etc., was not obtained because the therapist considered such exploration too threatening to the patient. Therapy, therefore, is based on the patient's having evolved gradually a strong feeling of attachment to the hospital and clinic as well as a sense of loyalty and friendship to his psychiatrist. The discussion of reality topics of mutual interest strengthens both identification and the ties to reality. This enables the patient without an interpretation by the therapist to see himself through identification as a man and as an independent entity in the world. As his psychotherapist described this treatment, "...it is an active interchange of ideas between two people who might just as easily be sitting side by side at a bar."

Friendship therapy might very well be the classification of the treatment used in this case.

Jane

PROBLEM:

Jane is a 39-year-old, married woman who has been drinking heavily since age 16. Although from the first drink she realized something was wrong with her response to alcohol, only in the preceding ten years has she admitted she was alcoholic. AA membership of seven years has not helped her to control her drinking. Three years ago she came into psychotherapy because she felt "psychiatry was my only hope in avoiding total ruin."

MEDICAL DATA:

In spite of heavy alcohol intake for 23 years, Jane enjoys good health.

FAMILY BACKGROUND:

Both Jane's parents are living and well. Her father is a prominent New York banker who has amassed a great fortune. Jane describes him as a passive, unaccessible, unaffectionate, and solitary figure with but two life interests: his work and making sure that his wife is not grieved by the behavior of the children. Whenever an altercation occurs between his wife and the children, the father will intervene with the patient or her only brother "to apologize to mother." Outside of this action, he withdraws and plays no obvious active role in his family life.

Jane's mother, on the other hand, is an aggressive, demanding, controlling, and powerful family force. Not only is she "Harriet Craigish" in her outlook ("every item is always just where it belongs and the whole house is antiseptic"), but she insists on treating Jane and her brother as though they were still small children. As long as Jane can remember, her mother used illness or the threat of her own death as the weapons to control her children's behavior. The mother lives not too far from the patient's home in a fashionable New York suburb and intimately affiliates herself with the patient's household by expending great sums of money on Jane and her brood and delivering pronouncements to the family on behavior.

Jane's brother, seven years her senior, also lives close by the parental home. He is a weak, passive man who has a high and responsible executive position in a major industry. However, according to the patient, outside of his profession he is driven to distraction and depression by his mother. His marriage to a "wonderful gal" is terrible because of maternal influence, and the patient is incredulous when she describes how this important executive becomes a cringing, distraught little boy in the face of his mother's emotional onslaughts. He suffers from a duodenal ulcer and hypertension.

Jane's husband epitomizes the proper, upper-class male. Three years his wife's senior, her husband attended fashionable private schools and graduated from Princeton. He is aloof, restrained, and unemotional. Following graduation, he entered his father's manufacturing business where he is a vice president. His contribution to the business is limited. Although he is paid well, he drinks heavily and avoids responsibility, and there is often financial turmoil in the family. As with almost half of the women alcoholics we have seen, Jane, too, had married an alcoholic. Her husband has had numerous extramarital affairs, although he has limited sexual interest in his wife.

Jane married at age 19 after one year's courtship. She idolized her "handsome, all-American" husband, but though she was excited and thrilled by their premarital sexual activity, a striking change ensued following marriage when her husband appeared to lose all interest in sex. In spite of her disappointment in her marital sex life and the absence of the affection she craved, she tried hard to make the marriage work. A year after their marriage, while the husband was stationed in New Orleans, Jane and her husband entertained his best friend in their apartment. There was much drinking, and after the husband returned to his military station later that night, Jane and the friend continued to drink and eventually ended up in bed. The shame she associated with her lack of faithfulness caused Jane to drink more and more, resulting frequently in extramarital sexual activity. Only at the time of her first pregnancy did she stop drinking, and until the baby was born she did not drink at all. This behavior she followed through each of her five pregnancies.

Jane describes herself as a model child who was always clean and good. She never disobeyed her parents and tended to be shy and withdrawn. However, following her sixteenth birthday, she was at a party with some of her friends when a bottle of liquor was produced. She took a drink (although she had been all her life strictly admonished about the evil effects of alcohol by her mother), loved the effect it had on her, and could not get enough. Alcohol's influence produced a striking change in Jane. Whereas before she was quiet, sad, proper, and a bit withdrawn, with alcohol she became gay, seductive, and "the life of the party." Always her response was the same: "I could not get enough."

Following the birth of her children and the resumption of her pathological drinking, Jane tried desperately to stop drinking. She became an active AA member but could refrain from drinking only for short periods of time. She revealed that whenever she became anxious about anything, her husband would "feed" her alcohol to calm her. Only when her whole life seemed on the verge of disintegration did Jane seek psychiatric help.

TREATMENT:

The course of Jane's treatment involved two broad areas. On one hand it was necessary to have her develop a warm, supportive relation with her therapist, (a man,) which was not sexual, while on the other hand, her highly sexualized emotions had to be examined and fitted into the larger context of her emotional ties to all people.

In the early stages of therapy, she was very seductive. She was an attractive young lady in face and figure, and her clothes and posture were suggestively designed and executed. It was as though this woman felt that the sexual way was the only way a man could be interested in her. Only after many months of treatment where the psychotherapist gently pointed out his interest in her as an individual, not as an object of sex, and only after she tested out his failure to respond to her seductiveness could she relax and begin to feel safe enough to explore her inner self.

In time as therapy progressed, the patient was able to see how she had always expected her father to take her side against her mother—which he never did. Following such frustrations, she would drink heavily and ultimately end by having a sexual affair. Although they were initially gratifying, inevitably disappointment would occur, thus symbolically repeating her failure to relate to her father. Even her sexual life with her husband was unsatisfactory, for she always felt as though she was used as an object to gratify his sexual urges rather than loved for herself. Her husband's attitude toward her she often likened to that of her mother, and she responded by alternately being attracted to and repelled by both of them. Her brother was seen as an external personification of her conflict with her mother and viewed with pity. With Antabuse to control impulsive drinking, the patient was able to gain some control over her drinking and clarify a good many of her conflicts as to her identity, her ties to her family, and her relation to her environment.

DISCUSSION:

This patient illustrates the alcoholic who on the surface has had every advantage of life and who on more careful examination was an emotionally deprived individual. Her parents provided material needs, but no love or comfort. At no time did she feel loved or wanted. Her sexual actions were an "acting out" of her desire to be loved by her father, with the certain result that she was rejected. The similarity of behavior between her mother and husband in the patient's eyes produced a deep and frightening anxiety about her possible homosexuality. This further necessitated her being attractive to men to reassure herself of her femininity. The illness and incapacity derived from her excessive drinking gratified her dependency wishes. The gain she received from her alcoholic illnesses in her mind was more than enough to compensate for the destruction her drinking caused. Only when she saw that the total break-up of her immediate family was imminent, where she might lose her five young children (and the dependency gratification she achieved vicariously from their dependent state) was she forced to come for help. Her drinking also was an attempt at revolt against the mother. It is interesting that she and her brother used diverse, unsuccessful methods of coping with their domineering mother. The mother's strong opposition to alcohol influenced Jane's symptom choice. We can also see that Jane had a pathological response to alcohol from the very first drink.

Her psychiatrist reports that her therapy has been tortuous and difficult. Many times she has been fearful that psychiatric treatment would push her over the edge into a frank psychosis. However, by acting constantly as a confronter of reality, her therapist has succeeded in lending her the emotional support essential for her to go on in self-exploration. The patient when able to feel emotionally free of all the people in her life, and to see herself as a human being who requires respect, gives up her pathological drinking. However, she still has periods where she becomes emotionally upset and begins to drink again. These "slips" are usually managed in a few subsequent therapy sessions. Her treatment would have been more manageable had her husband accepted treatment also.

Jim

PROBLEM:

Jim is an 18-year-old state ward of Italian descent, who was referred to an alcoholism center for treatment. The patient was brought to the agency by a social worker after having been picked up by the police on a number of occasions for assaultive behavior while heavily intoxicated.

MEDICAL DATA:

Jim has enjoyed excellent health, with only the usual childhood diseases.

BACKGROUND:

The patient as a state ward was placed in the home of his present foster parents when he was three years of age. He knows nothing about his real parents. Jim's foster mother is 43 and is described as a "nice" person who is occasionally affectionate. The foster father is 45, "a big, fat, kind guy," whom the patient sees only on week ends. At times, Jim will help his foster father with work about the house, but more often there is little direct contact with him. Although Jim has maintained a reasonable relationship with his foster parents, there is no evidence that any bonds of warmth or closeness exist. The foster father does on occasion become intoxicated both at home and away. These drunken episodes result in the foster mother's becoming extremely angry with her husband's alcoholic excesses. As a consequence Jim sees his foster mother as an aggressive, controlling power in the household. There are six other foster children in the house, and Jim gives evidence of rivalry feelings with them without evidence of any warm ties.

Little information is available about Jim's early years. Despite having repeated the first and third grades of school, he focused most of his talk during therapy upon his goal of completing high school and upon his part-time job. A below-average student, Jim describes his classmates as strangers. School work has always been difficult, and he complains of not being able to retain material studied. He hoped that by completing his home work and behaving in school he might be able to graduate from high school. His part-time work is in a pharmacy, and he feels close to his boss. As a result of his admiration for his employer, he has entertained ideas of possibly becoming a pharmacist. He recognizes, however, that there is little likelihood of achieving this goal. Jim often feels depressed.

Jim's drinking history is only of three years' duration. He reports having taken his first drink at age 15 on New Year's Eve at a friend's house. He consumed too much beer and became intoxicated. On his way home from his first drinking experience, he was picked up by the police and placed in jail overnight. Appearing in court the next day, the foster mother bailed out the patient. Following this initial episode, there were other bouts of intoxication of increasing frequency and severity. In time he was again arrested by the police, placed in jail, and again released to the custody of his foster mother. After this episode, however, he was placed on probation to be seen by a probation officer weekly. Within two weeks, he was again intoxicated and arrested with friends for breaking windows. The patient contends that he was not responsible for the acts of violence, but that the police blamed him. His probation was then extended to nine months.

According to the patient, once he begins to drink he cannot stop. Alcohol makes him exhilarated. Only after the intoxication has been dissipated does Jim begin again to feel depressed.

Jim likes the happiness alcohol brings him; the good feeling about the world. When sober, Jim is shy and reticent. When intoxicated, Jim is freer, talkative, and gay. Now that he has suffered intoxication and arrest, he has developed a fear about drinking. He equates alcohol with arrest. The other major concern beside the drinking-police equation is a concern about his real parents. Much time is spent wondering who his real parents are, what his real parents are like, and why he was separated from them. These questions about his parents extend to his name and his ambivalence about it. His name is too long; it is difficult to pronounce; no one else has this name; it is not a popular name. He has thought about changing it but cannot do so because it would break his last possible tie with his real parents.

TREATMENT:

Treatment was directed toward establishing a relationship with this deprived, retiring youth, thereby permitting him to ventilate some of his emotions. As the relationship in psychotherapy evolved, it became apparent that his passivity was an emotional defense against his hostile aggressive feelings. As he gradually was able to verbalize and clarify some of these feelings, he began to feel freer and happier. Previously he found release only through intoxication, which ultimately led to difficulties with the law. These events only served to cause him to withdraw deeper into his passivity or deeper into intoxicated states.

With six months of treatment, Jim successfully completed

high school, gave up alcohol, and found gainful employment. Although it is impossible to predict the future for this boy, the fact he received effective treatment early for his alcohol problem increases his potential for achieving a useful social role in the community.

DISCUSSION:

The case history of Jim illustrates a number of points pertinent to alcoholics in general. For Jim, emotional deprivation began early in his life and was sustained. Evidence of early failure is demonstrated by his grade-school setbacks. As is common with some alcoholics, he came from a matricentric home with the father absent from the home much of the time. He also had an alcoholic role model in his foster father (the foster father used alcohol excessively to deal with his life). Jim showed evidence of interpersonal difficulties in his inability to relate to his peers, foster siblings, and classmates.

Jim's first drinking experience was unhealthy. He had his first drink away from home, became intoxicated at the very first, and was arrested. Therefore his problem with alcohol was immediate and abrupt. We can also see how the pharmacological effect helped Jim relieve his inhibitions.

In conclusion we should like to point out that the two school failures in the first three grades of school should have alerted a child-guidance facility to the potential problem and early intervention.

Joe

PROBLEM:

From the New York area, we have the case of a 37-year-old male, Joe, who has a twenty-year history of alcoholism that has resulted in numerous arrests for loitering, drunkenness, and disorderly conduct.

MEDICAL DATA:

The patient enjoys good health and has never suffered a major illness or operation.

FAMILY BACKGROUND:

Joe's mother and father are both living and well. The only other sibling, a younger brother, also enjoys good health. Both parents were born and raised in Ireland. The mother is a housewife; the father works in a factory. Although alcohol is kept in the home for festive occasions, neither parent drinks heavily. Joe's image of his parents is that they misunderstand him and always have. Joe's impression of his parents is that they are "conventional" Irish-Americans, living close to the church and within a community of similar people. The father is described as passive and guided by the wishes and pronouncements of the wife; he has never given Joe advice or guidance. The mother, on the other hand, is the dominating household influence. Her dominance, however, is achieved not through strength but by acting hurt, sad, and sorry whenever any of her three "boys" behaves contrary to her wishes. The father has dealt with this wifely onslaught by keeping out of the way and always remaining neutral. The younger brother deals with the home situation by alcoholism and women. In other words, the brother can only stay away from the gravitational pull of the mother when drunk or fornicating. The patient, Joe, responds more often as the father does, content to live at home, unmarried, spending his days at work. At night he departs from the father's routine by becoming intoxicated.

Joe in his early years was apparently a well-integrated member of his environment. After graduation from parochial high school, he joined the Merchant Marine. To achieve this, Joe had to rebel against parental wishes, especially those of his mother. This act is one of the few healthy sparks of rebellion against the matriarchal influence enmeshing the males of the family. With this act, Joe succeeded in seemingly separating himself from his mother, a step never taken by his father and only rarely by his brother.

During Joe's early years, there was no evidence of disturbed behavior. He had companions, was active in sports, and achieved average grades in school. Joining the Merchant Marine was meaningful to Joe for many reasons. He liked the idea of being an independent man, and the possibilities for adventure were appealing. This period of life is recalled with great pleasure. There was ample opportunity for reading during the long hours at sea, and in time, Joe had acquired a vocabulary and knowledge far beyond his formal education. He delighted in listening to the tales of the old mariners and repeated many of them with relish during his therapy. Joe pursued this life during the war and thereafter, eventually achieving the position of third mate. The interest which provided the impetus for attaining the higher rank was apparently based upon his romanticized image of sea life, since he was little interested in the mechanical and administrative aspects of ships. Irrespective of motivation, the fact of promotion indicates his capacity to perform. After about eight years, disillusionment and the end of World War II set in and he found himself drinking more and more while in port, and getting into more and more trouble. At times he would become belligerent while drinking and get into fights. Mainly, however, his troubles stemmed from becoming drunk, passing out, and then being arrested on a drunkenness charge. Interestingly, the greatest number of episodes of intoxication occurred in his home port of New York, while closest to his mother.

Following his decision to leave the sea, his alcoholism became more severe. He tried a succession of jobs without success. More and more often he frequented barrooms. However, when the Korean crisis developed, he was an early enlistee in the Marines. The romantic, juvenile image of the Marines as the ideal of men induced him to join. He responded well. His drinking diminished; his life became more orderly; he was a good marine. During the Korean action he acquitted himself in an effective and honorable way, earning commendations for his courage. When the fighting ended and occupation duty followed, the most alarming of his drinking bouts ensued. Not a day passed without his being drunk. His discharge from service was followed by heavier alcohol intake. Despite his pathological drinking, he enrolled in a night course at college. Only when his alcoholism began to interfere with his college studies did he seek help for his problem.

TREATMENT:

At the first interview, Joe was in terrible shape. He was recovering from a hangover, was withdrawn and almost mute, and was able to control his shaking only by holding his head in his hands. The therapist actively started talking to him. His response to this approach was to request Antabuse. The therapist gratified his request and wrote a prescription. However, the patient never actually used the medication. Wisely, the therapist never commented on the request or on the patient's continued drinking. He recognized the request for Antabuse as a desire for control and a testing of the therapist. What quickly emerged in the therapy was Joe's loneliness and isolation. Most women were strangers to him, since he had only associated with barflies and prostitutes. He felt unworthy of women he might have married. In social situations in the presence of women, Joe was tense and shy. To counter his fear of women, he sought courage in drink, only to end up sullen and nasty to them instead of, as he sought, charming.

During the earliest weeks of therapy, the interviews were overtly chatty and superficial, but nevertheless supporting. When the therapist finally began to inquire about background material, this was asked in a friendly rather than clinical way. Although Joe had traveled widely and had many experiences, he was unable to talk about them early in his treatment. He rather focused on the present situation—his alcoholism and his unworthiness. During an interview where Joe was intensely expressive of his unworthiness, the therapist reacted by asking him about his life at sea and in Korea. Joe responded with surprising tales of adventure which thoroughly delighted the therapist. The therapist in turn responded by equating Joe's experiences with those of William McPhee, Joseph Conrad, and Stephen Crane. This served to emphasize that the patient had far from misspent his life, and it offered acceptable role models. Further, the therapist stressed that Joe had lived experiences most would envy. At first, Joe was reluctant to elaborate about his pleasant experiences, but the therapist persisted. As Joe warmed up to his subject during subsequent interviews, there was a sharp falling off of drinking, and his grades improved. With a strengthening of the therapeutic relationship, the therapist, after four or five months of treatment, began to talk about his own background. Since the patient and doctor shared certain cultural similarities, their bond was strengthened. Joe spontaneously told more and more about his family. How dreary and drab it was living with them; how much he wanted a job and financial independence. The latter would permit him to move away from the family and, he hoped, eventually to marry. The therapist encouraged and supported these hopes, and within a month the patient had secured a job and rented an apartment (just two blocks from his therapist). Drinking stopped. He continued to visit a bar on occasion, but ordered a Coke without misgiving. Although an attempt for a better job resulted in legitimate frustration, he handled the disappointment well. As therapy progressed, the doctor separated out the reality image of Joe from that held by the patient of himself: an undeserving, unworthy person; a pretender to a society that would not accept him. Joe felt that he contained none of the good and all the bad qualities of an Irish-American: seaman, alcoholic, uneducated, and low-born. This contrasted with the reality: becoming a third mate, going to college, performing well in school, traveling around the world, and undergoing combat without emotional breakdown. This positive emphasis was combined with interpretations of his erotic yet fearful attachment to his mother, his disgust for, but identification with, his father, and his love of, but hostility toward, his Irish-Catholic culture.

Joe was helped to see how the company of men, the avoidance of women, and socially acceptable aggressive situations made him feel more comfortable. The focus was to give him a masculine identity and a feeling of worthiness.

DISCUSSION:

The ego assets have already been noted. Basically, the patient's passivity and hostility toward an aggressive, dominating mother were reinforced by the passive role assumed by his father and brother. Only when the patient has succeeded in being aggressive, assertive, and ambitious can he function without alcohol and at a high level. His sexual problems have manifested themselves to date in his inability to relate to women and to marry. The women he considers good he equates with his mother, since they restrict him, dominate him, possess him, but yet offer him no love. This is the mother image he runs toward and away from in his ambivalent dance.

This case illustrates ideally the Irish-alcoholic configuration described in Chapter 4. There is in Joe's family another alcoholic sibling. Joe also does well in a protected, masculine setting with clear-cut goals, and he typifies the feeling of many alcoholics of their own total unworthiness. Thus, the male drinking, working, and thriving in the company of men, caught in the maternal web, attempts to escape by that image glorified in his folklore—the drunken Irishman.

Charles

PROBLEM:

Charles has had a problem with periodic drinking sprees for many years, but the problem became more serious in the last ten years, when sprees occurred more often and resulted in physical incapacitation necessitating hospitalization.

MEDICAL DATA:

Charles has suffered no serious illnesses. He, however, describes his general level of health as poor, reporting frequent head colds, generalized aches and pains, and frequent superficial injuries in the course of his work. Other complaints are: nervousness, restlessness, boredom, insomnia, and obesity. His prime dissatisfaction with physicians is their failure to provide sedatives for his insomnia, and their insufficient interest in his weight problem.

FAMILY BACKGROUND:

The patient's mother died two days after his birth from the complications of childbirth. He was raised by an elderly aunt and uncle who had no children of their own. According to the patient, his aunt and uncle provided the material necessities of life even to a point of overindulgence, but neglected the love, attention, and understanding he craved. Severe and rigid standards of behavior were set for him, and if he failed or misbehaved he was severely punished. Despite the severity of their standards and their punishment, Charles feels they did not ask or permit him to assume independent responsibility. Although he maintains that he was without love and respect for them, he stoutly denies feelings of anger and hostility. Apparently, because his material needs were so adequately met and his responsibilities negligible, Charles continued to live with his aunt and uncle until his twenty-third birthday despite his lack of rapport with them.

With his father, Charles had no emotional ties. At the mother's death, disintegration of the family unit was immediate. Two older sisters were farmed out to interested relatives, while the father moved from boarding house to boarding house, wherever his lumbering work and alcoholism carried him. Father and son seldom sought each other out. The only tangible contact Charles had with his father was through some limited financial support the latter provided for his care. Charles has always been sure that he bore the burden of his father's resentment. The patient attributes this resentment to his mother's death at his birth. Although Charles will discuss his father's resentment and will describe the coolness and casualness of their limited contacts, he denies anger and hostility toward his father. He even denies any desire to have had a more satisfactory relationship with a father than he experienced.

Charles has limited contact with his two older sisters and has never been or felt close to them.

The patient was first married at age 25. After three or four years of marriage, he and his wife "just drifted apart," ultimately divorcing. It is difficult to ascertain Charles's relationship to this first wife. He reports no arguments, no serious trouble, just that "we drifted apart." Although he admits not having been in love with her, he contends he respected and liked her very much. From this union, one son was born. Following the divorce and the wife's eventual remarriage Charles lost complete contact with her and with his son. At no time did he feel any curiosity or expend any energy to find out about them. When the patient learned of her death a few years ago, while he was in treatment, he responded by reiterating his fondness and friendship for her and again exonerated her of all blame for the rupture of the marriage. "If I had amounted to anything," he said, "the marriage might have worked." Since her death he occasionally considers searching for his son but then does not follow through, admittedly because he is not really interested.

When in his early thirties Charles remarried. Shortly thereafter he entered military service. On his return from the army, his wife informed him of her interest in another man and her desire for a divorce. When the divorce was final, Charles lost complete contact with this wife. There is no ill feeling toward her, just a sense of relief and disappointment at realizing the sort of woman she was. Anger and hostility toward this wife is also denied. Instead, there is a passive, hopeless attitude toward his two wives and two marriages. He admits an absence of love on his part for these women and shoulders the responsibility for the marital break-ups. There is certainty in his mind that there was nothing that he could have done to alter the outcome of these marriages.

Although Charles has not remarried, he has developed a long-time relationship with another woman. This relationship is of twelve years' duration. According to the patient, this woman has been "maternal" and "romantic," and their relationship has been without sexual intimacy. In earlier years, they had formal dates; but now she often provides his food, shops for his clothes, and manages his finances. To Charles this relationship is "brother-sister" or maybe "the kind you have with a mother." Charles has refrained from dating other women for fear of hurting this woman who is so kind to him. To the patient this relationship "just happened and perhaps it's for the better." In his view he would not be good for any woman and it would not be right for him to become serious about anyone because of his drinking.

In all these relationships: his aunt and uncle, his father, his two wives, his girl friend, he says, "I don't want to blame anyone; it was my own fault."

Charles is a lonely being. He has no close friends. He will readily admit his "boredom" and his "loneliness." On the other hand, the patient does like the freedom to do just as he wishes and has no expressed desire to enter relationships which would entail obligations.

In contrast to his adult state of solitude and inaction, Charles was an active teen-ager. Until his first marriage he was involved in sports and had the leadership qualities to become a local baseball manager. He reports that he drank socially, dated girls, and enjoyed life. From the day of his first marriage, Charles lost his capacity for an active, enjoyable life.

For the past twelve years, Charles has worked as an attendant at a state hospital, achieving the rank of "licensed attendant." Although he resents the dullness and lack of future in his hospital job, the patient is pleased with its ease and security. The hospital provides his living quarters, food, and medical care and presents him with a check and no responsibilities. The patient states, "I think this is a good job for a fellow like me." By this, he means that since he is unskilled and untrained, he could not obtain better work. More likely, Charles is employed in the type of job which satisfies all his dependency needs (his unconscious desires to be taken care of). When Charles has occasionally attended a sports event, he has usually had to depart before its conclusion because of his "nervousness and boredom." The limits of the patient's life and his activity are defined by his work and his room in the hospital.

In 1954 Charles was treated by a psychiatrist in a local alcoholism clinic. With Antabuse, he was able to abstain for six months. Inadvertently, however, he tasted some alcohol, and, experiencing only a minimal Antabuse reaction, decided to discontinue the drug and return to his old pattern of drinking.

TREATMENT:

Following a severe drinking episode, Charles found himself cared for in the emergency ward of a hospital, which offered him treatment in its alcoholic clinic. His present psychotherapy is of four years' duration. The major roadblocks during the course of therapy were his underlying hostility and anger, his inability to form an emotional relationship, and his inability to express feelings. His hostility was manifested by his sullen manner, a wry smile, and even by caustic comments. He tended to guard against revealing information emotionally meaningful about himself. He preferred to offer "I don't know" or stereo-typed, meaningless phrases. Discussions about his life were mechanical rather than emotional. Although he stressed his loneliness, he would not consider action to alleviate this state. He was concerned about his obesity and insomnia; but instead of dealing with the problem, he preferred inaction and com-plaints of disinterest on the part of caretakers. He drinks ten cups of coffee daily and uncountable Cokes and ginger ales. Whenever annoyed and irritated by people he turns to alcohol and then communicates with them and enjoys their company.

His therapy has been mainly directed toward establishing a relationship. By so doing, the therapist has been able to mobi-lize slowly some of the hostility and anger present in this patient. He is most conscientious about his treatment appoint-ments and has gone for four and five months at a time without alcohol. Even when there has been a slip, he has been able to stop drinking of his own volition in a day or two without be-coming desperately ill. Although Charles continues to have rare drinking bouts, the pattern of his drinking behavior has been changed for the better. He has achieved some alleviation of his psychological difficulties at a level within his limited capacity.

DISCUSSION:

In this patient, the early deprivation is striking: the loss of his mother when he was but two days old followed by a life pattern of severe emotional deprivation. The early and continuous deprivation resulted in overwhelming hostility, anger, and mistrust in all relationships. A passive life situation of acceptance of whatever happens as well as a need to seek out situations of maximal dependent gratification is the pattern of existence for this solitary figure. Only when he drinks can he experience some closeness and relatedness to people. For him alcohol serves a dual purpose: symbolically, he is loved when he is drinking; and when he becomes ill from drink, someone will take care of him. At the same time, he can punish himself for maintaining his infantile wishes by being an alcoholic and in the last analysis "no good."

This patient illustrates vividly the classical reaction to intense early deprivation in seeing the world as continually depriving and rejecting him. He then unconsciously molds the action and goal of his life to regain that of which he was deprived.

Viewed as a whole, we must conclude that Charles's life was a life of failure. Two days after he entered this world his mother was dead. His two marriages were unsuccessful, and he has achieved minimal occupational goals. Charles's relationship to his older woman friend is a substitute for the mother he missed. As is commonly seen in alcoholics, Charles achieved his peak early, while in adolescence. When responsibility threatened Charles he disintegrated, and after his first marriage he was never again able to maintain a relation involving responsibility. He had a possible role model in his alcoholic father, and he handled his hostility by turning it inward onto himself.

Charles survives in a limited way only in a protective environment. This protective environment consists of the older woman, who takes care of his needs, and his place of residence and work in the hospital. Even this much protection and support was not enough for Charles. Only after the addition of Antabuse, the clinic, and the therapist was sufficient support afforded to help Charles gain greater control over his drinking. This case history emphasizes that the goals of therapy must be confined within the limits of the patient's capacity.

Mabel

PROBLEM:

Mabel is a 42-year-old married woman who began having serious drinking problems five years ago following a hysterectomy. Although she had been drinking heavily since age 18, she had previously been able to fulfill her responsibility to her family and community. Associated with the loss of control over her alcohol intake, Mabel became sexually promiscuous with many men. Only when it became clear that her marriage would be destroyed by her behavior did she seek psychiatric help.

MEDICAL DATA:

Mabel had tuberculosis at age seven and was hospitalized in a sanatorium for one year. Her hysterectomy at age 37 was performed because of benign tumors in her uterine tissue. Outside of these two medical episodes, Mabel has been physically active and well.

FAMILY BACKGROUND:

The third of four children, Mabel had a tuberculous and alcoholic father. When she was three or four years old, he was hospitalized in a tuberculosis sanatorium for one year, and when she was seven her mother "threw him out for good because of his drinking." Although her father continued to live in the same farm community in Iowa as the patient, she rarely saw him. He died from complications associated with his alcoholism when the patient was thirteen. Her mother is alive and is described as a gentle, kind person whose only "two hates" in the world are "men and drink." In spite of her feelings about men, when the patient was ten her mother conceived a child out of wedlock. This child was outwardly accepted as a full-fledged family member, although his physical differences were always obvious. Although Mabel loves her mother, she has never quite forgiven her for ridding herself of the father and bearing a child by another man.

Mabel's older sister is an alcoholic married to an alcoholic who lives in abject poverty and squalor. Mabel has often blamed herself for not somehow helping her sister to overcome her difficulties.

Mabel's husband is a successful journalist who has amassed a great deal of money in the stock market. He and the patient were childhood sweethearts but from the time of their marriage, he has suffered from asthma, hypertension, and ulcers and has required much care from his wife. They live in a wealthy community in upstate New York and their three sons attend private schools. There has been to date no apparent difficulty in the children.

TREATMENT:

From the start of therapy, Mabel was skittish about psychiatry. She reported one previous experience with a psychiatrist where she had feelings that the doctor had sexual designs upon her and she quickly interrupted treatment. She also felt she was beyond help and frequently found one excuse or another to cancel her appointments. Whenever she did manage to arrive for her therapy, she expected to be dismissed. Mabel, whenever drinking, would express hostility toward her therapist by calling him "cold," "an iceberg," "not really interested in her."

These outbursts and her therapy absences were met by gentle reassurance to the patient that she would not be "thrown out" of treatment, and that the psychiatrist had no doubts that she was a woman.

During the first four months of psychotherapy, Mabel attempted unsuccessfully to stop drinking. She frequently tested her relation with her psychiatrist. One day when she came for treatment, she had been drinking heavily and reported that she drove to the appointment at "100 miles per hour." The therapist pointed out the obvious self-destructive motive and offered to hospitalize her for a day so that she might drive home safely. The patient refused, reassuring the therapist she would be careful. Mabel returned to her home and that day stopped drinking, and the abstinence was maintained throughout the remainder of her treatment.

Relatively quickly, thereafter, she worked out her problems concerning her fear of her loss of femininity following hysterectomy, her resentment about being rejected by her mother and her father, and her anger toward her husband's lack of masculinity.

DISCUSSION:

Mabel's psychotherapy points out that with some emotional support early in life, in spite of a disturbed early history, a good deal of healthy emotional functioning can ensue. Although Mabel felt resentment toward her mother on three major scores (permitting Mabel to go to a sanatorium, throwing her father out, and having an illegitimate child), she nevertheless had always felt that she was close to and had support from her mother. Missing was a relation to a masculine figure, and for this reason an early attachment to a boy evolved, which in time culminated in marriage. However, like her father, her husband was a sickly, unmasculine person, and she found herself as mother rather than as wife. When the hysterectomy threatened her identity as a woman, Mabel responded to the severe stress by alcoholism (her identification with her father) and by promiscuity, constantly seeking reassurance as to her desirability as a woman. The mother's hostility toward alcohol and men reinforced the patient's unhealthy behavior when her equilibrium was shattered.

In therapy, she re-experienced some of her conflicts. The therapist, in spite of her efforts to have him reject her, maintained a continuous interest in her. In spite of this interest, no sexual threat occurred, and again and again, it was pointed out to her that it was unnecessary for her to act out sexually to demonstrate her femininity. Major progress occurred after the therapist had actively expressed concern and offered active support when she was in a self-destructive state.

Mabel is an example of a reactive alcoholic who as a consequence of her close positive emotional contact with her mother early in life, overcame many traumatic experiences and adjusted adequately. When the hysterectomy resulted in an uncontrollable situation, early intervention in her pathological drinking behavior produced a good treatment result.

Alex

PROBLEM:

Alex is a 47-year-old male who was referred for treatment of alcoholism from a mental institution. The patient had been hospitalized after having attempted suicide while intoxicated.

MEDICAL DATA:

The patient now enjoys good health. When age six, he was confined to a tuberculosis sanatorium for one year for a "spot on the lung," and at age 12 he suffered a compound fracture of the left elbow. Alex has been hospitalized in mental hospitals on a number of occasions because of his reaction to excessive alcohol intake.

FAMILY BACKGROUND:

Alex's mother is in her seventies and is living and well except for a mild diabetes diagnosed two years ago. The patient does not discuss his mother often in therapy, and only visits her a few times a year, although she lives nearby. His father died at age 44 when Alex was but four years old. The cause of the father's death is unknown. Alex has a brother four years older who is living and well, and a younger alcoholic brother, 45, unmarried and living with his mother.

Alex lives at home with his wife and 16-year-old daughter. His two older children, both boys, are married and live away from the patient's family orbit. Much of the material in treatment has focused upon Alex's relationship to his wife and daughter. A major source of concern was the daughter's poor school performance and the low reputation of her close friends. Beyond this, Alex is concerned and guilty about the child's health. At age 4 the daughter developed diabetes. Prior to the diagnosis, an event took place which led to Alex's guilt. Alex was washing the car, while his daughter and a playmate were inside. Suddenly, the car began to move. In some way, Alex was sure his daughter had dislodged the hand brake, and while in the process of rescuing the children, he bumped his child's head on the door of the car. Three days later, she became irritable, restless, and lost her appetite. A medical examination at that time revealed diabetes, and because the doctor in the course of his questioning had asked about head injuries the patient became convinced that he was responsible for her condition. As a consequence, Alex has had much ambivalence in his dealings with his daughter. On one hand, he wants to control her and on the other he feels he is overcontrolling. He loses his temper with her easily and at times has struck her and then felt very guilty. He feels that his daughter's main drive is to be free of her parents, which will cause her to run off and marry hastily. As Alex makes attempts to become closer to his daughter or to discipline her, he senses that his wife tends to withdraw, leaving him a clear field, which frightens him. He identifies with his daughter's condition, likening her diabetes to his lung problem. The history of his spot on his lungs caused him to limit his physical activities throughout school, and because of his history he was dropped from a varsity athletic team to which he had been named. The possibility of being sick and different had made him indifferent and carefree. Alex sees a similar indifference and lack of drive in his daughter as a result of restrictions due to diabetes. He is also certain that his alcoholism drove his two sons to leave school prematurely and flee into marriage and lives of their own.

Alex's own youth was disruptive. Following his father's death when Alex was four and after his hospitalization for tuberculosis when he was six, Alex lived with a paternal aunt and uncle. He continued to live with them until his marriage. Why he did not at any time return to live with his own mother we do not know. All Alex can remember of those early years is his life in the sanatorium. He was cared for by nurses, he felt lonely—"just another patient"—and without affection. He could recall his early memory that his father and mother did not visit often. Following discharge, he attended parochial schools. Of these schools, he recalls only the "harshness" of the nuns, and the "strictness" of the discipline. Somehow his loneliness increased whenever he realized that both his brothers continued to live with their mother while he did not. Toward the end of his parochial school education he decided to marry a fellow student and did so.

TREATMENT:

Although Alex began to drink at age 18, about the time of his marriage, his drinking did not become a serious problem until he was 42 or so. The problem with alcohol became obvious when he was less able to work, lost jobs, or suffered physical or emotional abuse as a result of drinking. Whenever Alex has become hopelessly entangled in the web of his alcoholism, suicidal thoughts become prominent. The history of the development of his alcoholic bouts is important. Alex would go without a drink for two to three months, and then on the way home from work would have two to four drinks. He would maintain this level of intake for several days until his wife ascertained that he had been drinking. She and the children would withdraw from the patient and become cold and uncommunicative. Alex would become depressed, feel sorry for himself and angry with his family, and in defiance continue and increase his drinking. Then his intoxication was sustained with almost constant drinking, and he would stay away from home. These drinking debauches usually lasted one or two weeks and ended with sickness. He recovered within a day or two and would go back to his job.

When the patient was seen initially, he was tense and anxious. He related his nervousness to being unable to perform well any tasks following his suicidal attempt and consequent mental hospitalization. He talked about how his nervousness caused him to be irritable and how on occasions he fled his home area, traveling far into the South. These excursions were never planned but impulsive. They always occurred when he was intoxicated. He would begin to feel his unworthiness, and convinced himself that a different climate and locale might allow him to establish himself successfully. When he sobered up and recognized the significance of his acts, he would begin to feel desperate, panicky, and fearful of being alone. Although he had always been certain that his family would be better off without him, he terminated his bouts of fleeing by immediately contacting his family and returning home. Each such episode made him feel increasingly worse because he was certain that he lost the "family's respect." He felt that the loss of respect was because he had set so bad an example for his children, and that he had diminished his authority as head of the household. He became more aware of his increased depression and feelings of isolation and had difficulty in sleeping at night. Alex also felt that his problem has been complicated by his boss. Alex is a machinist; his boss a designer. To the patient, the boss is a tyrant and an impossible individual to get along with. "The boss grasps what he wants, when he wants and despite whoever is in his way." Only Alex has been able to tolerate him. As a consequence, the boss has eliminated many of the technicians who ordinarily would perform steps in the operation between original design and ultimate manufacture. Because Alex has more to do, he is certain that his strong boss is taking advantage of a weak inferior. He was certain the feelings of weakness and of being drained were the causes of his drinking. Often he would describe his terror on Monday mornings when, on seeing the boss's car in the parking lot, he could not bring himself to go to work.

Alex's fear of his boss and his concern with his own depression often led him to discuss in treatment his thoughts about existence and the meaning of life. Much interview material was centered about this theme. In this connection, he expressed his avid preference for literature about famous men. He had read extensively about Lincoln, Churchill, Van Gogh, and many others. Van Gogh he was unsympathetic to because he drank himself to "insanity and suicide." Clarence Darrow, who defended the underdog, and Lincoln were his heroes. Caesar, Mussolini, Napoleon, and Hitler, who signified sin and inhumanity, were disparaged. Although reared as a Catholic, Alex had renounced Catholicism because he believed it to be a religion based primarily on fear. In this connection he mentioned often how nothing was meaningful; there was just no rhyme nor reason to life. To Alex, man was just a "higher type of animal," and he thought that certainly in the universe there are people cleverer than man as we know him today. God is to be believed in only if actually seen; there is no love, no hereafter. He was concerned with who was responsible for world events and expressed concern over his feelings of responsibility for his family and their difficulties. His therapist had the impression that Alex formulated some of his ideas in relation to his own sense of omnipotence.

DISCUSSION:

The therapeutic approach was at the first directed toward offering emotional support designed to elevate the self-esteem of the patient. His preoccupation with unusual injustices was related to his depression, and by exploring these feelings of discrimination, unfair play, etc., he came to see their correlation with his depression. His concern with his passivity as evidence of inadequate masculinity was explored. From this exploration he began to see how his drinking was his defense against the overwhelming fear of his passivity. He worked out his passive identification with his dead father and uncle and his image of all women as dominant and aggressive. Along with these passive wishes, the patient was able to uncover that his fear of passivity was responsible for his inability to get close to people because of his fear that he would be destroyed. Even competitive games with physical contact became abhorrent to him. Only when drinking did Alex feel aggressive, masculine, and purposeful. With drink, he could rid himself of his intellectual defenses, alleviate his depression, and begin to feel masculine. After two years of psychotherapy, the patient has not had any alcohol, works successfully, and has become the dominant member of his household. He quite correctly contends that his wife seems to enjoy life more now that she has a man around the house.

This patient has achieved the maximum available goal in the psychotherapy of alcoholism. His underlying emotional and intellectual strength was sufficient to direct therapy toward an exploration of unconscious motivations and to a resolution of transference problems.

Bibliography

Chapter 1

1. Bernard, C. *Introduction to the Study of Experimental Medicine* (translated by H. C. Greene and L. J. Henderson). Macmillan, New York, 1927.

2. Cannon, W. B. *Bodily Changes in Pain, Hunger, Fear and Rage*, 2nd ed. Appleton, New York, 1929.

3. Demone, H. W. Is education the answer to alcohol problems? In *Alcohol Education: What Does a Teacher Need to Know To Teach?* Vermont State Dept. of Education, Montpelier, 1960.

4. Himwich, H. E. The physiology of alcohol. J.A.M.A. **163**:545-9, 1957.

5. Horace quoted in Goodman and Gilman, *The Pharmacological Basis of Therapeutics*. Macmillan, New York, 1941.

6. Horney, K. *Our Inner Conflicts*. W. W. Norton, New York, 1945.

7. James, W. H. *The Varieties of Religious Experience: A Study in Human Nature*. Longmans, Green, New York, 1902.

8. Roueche, B. *The Neutral Spirit: A Portrait of Alcohol*. Little, Brown, Boston, 1960.

9. Wiener, N. *Cybernetics*. John Wiley, New York, 1948.

Chapter 2

1. Montague, A. Constitutional and prenatal factors in infant and child health. Symposium on the Healthy Personality, Transactions of Special Meetings of Conference on Infancy and Childhood, June

8-9 and July 3-4, 1950, New York. Supplement II: Problems of infancy and childhood. Transactions of Fourth Conference, March 1950. Sponsored by Josiah Macy, Jr. Foundation. 1950.

2. Pavlov, I. P. in H. Wells, *Toward a Scientific Psychology and Psychiatry*. International Publishers, New York, 1956.

3. Seitz, P. Infantile experience and adult behavior in animal subjects: II. Age of separation from the mother and adult behavior in the cat. Paper read at the American Psychosomatic Association meeting, March 29 and 30, 1958, Cincinnati, Ohio.

Chapter 3—Section a

1. Alcoholism (queries and minor notes). J.A.M.A. **165**:312, 1957.

2. Bacon, S. D. The social impact of alcoholism. Conn. St. Med. J. **12**:1105-10, 1948.

3. Barham, P. C. The treatment of alcoholism. Med. Practice. **194**: 570-74, 1937.

4. Brocklehurst, T. Alcoholic addiction—its classification and cure. S. Afr. Med. J. **23**:771-4, 1949.

5. Coriat, I. H. The psycho-pathology and treatment of alcoholism. Brit. J. Inebr. **9**:138-47, 1912.

6. Ernst. N. Klinische Beobachtungen an Alkoholikern (Clinical observations on alcoholism). Klin. Wschr. **12**:1829-32, 1870-72, 1933.

7. Fleming, R. The treatment of chronic alcoholism. New Eng. J. Med. **217**:779-83, 1937.

8. Goldberg, L. Quantitative studies on alcohol tolerance in man. Acta. Physiol. Scand. **5** (Suppl. 16):1-128, 1943.

9. Isbell, H. and M. W. White. Clinical characteristics of addictions. Am. J. Med. **14**:558-65, 1953.

10. Izikowitz, S. Om alkoholismens medicinska terapi och terapi och profylax, nagra synpienkter och erfarenheter (On the medical therapy and prophylaxis of alcoholism: Some viewpoints and experiences). Nor. Med. **31**:2039-48, 1946.

11. Jellinek, E. M. *The Disease Concept of Alcoholism*. Hillhouse Press, New Haven, 1960.

12. Knight, R. P. The psychodynamics of chronic alcoholism. J. Nerv. Ment. Dis. **86**:538-48, 1937.

13. Lemere, F. What causes alcoholism? J. Clin. Exp. Psychopath. 17:202-6, 1956.

14. Maudsley, H. *The Pathology of Mind.* Macmillan, London, 1879.

15. Menninger, K. A. *Man Against Himself.* Harcourt, Brace, New York, 1938, pp. 160-84.

16. Mitscherlich, A. *Vom Ursprung der Sucht. Eine pathogenetische Untersuchung des Vieltrinkens* (On the origin of addiction. A pathogenetic study of polydipsia). Ernest Klett, Stuttgart, 1947.

17. Pfeffer, A. Z. The natural history of alcoholism. 1. Its onset and course. In *Alcoholism as a Medical Problem.* H. D. Kruse (ed). Hoeber-Harper, New York, 1956, pp. 68-78.

18. Seliger, R. V. The psychiatric treatment of the alcohol addict. J. Crim. Psychopath. 3:78-89, 1941.

19. Simmel, E. Alcoholism and addiction. Psychoanal. Quart. 17: 6-31, 1948.

20. Wexberg, L. E. Psychodynamics of patients with chronic alcoholism. J. Clin. Psychopath. 10:147-57, 1949.

21. Wikler, A. A psychodynamic study of a patient during experimental self-regulated re-addiction to morphine. Psychiat. Quart. 26:270-93, 1952.

22. Wikler, A. and R. W. Rasor. Psychiatric aspects of drug addiction. Am. J. Med. 14:566-70, 1953.

Chapter 3—Section b

1. Abraham, K. L. The psychological relations between sexuality and alcoholism: *Selected Papers, Institute of Psychoanalysis.* Hogarth Press, London, 1927.

2. Adler, A. The individual psychology of the alcoholic patient. J. Crim. Psychopath. 3:74-7, 1941.

3. Ansbacher, H. and R. Ansbacher. *The Individual Psychology of Alfred Adler.* Basic Books, New York, 1946.

4. Björk, S. Alcoholism from the psychological viewpoint. Svenska Lakartidn. 47:1018-26, 1950.

5. Duchêne, H., M. P. Schutzenberger, J. Biro, and B. Schmitz. Particularites de l'ecart d'age des couples dont le mari est alcoolique (Details of age differences among couples in which the husband is an alcoholic). Bull. Inst. Nat. Hyg. 7:609-12, 1952.

6. Freud, S. Contributions to the psychology of love. The most prevalent form of degradation in erotic life (1912), in *Collected Papers*. Hogarth, London, vol. 4, pp. 203-16, 1925.

7. Freud, S. Mourning and melancholia (1917), in *Collected Papers*. Hogarth, London, vol. 4, pp. 152-70, 1925.

8. Freud, S. *Three Contributions to the Theory of Sex*, 4th ed. Nervous Mental Diseases Publishing House, Washington, D. C., 1930.

9. Gibbins, R. I. *Chronic Alcoholism*. Brookside Monograph, No. 1, Alcoholism Research Foundation, Ontario, 1953.

10. Jellife, S. E. Alcoholism and phantasy life in Tolstoi's drama "Redemption." N. Y. Med. J. 109:92-7, 1919.

11. Jellinek, E. M., H. Isbell, G. Lundquist, H. M. Tiebout, H. Duchêne, J. Nardones, and L. D. MacLeod. The "craving" for alcohol; A symposium by members of the WHO Expert Committees on Mental Health; Alcohol. Quart. J. Stud. Alc. 16:34-66, 1955.

12. Knight, R. P. The dynamics and treatment of chronic alcohol addiction. Bull. Menninger Clin. 1:233-58, 1937.

13. Knight, R. P. The psychodynamics of chronic alcoholism. J. Nerv. Ment. Dis. 86:538-48, 1937.

14. McCord, W., J. McCord, and J. Gudeman. Some current theories of alcoholism: A longitudinal evaluation. Quart. J. Stud. Alc. 20:727-49, 1959.

15. Meerloo, J. A. M. Artificial ecstasy. A study of the psychosomatic aspects of drug addiction. J. Nerv. Ment. Dis. 115:246-66, 1952.

16. Menninger, K. A. Alcohol addiction. In *Man Against Himself*. Harcourt, Brace, New York, 1938, Chap. 3.

17. Navratil, L. Die Rolle der Ehefrau in der Pathogenese der Trunksucht. (The role of the wife in the pathogenesis of alcoholism). Wien. Z. Nervenheilk. 14:90-97, 1957.

18. Parland, O. Alkolismi ja homoseksualisni (Alcoholism and homosexuality). Alkoholipolitiikka Hels. 4:119-24, 1957.

19. Schilder, P. The psychogenesis of alcoholism. Quart. J. Stud. Alc. 2:277-92, 1941.

20. Strecker, E. A. Chronic alcoholism: A psychological survey. Quart. J. Stud. Alc. 3:12-17, 1941.

21. Tiebout, H. M. The ego factors in surrender in alcoholism. Quart. J. Stud. Alc. **15**:610-21, 1954.

22. Zwerling, I. Psychiatric findings in an interdisciplinary study of forty-six alcoholic patients. Quart. J. Stud. Alc. **20**:543-54, 1959.

Chapter 3—Section c

1. Conger, J. J. Alcoholism: Theory, problem and challenge. II. Reinforcement theory and the dynamics of alcoholism. Quart. J. Stud. Alc. **17**:296-305, 1956.

2. Dollard, J. and N. E. Miller. *Personality and Psychotherapy: An Analysis in Terms of Learning Thinking and Culture.* McGraw-Hill, New York, 1950.

3. Himwich, H. E. Views on the etiology of alcoholism. I. The organic view. In *Alcoholism as a Medical Problem,* H. D. Kruse (ed.). Hoeber-Harper, New York, 1956, pp. 32-9.

4. Kinghan, R. J. Alcoholism and the reinforcement theory of learning. Quart. J. Stud. Alc. **19**:320-30, 1958.

5. Lester, D. and L. A. Greenberg. Nutrition and the etiology of alcoholism. The effect of sucrose-saccharin and fat on the self-selection of ethyl alcohol by rats. Quart. J. Stud. Alc. **13**:553-60, 1952.

6. Mardones, R. J. On the relationship between deficiency of B vitamins and alcohol intake in rats. Quart. J. Stud. Alc. **12**:563-75, 1951.

7. Masserman, J. H., K. S. Yum, M. R. Nicholson, and S. Lee. Neurosis and alcohol. An experimental study. Am. J. Psychiat. **101**: 389-95, 1944.

8. Masserman, J. H. and K. S. Yum. An analysis of the influence of alcohol on experimental neurosis in cats. Psychosom. Med. **8**:36-52, 1946.

9. Masserman, J. H. Alcohol and other drugs as preventives of experimental trauma. Quart. J. Stud. Alc. **20**:464-6, 1959.

10. Popham, R. E. A critique of the genetotropic theory of the etiology of alcoholism. Quart. J. Stud. Alc. **14**:228-37, 1953.

11. Randolph, T. G. The mechanism of chronic alcoholism. J. Lab. Clin. **36**:978, 1950.

12. Richter, C. P. Loss of appetite for alcohol and alcoholic beverages produced in rats by treatment with thyroid preparations. In *Alcoholism, Basic Aspects and Treatment,* H. E. Himwich (ed.).

American Association for the Advancement of Science, Washington, D. C., 1951.

13. Shoben, E. J., Jr. View on the etiology of alcoholism: The behavioristic view. In *Alcoholism as a Medical Problem*, H. D. Kruse (ed). New York, Hoeber-Harper, 1956.

14. Smith, J. J. A medical approach to problem drinking. Quart. J. Stud. Alc. 10:251-7, 1949.

15. Ullman, A. D. The psychological mechanism of alcohol addiction. Quart. J. Stud. Alc. 13:602-8, 1952.

16. Weiss, Mildred. Alcohol as a depressant in psychological conflict in rats. Quart. J. Stud. Alc. 19:226-38, 1958.

17. Westerfield, W. W. and J. Lawron. The effect of caloric restriction and thiamin deficiency on the voluntary consumption of alcohol by rats. Quart. J. Stud. Alc. 14:378-84, 1953.

18. Wexberg, E. Ursachen und Symptome des Arzneimittelsucht und des Alkolismus (Causes and symptoms of drug addiction and alcoholism). Z. Psychother., Stuttgart. 1:227-35, 1951.

19. Williams, R. J., L. J. Berry, and E. Beerstecher Jr. Biochemical individuality. III. Genetotropic factors in the etiology of alcoholism. Arch. Biochem. 23:275-90, 1949.

20. Williams, R. J. Biochemical individuality and cellular nutrition. Prime factors in alcoholism. Quart. J. Stud. Alc. 20:452-63, 1959.

Chapter 4—Section a

1. Berreman, G. D. Drinking patterns of the Aleuts. Quart. J. Stud. Alc. 17:503-14, 1956.

2. Devereux, G. The functions of alcohol in Mohave society. Quart. J. Stud. Alc. 9:207-51, 1948.

3. Horton, D. The functions of alcohol in primitive societies. A cross-cultural survey. Quart. J. Stud. Alc. 4:199-320, 1943.

4. Lemert, E. M. The use of alcohol in three Salish Indian tribes. Quart. J. Stud. Alc. 19:90-107, 1958.

5. Mangin, W. Drinking among Andean Indians. Quart. J. Stud. Alc. 18:55-66, 1957.

6. Sandoval, L. R. Drinking motivations among the Indians of the Ecuadorian Sierra. Primitive Man. 18:39-46, 1945.

7. Sayres, W. C. Ritual drinking, ethnic status and inebriety in rural Colombia. Quart. J. Stud. Alc. 17:53-62, 1956.

8. Simmons, O. G. Drinking patterns and interpersonal performance in a Peruvian Mestizo community. Quart. J. Stud. Alc. **20:** 103-11, 1959.

9. *The Columbia Encyclopedia,* 2nd ed. Columbia Univ. Press, New York, 1956.

Chapter 4—Section b

1. Asbury, H. *A Methodist Saint: The Life of Bishop Asbury.* Knopf, New York, 1927.

2. Bacon, S. Social settings conducive to alcoholism. J.A.M.A. **164:**177-81, 1957.

3. Bales, R. F. The "Fixation Factor" in Alcoholic Addiction: An Hypothesis Derived from a Comparative Study of Irish and Jewish Social Norms. Doctoral dissertation, Harvard University, 1944.

4. Bales, R. F. Cultural differences in the rate of alcoholism. Quart. J. Stud. Alc. **6:**482-98, 1946.

5. Chopra, R. N., G. S. Chopra, and I. C. Chopra. Minor drug habits of India. Indian Med. Gaz. **77:**34-41, 1942.

6. Chopra, R. N., G. S. Chopra, and I. C. Chopra. Alcoholic beverages in India. Indian Med. Gaz. **77:**224-32, 290-96, 361-7, 1942.

7. Christensen, H. T. Student views on mate selection. Marriage and Fam. **9:**85-8, 1947.

8. Colvin, D. L. *Prohibition in the United States.* George H. Doran Co., New York, 1926.

9. Glad, D. D. Attitudes and experiences of American-Jewish and American-Irish male youth as related to differences in adult rates of inebriety. Quart. J. Stud. Alc. **8:**406-72, 1947.

10. Hooton, C. *What Shall We Say about Alcohol?* Abingdon Press, New York, 1960, p. 127.

11. Horton, O. The function of alcohol in primitive societies. A cross-cultural survey. Quart. J. Stud. Alc. **4:**199-320, 1943.

12. Hyde, R. W. and R. M. Chisholm. Studies in medical sociology. III. The relation of mental disorder to race and nationality. New Eng. J. Med. **231:**612-18, 1944.

13. Jackson, D. *Stumbling Block.* Joint Section of Education and Cultivation. Board of Missions of the Methodist Church. New York, 1960.

14. Jones, E. Student Drinking in the High Schools of Utah. Thesis, University of Utah, 1957.

15. Lane, E. W. *Arabian Society in the Middle Ages*. London, 1883, pp. 148-59.

16. Lolli, G., E. Serianni, Grace M. Golder, and P. Luzzatto-Fegiz. *Alcohol in Italian Culture. Food and Wine in Relation to Sobriety among Italians and Italian Americans*. New Haven, Publications Division, Yale Center of Alcohol Studies; and Glencoe, Ill., Free Press, 1958.

17. Methodists. Contact. 2 (No. 10). June 1, 1960.

18. Myerson, D. J. An approach to Skid Row problems in Boston. New Eng. J. Med. 249:646-9, 1953.

19. Percival, R. J. Alcohol and alcoholism in the Republic of Ireland. Int. J. Alc. Alcsm. 1:146-55, 1955.

20. Rosenman, S. Pacts, possessions and the alcoholic. Amer. Imago. 12:241-74, 1955.

21. Skolnick, J. H. A study of the relation of ethnic background to arrests for inebriety. Quart. J. Stud. Alc. 15:622-30, 1954.

22. Skolnick, J. H. The Stumbling Block. A Sociological Study of the Relationship between Selected Religious Norms and Drinking Behaviour. Doctoral dissertation, Yale University, 1957.

23. Snyder, C. R. *Alcohol and the Jews: A Cultural Study of Drinking and Sobriety*. New Haven, Publications Division, Yale Center of Alcohol Studies; and Glencoe, Ill., Free Press, 1958.

24. Straus, R. and S. D. Bacon. *Drinking in College*. Yale Univ. Press, New Haven, 1953.

25. India, looking backward. Time, Nov. 28, 1960, p. 25.

26. Wesley, J. *Works*. Wesley Conference Office, London, vols. VI, VII.

27. Malzberg, B. *The Alcoholic Psychosis*. New Haven, Publications Division, Yale Center of Alcohol Studies; and Glencoe, Ill., Free Press, 1960.

28. Yivo Annual of Jewish Social Science. Vol. X, p. 282, 1955.

Chapter 5

1. Horton, D. The functions of alcohol in primitive societies. A cross-cultural survey. Quart. J. Stud. Alc. 4:199-320, 1943.

2. Lolli, G., E. Serianni, G. Golder, and P. Luzzatto-Fegiz. *Alcohol in Italian Culture. Food and Wine in Relation to Sobriety among Italians and Italian Americans.* New Haven, Publications Division, Yale Center of Alcohol Studies; and Glencoe, Ill., Free Press, 1958.

3. Strecker, E. A. Chronic alcoholism: A psychological survey. Quart. J. Stud. Alc. 3:12-17, 1941.

Chapter 6

1. European Seminar and Lecture Course on Alcoholism. WHO Regional Office for Europe, Palais des Nations, Geneva, Copenhagen, Denmark, Oct. 22–Nov. 3, 1951.

2. Georgia. Acts of 1951, Senate Bill 53.

3. Kantor, D. and H. W. Demone. The concept of coordination by a state-sponsored alcoholism program. Realizing the potential in state alcoholism programs. Proceedings of the Northeast States Conference on Alcoholism, New Haven, Conn., May 18–20, 1959.

4. Lundquist, G. Alkoholismus als medizinisches und soziales Problem (Alcoholism as a medical and social problem). Nervenarzi. 22:373-5, 1951.

5. Lipscomb, W. Alcoholism—the chronological background leading to California's present program. Calif. Medicine. 88:133-9, 1958.

6. Massachusetts. Acts of 1959, Chap. 418.

7. McKinlay, A. P. Ancient experience with intoxicating drinks: Nonclassical peoples. Quart. J. Stud. Alc. 9:398-9, 1948.

8. Moore, M. Chinese wine—some notes on its social use. Quart. J. Stud. Alc. 9:276, 1948.

9. Office of the Commissioner on Alcoholism, Mass. Half-way Houses for Alcoholics: A Report to the Hon. Foster Furcolo, Governor of the Commonwealth of Mass., 1958.

10. Philp, J. R. Alcoholism in California—the experience of the California State Dept. of Public Health. Amer. J. Pub. Health. 49:322-6, 1959.

11. State Board of Health of California: First Biennial Report of the Permanent Secretary, Sacramento, 1870-71.

12. Roper, L. J. Virginia state program for the treatment of alcoholics. Quart. J. Stud. Alc. 10:176, 1949.

Chapter 7

1. Bacon, S. D. Communication of research—role of the Yale Center of Alcohol Studies. Alumni News of the Yale Summer School of Alcohol Studies. **XV**, 1, 1959.

2. Bacon, S. D. Welcome Address. Yale Summer School of Alcohol Studies, 1959.

3. Jellinek, E. M. Notes on the first half year's experience at the Yale Plan Clinics. Quart. J. Stud. Alc. **5**:279-80, 1944.

4. Keller, M. Personal Communication, Sept. 26, 1959.

5. McCarthy, R. G. A public clinic approach to certain aspects of alcoholism. Quart. J. Stud. Alc. **6**:500-514, 1946.

6. The Yale Center. Social Progress. **XLV**, No. 7, 1955.

Chapter 8

1. Annual Report, 1951. The National Committee on Alcoholism, Inc., New York.

2. Annual Report, 1952-53. The National Committee on Alcoholism, Inc., New York.

3. Annual Report, 1957. The National Council on Alcoholism, Inc., New York.

4. Annual Report, 1959. The National Council on Alcoholism, Inc., New York.

5. Levy, D. Massachusetts marks eight years of progress. Children Limited. 25, August–September, 1960.

6. Mann, M. Attachments to Policies of the National Council on Alcoholism.

7. Mann, M. *New Primer on Alcoholism.* Rinehart & Co., New York, 1959.

8. Mann, M. Personal Communication. October 17, 1960.

9. National Agency Information for the National Budget Committee. The National Council on Alcoholism, Inc., New York, 1958.

Chapter 9

1. Alcoholics Anonymous. *Alcoholics Anonymous Comes of Age: A Brief History of A.A.* A.A. Publishing, Inc., New York, 1957.

2. Alcoholics Anonymous. *Alcoholics Anonymous.* Works Publishing Co., New York, 1939.

3. Alcoholics Anonymous. *Twelve Steps and Twelve Traditions.* Alcoholics Anonymous Publishing Co., New York, 1952.

4. Bacon, S. D. A sociologist looks at Alcoholics Anonymous. Minn. Welfare. **10**:35-44, 1957.

5. Hanfmann, E. The life history of an ex-alcoholic. Quart. J. Stud. Alc. **14**:468-85, 1951.

6. Lemert, E. W. *Alcohol and Northwest Coast Indians.* Univ. of Calif. Press, Berkeley, 1954.

7. Trice, H. M. Alcoholics Anonymous. Annals Amer. Acad. Pol. and Soc. Science. **315**:108-16, 1958.

8. Trice, H. M. The affiliation motive and readiness to join A.A. Quart. J. Stud. Alc. **20**:313-20, 1959.

9. W., Bill. An address to the 11th annual meeting of the North American Association of Alcoholism Programs. Banff, Alberta, 1960.

10. W., Bill. Let's keep it simple—but how? The A.A. Grapevine. **17**:2, 1960.

Chapter 10

1. MacDonald, D. E. Mental disorders in wives of alcoholics. Quart. J. Stud. Alc. **17**:282-7, 1956.

2. Myerson, J. J. An active therapeutic method of interrupting the dependency relationship of certain male alcoholics. Quart. J. Stud. Alc. **14**:419-26, 1953.

3. Straus, R. and S. D. Bacon. Alcoholism and social stability: A study of occupational integration in 2,023 male clinic patients. Quart. J. Stud. Alc. **12**:231-60, 1951.

4. The Al-Anon Family Groups. A guide for the families of problem drinkers. Al-Anon Family Group Headquarters, Inc., New York, 1955.

Chapter 11

1. Bales, R. F. Cultural differences in rates of alcoholism. Quart. J. Stud. Alc. **6**:480-99, 1946.

2. Berreman, G. D. Drinking patterns of Aleuts. Quart. J. Stud. Alc. **17**:503-14, 1956.

3. Brusch, C. A., C. M. Cerrato, P. N. Papas, and F. A. Straccia. Clinical and laboratory evaluation of alcoholic beverages. Am. J. Proctology. 6:140-44, 1955.

4. Chans Caviglia, J. C. Resultados de una enenesta medica sobre alcoholism (Results of a medical inquiry about alcoholism). Rev. Psiquiat, Uruguay. 7:51-2, 1942.

5. Damrau, F. and E. Liddy. A psychological study of moderate social drinkers. Exp. Med. Surg. 17:291-6, 1959.

6. Demone, H. W., Jr. Is education the answer to alcohol problems? In Alcohol Education: What Does a Teacher Need to Know To Teach? Vermont State Dept. of Education, Montpelier, 1960.

7. Devereux, G. The function of alcohol in Mohave society. Quart. J. Stud. Alc. 9:207-51, 1948.

8. Dresel, E. A. Über die biologischen und sozialen Floagen des Alkoholismus (On the biologic and social consequences of alcoholism). Versorgunsw. 2:334-5, 1922.

9. Glad, D. D. Attitudes and experiences of American-Jewish and American-Irish male youth as related to differences in adult rates of inebriety. Quart. J. Stud. Alc. 8:406-72, 1947.

10. Haag, H. B., J. K. Finnegan, P. S. Larson, and R. G. Smith, Jr. Studies on the acute toxicity and irritating properties of the congeners in whiskey. Toxicology and Applied Pharm. 1:618-27, 1959.

11. Haggard, H. W., L. A. Greenberg, and L. H. Cohen. The influence of the congeners of distilled spirits upon the physiological action of alcohol. Quart. J. Stud. Alc. 4:3-56, 1943.

12. Jellinek, E. M. The problems of alcohol. In Alcohol, Science and Society. Quart. J. Stud. Alc., New Haven, 1945.

13. Jellinek, E. M. Immanuel Kant on drinking. Quart. J. Stud. Alc. 1:777-8, 1941.

14. Knupfer, G. Use of alcoholic beverages by society and its cultural implications. California's Health. 18:18, 1960.

15. Lemert, E. M. Salish Indian drinking. Quart. J. Stud. Alc. 19:90-107, 1958.

16. Mangin, W. Drinking among Andean Indians. Quart. J. Stud. Alc. 18:55-66, 1957.

17. McCarthy, R. G. Alcohol problems: their impact on school and community. In Alcohol Education. What Does a Teacher Need To Know To Teach? Vermont State Dept. of Education, Montpelier, 1960.

18. McCarthy, R. G. *Drinking and Intoxication*. The Free Press, Glencoe, Ill., 1959.

19. McCarthy, R. G., and E. M. Douglass. *Alcohol and Social Responsibility—A New Educational Approach*. Crowell, New York, 1949.

20. McKennis, H. Jr. and H. B. Haag. On the congeners of whiskey. J. Am. Geriatrics Soc. 7:848-58, 1959.

21. Parreiras, D. Conditions actuelles de la prevention de l'alcolisme en Bresol (Present status of alcoholism prevention in Brazil). Int. J. Alc. Alcoholism 1:134-45, 1955.

22. Pasciutti, J. New directions in alcohol education. In *Mental Health Aspects of Alcohol Education*. Massachusetts Office of the Commissioner of Alcoholism, Boston, 1958.

23. Rosenman, S. Pacts, possessions and the alcoholic. Amer. Imago. 12:241-74, 1955.

24. Roueche, B. *The Neutral Spirit: A Portrait of Alcohol*. Little, Brown, Boston, 1960.

25. Sandoval, L. R. Drinking motivations among the Indians of the Ecuadorian Sierra. Primitive Man. 18:39-46, 1945.

26. Sayres, W. C. Ritual drinking, ethnic status and inebriety in rural Colombia. Quart. J. Stud. Alc. 17:53-62, 1956.

27. Simmons, O. G. Drinking patterns and interpersonal performance in a Peruvian Mestizo community. Quart. J. Stud. Alc. 20: 103-11, 1959.

28. Snell, C. A. The congener content of alcoholic beverages. Quart. J. Stud. Alc. 19:69-71, 1958.

29. Sombor, J. A. The alcohol question with particular consideration of native conditions (Hungarian text). Orv. Hehl. 69:30-32, 1925.

30. Straus, R. and S. D. Bacon. *Drinking in College*. Yale Univ. Press, New Haven, 1953.

31. Tompkins, R. M. Fifty Years in the Teaching of Physiology and Hygiene in the Elementary Schools (with special reference to textbooks). Temple University Thesis, 1935.

32. Ungdomen och alkoholem (Youth and alcohol). Tirfing. 40: 27-31, 1946.

33. Ullman, A. D. Sociocultural backgrounds of alcoholism. Annals Amer. Acad. Pol. Social Sci. 315:48-54, 1958.

34. Williams, C. Should the young be educated in the use and abuse of alcohol? Brit. J. Addiction. 56:49-52, 1960.

35. World Health Organization Technical Report Series, No. 89. Expert Committee on Health Education of the Public. First Report, Oct. 1954.

Chapter 12

1. *A Basic Outline for a Company Program on Alcoholism.* The Christopher D. Smithers Foundation, New York, 1959.

2. Coe, F. E. The alcoholic on the payroll. Industry. 29-30, May 1959.

3. Cruckshank, W. H. Executive discusses industry's role in dealing with employee alcoholism. Alcoholism. 5:1-9, 1958.

4. Guttman, L. In *Measurement of Prediction, Studies in Social Psychology in World War II,* vol. 4, by Samuel Stouffer *et al.* Princeton University Press, Princeton, 1950.

5. Graves, M. Industry's fight to save the alcoholic. Success Unlimited. March 1959.

6. Haun, P. Alcoholism. Rocky Mtn. Med. J. 38:33-9, 1941.

7. Jackson, J. K. H-technique scales of preoccupation with alcohol and of psychological involvement: time order of symptoms. Quart. J. Stud. Alc. 18:451-67, 1957.

8. Jellinek, E. M. Phases in the drinking history of alcoholics. Analysis of a survey conducted by the official organ of AA (Memoirs of the Section of Studies on Alcohol, Yale Univ., No. 5). Quart. J. Stud. Alc. 7:1-88, 1946.

9. Jellinek, E. M. Phases of alcohol addiction. Quart. J. Stud. Alc. 13:673-84, 1952.

10. Jellinek, E. M. *The Disease Concept of Alcoholism.* Hillhouse Press, New Haven, 1960.

11. Levinson, H. Alcoholism in industry. Menninger Quart. 11: 1-20, 1957.

12. Llewellyn, J. A. Steel company forges alcoholism plan. Target. 7:1-2, 1958.

13. MacKay, J. Clinical observations on adolescent problem drinkers. Quart. J. Stud. Alc. 22:124-34, 1961.

14. Maxwell, M. Early identification of problem drinkers in industry. Quart. J. Stud. Alc. 21:655-78, 1960.

15. Mendelson, J., D. Wexler, P. H. Leiderman, and P. Solomon. A study of addiction to nonethyl alcohols and other poisonous compounds. Quart. J. Stud. Alc. 18:561-80, 1957.

16. Norris, J. L. Cost and remedy of the alcoholic hangover in industry. Industrial Medicine. 17:129-32, 1948.

17. Pfeffer, A. Z., D. J. Feldman, C. Feibil, J. A. Frank, M. Cohen, S. Berger, M. F. Fleetwood, and S. S. Greenberg. A treatment program for the alcoholic in industry. J.A.M.A. 161:827-36, 1956.

18. Spears, E. M. The chronic alcoholic in industry. Conf. Board Mang. Rec. 8:154-5, 1946.

19. Straus, R. and S. D. Bacon. Drinking in College. Yale Univ. Press, New Haven, 1953.

20. They're rehabilitating the alcoholic worker. The Wall Street Journal, April 28, 1958.

21. Trice, H. M. and J. R. Wahl. A rank order analysis of the symptoms of alcoholism. Quart. J. Stud. Alc. 19:636-48, 1958.

22. Ullman, A. D. To Know the Difference. St. Martin's Press, New York, 1960.

23. World Health Organization, Technical Report Series. Expert Committee on Mental Health, Alcoholism Subcommittee, Second Report. Annex 2, The phases of alcohol addiction. No. 48, Aug. 1952.

Chapter 13

1. Armstrong, J. J. and R. J. Gibbins. A psychotherapeutic technique with large groups in the treatment of alcoholics. Quart. J. Stud. Alc. 17:461-78, 1956.

2. Armstrong, J. D. The protective drugs in the treatment of alcoholism. Can. Med. Assoc. 77:228-32, 1957.

3. Bachet, M. Inhibitions de type hypnotique et inhibitions par l'ambiance en therapeutique psychosomatiques (Inhibition by hypnosis and through environment in psychosomatic therapy). Graz. Med. Fr. 60:847-60, 1953.

4. Baldwin, D. S. Effectiveness of case work in marital discord with alcoholism. Smith Coll. Stud. Soc. Work. 18:69-122, 1947.

5. Bales, R. F. Social therapy for a social disorder—compulsive drinking. J. Social Issues. 1:14-22, 1945.

6. Bell, R. G. Treatment and rehabilitation of alcohol addicts. Ontario Med. Rev. **18**:23-5, 1951.

7. Bensoussan, P. A. Quelques caracteres particuliers des familles d'alcooliques et leur consequences therapeutiques. (Some special characteristics of the families of alcoholics and their therapeutic implications). Rev. Med. Prat. **4**:489-95, 1958.

8. Bloomberg, W. Use of benzedrine as an adjuvant in the treatment of chronic alcoholism. Amer. J. Psychiat. **98**:562-6, 1941.

9. Brunner-Orne, M. and M. T. Orne. Directive group-therapy in the treatment of alcoholics: technique and rationale. Int. J. Group Psychother. **4**:293-302, 1954.

10. Brunner-Orne, M. The role of a general hospital in the treatment and rehabilitation of alcoholics. Quart. J. Stud. Alc. **19**: 108-17, 1958.

11. Carlson, A. J. The conditioned reflex therapy of alcohol addiction. Quart. J. Stud. Alc. **2**:672-6, 1944.

12. Carver, A. E. T.E.T.D. in the treatment of alcoholics. Brit. Med. J. **2**:466-8, 1949.

13. Chafetz, M. E. Practical and theoretical considerations in the psychotherapy of alcoholism. Quart. J. Stud. Alc. **20**:281-91, 1959.

14. Chambers, F. T. Analysis and comparison of three treatment measures for alcoholism: Antabuse, the Alcoholics Anonymous approach, and psychotherapy. Brit. J. Addict. **50**:29-41, 1953.

15. Cork, R. M. Case work in a group setting with wives of alcoholics. Social Worker. **24**:1-6, 1956.

16. Cummins, J. F. and D. G. Friend. Use of chlorpromazine in chronic alcoholics. Amer. J. Med. Sci. **227**:561-4, 1954.

17. Dent, J. V. Apomorphine in treatment of addiction to "other drugs." Brit. J. Addict. **50**:43-5, 1953.

18. Feldman, D. J. Drug therapy in chronic alcoholism. Med. Clin. of N. Amer. **41**:381-92, 1957.

19. Forizs, L. Brief intensive group-psychotherapy for the treatment of alcoholics. Psychiat. Quart. Suppl. **29**:43-70, 1955.

20. Gelbman, F. and N. B. Epstein. Initial clinical experience with Antabuse. Can. Med. Assoc. J. **60**:286-8, 1949.

21. Glud, E. The treatment of alcoholic patients in Denmark with Antabuse. Quart. J. Stud. Alc. **10**:185-96, 1949.

22. Gottesfeld, B. H., L. M. Lasser, E. J. Conway, and N. M. Mann. Psychiatric implications of the treatment of alcoholism with tetraethylthiuram disulfide. Quart. J. Stud. Alc. 12:184-205, 1951.

23. Gottsegen, I. What hospitals can do about alcoholism. J. Amer. Hosp. Assn. 30:33-6, 1956.

24. Greenbaum, H. Group psychotherapy with alcoholics in conjunction with Antabuse treatment. Int. J. Group Psychother. 4:30-41, 1954.

25. Igersheimer, W. W. Group psychotherapy for nonalcoholic wives of alcoholics. Quart. J. Stud. Alc. 20:77-85, 1959.

26. Jacobsen, E. Biochemical methods in the treatment of alcoholism, with special reference to Antabuse. Proc. Roy. Soc. Med. 43:519-26, 1950.

27. Kant, F. Further modifications in the technique of conditioned reflex treatment of alcohol addiction. Quart. J. Stud. Alc. 5:229-32, 1944.

28. Kissin, B., V. Schenker, and A. Schenker. Adrenal cortical function and liver disease in alcoholics. Amer. J. Med. Sci. 238:344-53, 1959.

29. Kissin, B., V. Schenker, and A. Schenker. The acute effects of ethyl alcohol and Chlorpromazine on certain physiological functions in alcoholics. Quart J. Stud. Alc. 20:480-92, 1959.

30. Lemere, F. and W. Voegtlin. An evaluation of the aversion treatment of alcoholism. Quart. J. Stud. Alc. 8:261-4, 1950.

31. Macdonald, D. E. Group psychotherapy with wives of alcoholics. Quart. J. Stud. Alc. 19:125-32, 1958.

32. Myerson, D. J. The study and treatment of alcoholism: a historical perspective. New Eng. J. Med. 257:820-25, 1957.

33. Neveu, P. Narcoanalyses d'alcooliques (Narcoanalysis of alcoholics). Ann. Med. Leg. Paris. 30:364-5, 1950.

34. Oltman, J. E. and Friedman, S. Blood eosinophiles in alcoholic states. Arch. Neur. and Psychiat. 68:530-33, 1952.

35. Prout, C. T., E. I. Strongin, and M. A. White. A study of results in hospital treatment of alcoholism in males. Amer. J. Psychiat. 107:14-19, 1950.

36. Selzer, M. L. Hostility as a barrier to therapy in alcoholism. Psychiat. Quart. 31:301-5, 1957.

37. Shea, J. E. Psychoanalytic therapy and alcoholism. Quart. J. Stud. Alc. **15**:595-605, 1954.

38. Sinclair, A. The treatment of alcoholism. Med. J. Aust. **40**: 834-5, 1953.

39. Smith, J. J. The treatment of acute alcoholic states with A.C.T.H. and adrenocortical hormones. Quart. J. Stud. Alc. **11**: 190-98, 1950.

40. Strayer, R. Treatment of client and spouse by the same caseworker. Illustrated by the case history of an alcoholic outpatient. Quart. J. Stud. Alc. **20**:86-102, 1959.

41. Tiebout, H. M. The role of psychiatry in the field of alcoholism. With comment on the concept of alcoholism as a symptom and as disease. Quart. J. Stud. Alc. **12**:52-7, 1951.

42. Tiebout, H. M. The ego factors in surrender in alcoholism. Quart. J. Stud. Alc. **15**:610-21, 1954.

43. Tintera, J. W. and H. W. Lovell. Endocrine treatment of alcoholism. Geriatrics. **4**:274-80, 1949.

44. Usdin, G. L., P. C. Rond, J. Hinchcliffe, A. B. Arthur, and W. D. Ross. The meaning of disulfiram to alcoholics in group psychotherapy. Quart. J. Stud. Alc. **13**:590-95, 1952.

45. Voegtlin, W. L. The treatment of alcoholism with adrenal steroids and ACTH. Quart. J. Stud. Alc. **14**:28-37, 1953.

46. Walcott, E. and R. Straus. Use of a hospital facility in conjunction with outpatient clinics in the treatment of alcoholics. Quart. J. Stud. Alc. **13**:60-77, 1952.

47. Wallerstein, R. S. Comparative study of treatment methods for chronic alcoholism: the alcoholism research project at Winter V. A. Hospital. Amer. J. Psychiat. **113**:228-33, 1956.

48. Wenger, P. The treatment of alcoholism in veterans in an open psychiatric building. Quart. J. Stud. Alc. **16**:96-100, 1955.

Index

Note: Authors have been included only when their work has been discussed in the book.

313